Endorsements for *Love. Crash. Rebuild.*

"When the effectiveness of a couple's therapy process is validated by research and personal experience, which the authors of the PACER method have demonstrated, it should be shouted from the rooftop to every couple caught in their power struggle and to every therapist committed to helping them. That's what I am doing with my echo of the authors' recommendation for a Pause, Accountability, Collaboration, Experiment, and then Reset, Repair, and Renew."

Harville Hendrix, PhD and Helen LaKelly Hunt, PhD, co-authors of *NY Times* best seller *Getting the Love You Want: A Guide for Couples and Doing Imago Relationship Therapy in the Space Between*

"*Love. Crash. Rebuild is* a phenomenal book that should be on every couples' bookshelf! All couples fight, but the healthy ones use that breakdown to come back to intimacy and love better than ever. This book gives a simple step-by-step guide to doing just that! The authors have taken the best of psychoanalysis, family systems theories, narrative therapy, twelve-step couples recovery approaches, and behavior modification and created a couples healing process that really works. Definitely get this book—it could save your relationship or marriage!"

Dr. Diana Kirschner
Bestselling author and CEO of Lovein90Days.com

"The Borgs are a dynamic duo and their new book *Love. Crash. Rebuild.* positions them to be among the likes of John and Julie Gottman and Harville and Helen Hendrix. This relatable, easily digestible read offers couples concrete and simple steps to strengthen and save their long-term relationship or marriage. I will be referencing their ideas in my sessions with couples for a long time to come."

Hope Kelaher, LCSW
Author of the award-winning *Here to Make Friends: How to Make Friends as an Adult* and *The Resilience Workbook for Women*

"This book, written by a committed couple, therapists themselves, offers a compassionate instruction manual on how to weather and grow through the inevitable ups and downs of couple life. Their original PACER model introduces and demonstrates the use of invaluable skills no couple should go without. A crash course in relationship literacy!"

Suzanne Iasenza, PhD
Author of *Transforming Sexual Narratives:*
A Relational Approach to Sex Therapy

"*Love. Crash. Rebuild.* is a remarkable guide for couples who want to transform conflict into connection. You can immediately tell that Dr. Mark Borg and Haruna Miyamoto-Borg bring not only deep expertise as couples therapists, but also years of hands-on experience. The PACER model they offer is brilliantly grounded in interdisciplinary research—from psychoanalysis to recovery work—while remaining practical, accessible, and realistic for everyday use.

"Anyone recovering from a traumatic childhood who finds old wounds resurfacing in their romantic relationship will find this book immensely valuable. *Love. Crash. Rebuild.* is a compassionate, wise, and actionable roadmap for couples ready to move from rupture to repair."

Robyn Koslowitz, PhD
Clinical Psychologist and Author of *Post-Traumatic Parenting*

"Haruna and Mark's relationship model begins with the luminous idea that at the heart of every rupture lies a heartfelt yearning for reconnection. Even after the glow of the honeymoon phase fades, every repair—big or small— becomes an invitation to rekindle warmth and let love shine anew. Don't shy away from trouble; welcome it as love in action."

Faith Bethelard, PsyD

Love. Crash. Rebuild.

Love. Crash. Rebuild.

ALTERNATIVES *to* DISTANCE, DESTRUCTION, *and* DIVORCE

Mark B. Borg, Jr.
Haruna Miyamoto-Borg

C*RP

CENTRAL RECOVERY PRESS

LAS VEGAS

Central Recovery Press (CRP) is committed to publishing exceptional materials addressing addiction treatment, recovery, and behavioral healthcare topics.

For more information, visit www.centralrecoverypress.com.

Publisher: Central Recovery Press
             530 S 6th Street
             Las Vegas, NV 89101

30 29 28 27 26 25   1 2 3 4 5

Library of Congress Cataloging-in-Publication Data has been applied for.

Photo of Mark Borg and Haruna Miyamoto-Borg by Brittainy Newman.

Every attempt has been made to contact copyright holders. If copyright holders have not been properly acknowledged please contact us. Central Recovery Press will be happy to rectify the omission in future printings of this book.

Publisher's Note
This book contains general information about practical strategies and applications for self-care through caring for our most significant relationships. The book's counterintuitive lesson is simple: conflict is an inevitable ingredient of couple's life and resolving the conflict and turmoil of a relationship is really the foundation of great marriages.

Our books represent the experiences and opinions of their authors only. Every effort has been made to ensure that events, institutions, and statistics presented in our books as facts are accurate and up to date. To protect their privacy, the names of some of the people, places, and institutions in this book may have been changed.

Cover design by The Book Designers. Interior design by Deb Tremper.

Mark dedicates this book to

Joanna Murphy, Moonli Singha, and Rósa Guðmundsdóttir.
Sirens all, though unlike your mythological analogs, you guide me—
my heart, my soul, my love, especially my love—safely through my
own perilous historical compulsion to crash all approximations
of love upon the rocky shores of total annihilation!

Haruna dedicates this book to

Mark B. Borg Jr., Kata and Uta Borg, and my
parents, Yoko and Osamu Miyamoto.

Table of Contents

Introduction

In July 2011, we were in Istanbul working on a psychology paper studying how couples engage with each other when they are past the honeymoon period.[1] Our hope was that the paper would be a consolidation of the work we had already done as a couple in our own therapy and in our individual trainings. We wanted to use the lessons we learned about conflict, whether it was a small fight, a real battle, or even a period of war, to help couples reset into a different state of love.

It turns out that art was in fact reflecting reality, because war—a *love crash* par excellence—was exactly what we were going through in our villa. When we met in 2006, we had a honeymoon period like no other. We were crazy in love. For the first eighteen months of our relationship, we couldn't think straight. We were all over each other. Our life was exciting; we set up camp in New York City and traveled the world. And then, everything changed. Haruna got pregnant and received a cancer diagnosis. We wanted to sell our apartment and get a bigger one, but the deal fell through, and we were stuck with two pieces of expensive New York real estate—just as the real estate market crashed in 2008. These troubles, and myriad others, sent us from love's dizzying high to a catastrophic wipe-out, a bottoming out that quickly became chronic. We were fighting all the time, and it was ugly. We didn't know how to be vulnerable and human with each other and navigate the tragic circumstances. We didn't know how to disagree and accept our differences. We didn't know how to pick ourselves up after falling apart.

So that night in Istanbul we sat down and decided that we needed ground rules—for what would be our own *love-crash rehab*! What had we learned in

1. Mark B. Borg, Jr. and Haruna Miyamoto-Borg, "The Borderline Stage of Relationship," *Psychology Research*, 2 (2012): 1–13.

1

our years of marriage and through our roles as therapists (especially couples therapists) about how two adults navigate their own failures and successes? We realized we could boil all those experiences down to just two rules:

1) Keep the focus on yourself, and
2) Refer to Rule #1

In other words, "Keep the focus on yourself" is the royal road to conflict resolution. We use these rules not just for getting through conflict, but for doing everything that couples do. And from this cornerstone, we have been able to rebuild and maintain a foundation of *vulnerability, empathy, intimacy,* and *emotional investment* in our alliance as an expression of our love.

Does this mean that we're now the perfect couple? Hardly! We do, however, know a lot about couples and how they behave. As couples therapists who are also a couple, we've managed to work out some pretty serious kinks in our marriage and have done the same for so many of our clients. Mark's psychoanalytic training looks at person's history to see how unresolved wounds continue to play out in new relationships. Haruna's training as a family and couples therapist taught her how to identify people's issues and help couples bridge two perspectives in order to reconnect. In other words, Haruna focuses on helping folks connect while Mark focuses on the part of a person's past that interferes with those connections.

Couples come to see us because they know something's wrong with their relationship, but they don't know what it is or how to fix it. Some of our clients think the problem is that they're fighting or that they are not having sex as often as before (or ever). Other couples we meet are deeply in love yet have no idea how to build on their relationship or how to maintain a relationship. So, when life gets messy, so many of us automatically think of the worst-case scenario and believe that "this is just happening to me." In this case, our minds go to the far end of the spectrum: we chose the wrong partner and should get divorced.

Or we avoid dealing with our relationship problems by checking out in a variety of ways—so-called *acting out.* By "acting out" we usually mean either:

1) Doing something destructive (to self and/or other)
2) Doing something that distances ourselves from awareness of our most vulnerable emotions (e.g., pain, fear), and each other

How often is acting out the salve we put on our anxiety and agitation? How often do we medicate our discomfort with behavior that decreases our awareness of our emotional state but adversely increases our pain and fear and puts us in conflict with each other? Such "medication" effectively gets rid of our *awareness* of what underlies conflicts but does nothing to resolve the conflict itself. In fact, it is the road to ruin.

In contrast, the most successful couples take a completely opposite approach. They recognize that conflict is an inevitable part of marriage, and it can erupt at any time[2]. And, they get through the conflict, whether it is a major challenge or a small slight, by acknowledging the discord and working together to resolve it. The truth is all conflicts lead to periods of destabilization—a *rupture* in the status quo or the emotional wedge between two people—and can also bring couples closer together and lead to *repair*[3]. We believe, as do prominent researchers including neuroscientist Edward Tronick and child psychotherapist Janine Sternberg, that relational health occurs via the process of rupture and repair—rather than perfect

2.   According to renowned couples researcher/therapist, John Gottman (1999), "Marital conflict is shared by both happy and unhappy couples, and the rank order correlation of severity of problems is about 0.94 between the two groups (the maximum value is 1.00, so this is extraordinarily high)," 21.
3.   Though "rupture and repair" is a process researched and developed by Edward Tronick throughout his career as a developmental neuroscientist and clinical psychologist, this process is also called "rupture and mismatch." Succinctly put: "Repair is the crux of human interaction. Repair leads to a feeling of pleasure, trust, and security; the implicit knowledge that *I can overcome problems*. Furthermore, repair teaches a critical life lesson: The negative feelings that arise from mismatch can be changed into a positive feeling when two people subsequently achieve a match," (Tronick & Gold, 2020) 38.

attunement.[4,5,6,7] In fact, when couples repair their ruptures, it can bring them closer together.

The process of repair can also heal existing attachment issues.[8] People with secure attachment styles typically remain grounded during emotional disruptions and even during severe life crises. They experience emotions and go through life upsets without becoming profoundly disturbed and usually return to equilibrium relatively quickly. By contrast, a person with an insecure attachment style experiences the normal ups and downs of life as so intense, they can only function in relationships by avoiding anything that might trigger insecurity and anxiety or frantically forcing their partner to engage in solutions immediately. This may mean avoiding or controlling interpersonal connections altogether.

As we tell our clients all the time, the problem isn't that couples have ruptures; the problem is when ruptures do not lead to repairs. When we make use of rupture and repair, conflict can help your relationship evolve so that you can be more vulnerable, empathetic, intimate, and invested in each

4.   Edward Tronick developed the concept of *rupture and repair* early in his career through his studies that he termed the *Still Face Experiment.* The "still face" demonstrates how vulnerable we all are to the emotional or nonemotional reactions of the people we are close to. It demonstrates how babies who are just learning about their relational world try to achieve connection. Babies were once thought to be unable to understand emotions (Tronick & Gianino, 1986), 3–4.

5.   Edward Z. Tronick, "Emotions and Communication in Infants," *American Psychologist* 44, no. 2 (1989): 112–19.

6.   Edward Z. Tronick, *The Neurobehavioral and Social-Emotional Development of Infants and Children* (New York: W. W. Norton, 2007).

7.   Janine Sternberg, *Infant Observation at the Heart of Training* (London: Routledge, 2018).

8.   While high-functioning people may appear emotionally secure, those who have an adversarial relationship with the world lock down their emotions to conceal what clinicians call an *insecure attachment style* (Bowlby, 1969). This limits how well they access experience, and the way they perceive and relate within relationships is stunted. Research on attachment style finds a connection between limited dynamics in adults and how they related to their primary caregivers as children (Ainsworth, 1969). The greater your demand for intimacy as an adult, the more crucial your attachment style becomes. Attachment styles are generally classified as either secure or insecure (i.e., avoidant or anxious) depending on the quality of your childhood caregiving, innate factors with which you're born, and the fit between you and your caregiver's attachment styles (Bowlby, 1958). 364.

other—connected, rather than being a source of destruction and emotional distancing.

We know that creating and maintaining a great marriage, relationship, or partnership is hard work. And nobody teaches you how to do it. At best you may have been fortunate to grow up in a healthy and stable home where your parents set a good example. But even if that was the case, there is no guarantee that your partner did the same. Ironically, even clinicians like us were never taught how to do relationships the right way when we were in school training to be therapists—the professionals the rest of the world is supposed to turn to when their relationships go south.

So when our own ruptures weren't leading to repairs, we realized we needed help. Neither of us were able to get past blaming the other for everything that was not working. Our marriage got so contentious that one day Mark took off his wedding ring and Haruna took off hers as well and flushed them both down the toilet!

Then we went to couples therapy, a peer-support group, and went back to school to learn more about the latest couples therapy theories and practices. We tried every technique. We read self-help books. We wrote self-help books, blogs on *Psychology Today,* and academic articles. Ultimately, we came out on the other side as veterans of the experience and as a better couple. We took the best of everything we learned and created a model that encompasses psychoanalysis, family systems theories, narrative therapy, twelve-step couples recovery approaches, behavior modification, and other therapeutic techniques, and boiled them down to their most essential elements. And then added in the two rules.

Enter the PACER Model

Our counterintuitive lesson is simple: the conflict and turmoil and the intimacy of everyday life are the foundation great relationships are built on. However, we have seen, both personally and clinically, that couples have a much better shot at achieving long-lasting love if their relationship includes a codified process for dealing directly with—rather than medicating (i.e., acting out by distancing and destruction)—this same conflict.

We created a simple five-step process for reconciling differences, taking couples in crisis from rupture to repair. Our tool—the PACER model—can move any couple from rupture to repair within minutes. The model takes into account cultural differences, past hurts, and current crises. It is an opportunity for not just healing but for growth. And it is the core of what this book is providing for you: a way out of pain, numbing, or acting out and a way back into relationship.

The PACER model has five steps:

Pause: Rather than shutting down or escalating arguments when life gets tense, we teach readers how to create an empowered *Pause*, where each person puts down their weapons of offense and defense, takes a break, and allows for the space to remember their roles within a loving relationship. Couples are meant to be allies in a common process of living everyday together within the context of a love developed and shared. A Pause is not an "adult time out" because the intent is not a punishment or an opportunity to wallow. It is a productive break to take down the temperature of an argument.

Accountability: The crux of PACER is a simple phrase: "Keep the focus on yourself." It is an opportunity for self-awareness, so that individually we can identify and own the contributions we make to a conflict so that we can stop blaming our partner. In twelve-step programs, this process is called "taking inventory." We have found that the best way to *not* take your partner's inventory is to take your own. The goal of *Accountability* is a humble acceptance, willingness, and ability to account for flaws on your own. In this safe space we can think about the provocative, yet very helpful statement: "If my actions are not part of the problem, there is no solution." It is only by being accountable for our part of the problem that we can become empowered to contribute to the solution.

And in our Accountability there is real power: We begin to see and feel how we can contribute to our own healing—ours individually as well as to that of our relationship.

Collaboration: Ironically, *Collaboration* in this context doesn't mean working together, but it does hinge on our notion of the *two rules of healthy communication*. It is where we create a safe space together to share our insights about how we each contribute to the conflict. The Collaboration process is drastically different from traditional couples therapy, where one person talks, and then the therapist says to the other, "Now repeat to your partner what they said." Instead, we're asking you and your partner to participate in a unique, deep kind of listening. By creating a *meeting in the middle* (see Chapter Ten for a more in-depth discussion), each partner is going to bring their willingness to share what they discovered in Accountability (our method is a riff on the Chapter 9—Couples in Recovery Anonymous—practice called a "Meeting of Two"). Then they take ownership of their part of the problem, giving them a sense of responsibility over their part of the greater whole of the relationship: what we call their *us-ness* or the core of their *alliance*. Developing, building, and maintaining this alliance is the ultimate goal of the PACER model. Collaboration results in couples fighting far less frequently and, when they do fight, the arguments are less vicious and don't last as long. Ultimately, it creates an opportunity for empathy and a safe space where each is more likely to forgive.

Experiment: The *Experiment* is where couples use the incredible insights they've achieved in Collaboration and put them into action. The Experiment gives the rupture a name and includes developing a plan to resolve it. At the same time, couples develop new and creative ways of communicating and interacting. The goal of the Experiment is to rewrite the narrative of their relationship.

Reset: Couples can take a deeper look at what is lying underneath the initial rupture. It allows couples to gain a new insight, connecting the dots in a different way to allow for the possibility of finding other unresolved issues that are lurking below the surface. *Reset* leaves participants with a new level of accountability, and a healthier view of their relationship. Ultimately, it is the expression of going from rupture to repair and, in so doing, experiencing—accepting, taking in, and making use of—the healing elements of conflict resolution.

We put the PACER model into practice all the time, with our patients and absolutely in our own marriage. For instance, in 2021, we were going on a family trip to visit Mark's father in Puerto Peñasco, Mexico, near the border of Arizona. Our family had never spent much time with Mark's father and his stepmother, so the concept that this would in fact be a vacation was a little harrowing. But it was the first winter break during the pandemic, and the idea of being stuck in our apartment with our two kids seemed like an exercise in flawed parenting. So, we planned a trip that was predicated on a precise timetable: fly from NYC into Phoenix and landing around 2:00 p.m. That would be early enough in the afternoon so that we could have a meal, and then start off on what should have been about three-and-a-half-hour drive into Mexico while it was still light outside.

As usual, life didn't work out the way we planned. We got stuck on the runway in New York for about an hour and a half. By the time we got to Phoenix it was already 4:30 p.m. We all piled into a rental car, stopped for the meal, and then we started the drive. When we got to the border of Mexico at 8:18 p.m., we found out it closed: at 8:00 p.m. Dejected, we found a ratty hotel and fed the kids dinner at a Circle K convenience store that was also a gas station.

The next morning, we regrouped. The weather couldn't have been more perfect. We drove through the border into the Mexican desert, passing loads of pipe organ cactus, and as we were driving, we were becoming a little more optimistic with every mile—until one of our tires blew out. Remember, we live in New York City; we don't own a car and neither of us had ever fixed a flat tire. So, we took out the manual and an hour or so later we successfully swapped on the spare tire—a donut—working hard all the while to keep our cool. In fact, we were feeling good about ourselves and this accomplishment. Until an alarm in the car started going off, and we didn't know why. For Haruna, this unsettling noise was the proverbial last straw. Haruna started yelling, and in turn, our kids started screaming, "Mommy don't yell." Mark joined in with the kids and started telling Haruna *not to yell*. In less than forty-five seconds we were in a full blown, screaming battle. Things were really, really sucking badly. And we still had a couple of hundred miles to go before we got to Puerto Peñasco.

We kept driving. Haruna reminds Mark that the car's manual advised not to drive on the spare tire above forty-five miles an hour. But Mark kept going forty-seven, forty-eight. Haruna asked Mark to slow down, and Mark would yell back, "Don't tell me what to do." Finally, Mark pulled over, got out of the car, and told Haruna she could drive. We were as stuck as two people in a raging fight could possibly be.

Haruna drove in total silence; we hit *Pause*, which allowed us to calm down rather than acting out in all-out battle. Then, about a half an hour later, Mark reached out and grabbed Haruna's elbow and suggested that he could be *Accountable*, at least for his part of what had happened. We remembered the *rule of two*, and each kept the focus on ourselves. Mark knew he was wrong when he sided with his kids in an attempt to suppress Haruna's agitation over the car alarm. Haruna shared that although she realized her reaction was in fact, reactionary, it augmented the fight, which was not ideal. Mark related to what Haruna must have been going through to feel ganged up on by recalling an incident from his past when a group of friends turned on him in middle school—leaving him feeling ganged-up on, humiliated, and isolated. Through this experience, he empathized with Haruna's feeling that "everyone is against me" in the car, especially when her reaction to the emergency was quite legitimate after everything they'd been through. In turn, Haruna recalled feeling caught between her own parents' difficulties and, through this, empathized with Mark for feeling caught in the middle of what often felt like an impossible decision: to care for, love, and support either his wife or their kids. Haruna also recognized that just like she did, Mark also had a reaction to the car alarm and to the series of the unfortunate events since they landed in Phoenix.

Then, the *Collaboration* began. We kept the idea in mind that we are human and both of us will inevitably make mistakes. With this acceptance, we apologized to each other. A long time ago we developed a simple family slogan, so in the car we held hands for a minute and said aloud, "Just for today, no fighting." Once we did this, it was possible to start forward-thinking and *Experiment*—what we would each like to see happen during the rest of our trip. It didn't take long to resolve this fight, and when we did, we both *Reset* and felt that our relationship was in fact a third entity, an "us" that is separate from either individual and that we regained our alliance.

Going through the PACER model, in real time, when the rupture occurred, enabled us to enjoy the trip more. We were able to forgive each other, and ourselves individually, and move on. And we were able to find our way back to what we see as the four pillars of true love: intimacy, empathy, vulnerability, and emotional investment.

How This Book Works

Part I explores the typical ruptures couples have as well as the underlying anxieties and pain that cause them. Surprisingly, the problems are not what most couples come into therapy grumbling about or recognize on the surface. Many couples who come to see us complain that they are no longer talking to each other, no longer sexually intimate, or that they are just going through their day-to-day life of the marriage mindlessly. We first help them to see how these surface ruptures are masking deeper issues that can range from cultural differences to deep-seated fears and traumas. For instance, when working with couples we often see their failure in communication is tied to underlying issues having to do with acceptance of themselves, each other, and their day-to-day life *as is*. By using PACER when life gets tense, we can change the dynamic of everyday life from irresolvable conflicts to better communication and, in so doing, better alliances.

Part II features detailed instructions on the five steps of PACER. Within each step there are appropriate exercises and anecdotes so that you can see how the model works in real life. You'll meet dozens of our patients and come right into our own marriage to see how PACER has changed our lives. Most importantly, you'll see that by using the PACER model, each rupture becomes an opportunity for repair. And repair, as practiced in the everyday, becomes both the foundation for and the open road of love. The truth is, our mundane lives become the classroom for establishing and maintaining the four pillars of a healthy, loving, successful relationship: vulnerability, empathy, intimacy, and emotional investment. Using this tool, you will be able to resolve past hurts and current issues and find new joy in your marriage.

We cannot be sure why you picked up this book, but we believe there are alternatives to living with emotional distance and/or destructive behaviors that end in divorce, whether actual or a state of separation equally severe but less overtly obvious. The PACER model is one of those alternatives. By finding ways to manage the turmoil, stress, and anxiety of growth and development *together* in relationship, we can finally live in a growing, thriving state of loving and being loved.

PART I

Living in Real Life (IRL)

CHAPTER ONE

What Conflict Is Really About

It's no surprise that couples often have difficulty connecting, listening to each other, and understanding what the other person is experiencing at any given moment on any given day. It is inevitable in any intimate relationship that there will be conflict; whenever there are two people, one is bound to get upset about something. No matter what the conflict is about or how it is handled (what it looks like on the outside), it invariably leads to a destabilization—a *rupture* in the status quo.

Ruptures occur from the minute we're born and will continue to the end of our lives. According to infant development theory (especially those of Ed Tronick), ruptures begin when a parent is not attuned with their infants. This can be easy to imagine, as ruptures always occur in the context of a relationship. You could have upsetting feelings, such as, *I'm angry that I have so much work to do and I can't go outside and enjoy the beautiful weather*, but this emotional response is not a rupture. However, when you have too much work to do and yell at your partner because he's taking the day off, that's a rupture. You're taking the feelings that are going on inside of you and imposing them on somebody else and *enacting*[1]—*acting out emotions*

---

1.   Clinical enactments are broadly defined as moments or stretches of time in therapy where both the patient and therapist cannot put their conflicts into words, and instead act them out within the therapeutic milieu. An enactment is where you and I—in our relationship to/with each other (unconsciously communicating through the ways that we interact together, reengaging behaviors, thoughts, and feelings)—play out a dynamic

and unresolved dynamics from our relational histories—those emotions in the form of a conflict.

Conflict within a relationship is then the reaction that lets us know there has been a rupture. And, therefore, it is an opportunity for people in relationship to work together to fix whatever has gone wrong. Each and every time we go off the rails, we have both the challenge and opportunity to realign, reset, and heal—*rebuilding* one conflict at a time. It is easy to blame our partner when things go wrong, but when we think along the lines of rupture and repair, we can change the ways we experience conflict: it's not us against each other—it's us against the conflict.

Infant development theory shows us empirically that we have been in a state of rupture with our environment, which includes our primary caretaker (often our mother) from birth on. It's completely normal for couples to rupture, and we believe that ruptures are opportunities for us to pay attention to what is going on in the real life of our relationships. Therefore, ruptures can be seen as the equivalent of a call for help. In this exact sense, conflict is part of

---

pattern that repeats an essential early and unresolved conflict. Though the term enactment is a contemporary psychoanalytic concept that goes well beyond the scope of this book, it is necessary to give a brief definition to help understand the community dynamics explored in this chapter. One approach to understanding transference-countertransference interactions is by analyzing patient-analyst enactments. Hirsch defines these as "what happens when the analyst unwittingly actualizes the patient's transference and, together with the patient, lives out [the] intrapsychic configurations . . . [enactment] is viewed as the patient's unconscious effort to persuade or force the analyst into a reciprocal action: a two-party playing out of the patient's most fundamental internalized configurations." (Hirsch, 1998), 78. Similarly, Edgar Levenson believes that change in a system is created through a practitioner's "ability to be trapped, immersed, and participating in the system and then work his [or her] way out." (Levenson, 1972), 174. In its broadest sense, the enactment concept can also be used to describe and address how all interactions—in analysis as well as in our daily lives—are tainted by the unconscious dynamics of the enactors. This raises the question of whether enactments are so ubiquitous in our daily lives as to be increasingly useless (at least as special cases of unconscious material) in analytic settings. From this perspective, Lewis Aron (2003) asserts that "we are correct to ask, 'What is *not* an enactment?'" (623). However, he goes on to suggest that enactments "may well be a central means by which patients and analysts enter into each other's inner world and discover themselves as participants within each other's psychic life, mutually constructing the relational matrix that constitutes the medium of psychoanalysis." (ibid., 629).

a healthy relationship. It's trying to tell you that you're hurting each other's feelings or that you're missing each other or that you're lonely.

Most ruptures do not lead to relationship implosion. A rupture doesn't have to be the cataclysmic moment when you know you want a divorce; it can be any sort of tension, even a pinprick of hurt. Not being present in a relationship can be as much of a rupture as engaging in a full-blown affair. Something as quiet as turning away—or looking at your phone—while your partner is talking is a rupture, and so is ignoring problems that arise instead of dealing with them.

If you and your partner are really good at expressing each of your needs, wants, and especially feelings (which often are the signals that "something is not quite right"), then ruptures can be easily navigated. For instance, if Patty didn't do the dishes when it was her turn, and although Steve was annoyed, he reminded Patty, and Patty agreed that it was her turn to do the dishes, and then walked to the sink and did the dishes, that would be the end of the rupture. However, if you aren't as adept at expressing your needs, wants, and feelings, ruptures will come across with a lot of anger or hurt, and those emotions are harder to deal with, which is when longer lasting conflicts, and the negative behaviors associated with them, take hold.

It turns out that anger is a secondary emotion to more vulnerable, primary feelings like hurt, sadness, and fear. You can think about this relationship like a snail and its shell. The snail itself is the vulnerable feeling—the pain, sadness, fear—and shell is the anger. When you are in a rupture, anger is the armor that protects you from being honest with, or being open to, your own painful feelings in the presence of your partner. Think of it this way: it's a lot easier to be angry with your partner than show them how vulnerable you are when you are hurt.

When something in your relationship goes off the rails, whether it's your sense of security, familiarity, or peace, a rupture can start as soon as one of you begins to feel off balance. The imbalance itself can create the same primary vulnerable feelings: fear, hurt, insecurity, or sadness. Some people do not ever feel safe staying with those emotions, so they get angry as a way of protecting themselves even when they are alone. Others are more comfortable with their vulnerable feelings but have difficulty admitting they are having those feelings in front of their partners; and then they get angry, too.

For instance, our client John felt sad, lonely, and abandoned six months after his partner Anne took a new job that required her working longer hours. When Anne came home from work one evening, John expressed his anger and frustration about her work hours and criticized her for not spending time with him. "I am really upset that you prioritize your work now. Why don't you make time for us? You don't care about me anymore!"

However, the truth was that John knew he wasn't really angry at Anne; he was feeling left behind by his wife. He just wasn't able to say in the moment, "I miss you very much and miss spending time with you. I have been feeling lonely ever since you took this new job." His hostile feelings worked as the armor that protected him from admitting his more vulnerable feelings. Instead, John skipped the admitting part and flew straight to anger, creating a rupture Anne wasn't quite sure how to deal with.

Sometimes, by the time an imbalance creates real conflict, the initial cause of the imbalance often gets lost in the defense. You are so busy covering up your pain and defending yourself with anger that you can't circle back to the initial cause of the conflict. When this kind of rupture occurs, a couple ends up not listening to each other as both of them are busy defending themselves—rupture-palooza!

Trouble Is Our Teacher

The Buddha suggests that our troubles are our best teachers. Our conflicts—especially those we face together—can teach us:

- How we've protected ourselves through destructive and distancing behavior.
- How through our own difficulty in seeing and accepting our part in a conflict, we've usually taken up a defensive position and unexpectedly invited counterattacks.
- How to halt our defensiveness and live at peace—*relationship sanity*[2]—with each other.

2.   Throughout the *Irrelationship* series (Borg, Brenner, & Berry, 2015, 2018, 2022), Mark and his colleagues, John (Danny) Berry and Dr. Grant Brenner defined "relationship sanity" as a balance in the giving and receiving dynamic in relationship: "experiencing

- That we can influence our reactions and responses to each other in caring and loving ways.
- And that this transformative process can change our love and acceptance for each other—and ourselves.

Ruptures and Transitions

A transition can be any shift in the dynamic of the relationship caused by an external challenge that disrupts what we call *the intimacy of everyday life*. A transition could be a move or taking on a new job, a death in the family, birth of a child, a financial loss, physical health tragedy, or even a life-changing success. A transition can also occur as a subtle, emotional/psychological experience, as when one person is feeling confused, conflicted, and uncertain about the relationship.

At the most macro level, transitions can stem from the issues that affect the world around us. Every world event (that you know about) is going to affect your relationship: inflation, social media (and the associated FOMO, "compare and despair," etc.), war, and climate change. On the micro level, a transition can occur when you've been asked to join abruptly a new team at work and you bring an unsettled feeling home. You're feeling wounded and hurt because you weren't given a choice, so you act out on it (*it*, of course, being the painful scary emotion that you wind up expressing as defensive anger at your partner).

Transitions can easily become the primary contributor of a rupture. Many of us believe that we ought to be able to handle the small slights of life. But even the small slights can build on each other until they morph into a transition. For example, women going through perimenopause and menopause can have symptoms that impact sexual pleasure. While one woman may be going through this big physiological transition—and since she is a part of a relationship—the discomfort she may be experiencing during sex is creating an imbalance or transition in their relationship.

---

ourselves as being loving and lovable is a (if not the) relational definition of sanity" (Borg, Brenner, & Berry, 2018), 7.

The Continuums of Love Crashes:
Acute vs. Chronic, Distance vs. Destruction

We've seen, we've had, and we've survived many a *love crash*. And we believe the silver lining of each and every one of them is that we learn just a little bit more about ourselves, each other, our relationship, and the people who come to us for help. We've also learned that the way conflicts tend to manifest falls within four types:

- **Acute** conflicts generally develop suddenly and last only a short time, yet the damage can be extreme and long-lasting. Sometimes it can become the very evidence that is held onto and used as a rationale for defending oneself from taking emotional risks with the person who attacked acutely (and, sometimes, protecting our partner from the severity of our own attack on them).

- **Chronic** conflicts worsen over an extended period of time, and the severity of the conflict often expresses itself in passive, pervasive, and indirect ways that sometimes make it hard to recognize the underlying issues that are unresolved in the ongoing—and often disavowed—fight.

- **Distancing** conflicts can manifest in behaviors where one person or both partners move away from the other as a form of punishment and protection, creating either physical or emotional distance, or both.

- **Destructive** conflicts are the stereotype of couples' fights—where we attack and feel attacked verbally, emotionally, and sometimes physically.

Conflicts exist on a continuum with an extreme pole at one end that is *acute* and erupts, sometimes violently, into fights that are *destructive*. At the other end of the continuum is the pole where *chronic* conflict can be much more subtle, might go unaddressed for years, and tends to result in *distancing* behaviors. Distancing and destructive behaviors can, over the course of time, settle into *relationship habits*.

There are issues that are chronic—parenting, money, cultural influences—that can also appear in acute ways, almost right out of the blue. For instance, in our marriage we have agreed that there are some topics we can discuss with our parents and some that are off limits. These topics don't present much of an issue with Haruna's parents because they don't speak English and Mark doesn't speak Japanese. But there have been incidents when we have forgotten this agreement and brought up a topic with Mark's parents that has created chronic tension that can go on for years, as well as erupt into a fight in the moment that is extremely acute and destructive.

Ruptures and the Internal Conflict of Ambivalence

The kind of conflict that we have been referring to so far is the straightforward experience of fighting, squabbling, disagreement, clashing, and what some couples in extreme states refer to as *war*. But there is another, more subtle and internal conflict that individuals in every relationship can face, often without consciously realizing it (but acting it out nonetheless). This conflict is best expressed by Mark's song lyric: "I want you, I do—almost as much as I don't."

This type of conflict can be expressed as *ambivalence*. While many of us believe that true love and long-term relationships are founded on the resolution of mixed feelings—I either want you *or* I don't—we believe that being able to contain this internal conflict of I want you *and* I don't is the cornerstone of healthy relationships. In fact, we often tell our clients when they are having "mixed feelings" about someone, it means that they are beginning to emotionally invest in them and their heart is increasingly at risk. This is why it's perfectly natural to hold opposing feelings simultaneously.

In fact, working through this type of conflict means that contradictory emotions do not have to cancel each other out. Being in a love relationship is a dynamic activity where there is always an inherent risk of being disappointed, frustrated, or hurt (angry). In some ways your relationship is a car, and you and your partner are both driving it at the same time. There will be times where you love the way your partner drives, and there will be times when you won't. Sometimes, you'll wish that you could be the only driver. Having these thoughts doesn't mean that you are "out of love," it just means that you have conflicting thoughts, or are ambivalent, about your partner in real time.

Iconic couples therapist Esther Perel states, "Love rests on two pillars: surrender and autonomy. Our need for togetherness exists alongside our need for separateness."[3] Our own *pillars of love*—vulnerability, empathy, intimacy, and emotional investment—exist along such a continuum and delicate balance of togetherness and separateness. There are all sorts of scenarios where we move both closer to and farther away from actual intimacy or some approximation of it with each other. The first involves seeing the other IRL—in real life. The truth is, it's highly unlikely that anyone will ever find an absolutely perfect match (as many are now saying in reference to such popular dating sites like Match.com). We can't be absolutely crazy about someone, warts and all, all the time. But because we have been led to believe that love is all or nothing, the ambivalence that comes from seeing all sides of the one we love has to be navigated if we are to let someone into our hearts.

For instance, our client Tony came to see us because he wanted to fix his marriage. It's the second time he and his wife have been separated, and Tony told us, "Back when I was in my twenties, I never had a relationship that went longer than three months. Now I'm married for five years. I love my wife, but I'm feeling stuck." We pointed out to Tony that when he was younger, he was using his ambivalence as an off-ramp: he would end a relationship every time the honeymoon period ended. His hesitation to commit was actually his way of protecting himself from making the transition from honeymoon to everyday existence, which requires accepting lots of disappointment. Now that he was married, he was again trying to use his ambivalence about his wife in the same way. His only answer for having conflicting feelings about his wife were to categorize them as "feeling stuck again," and wanting to move on.

A second scenario for ambivalence arises during an external conflict when your partner is threatening to become even more significant to you than you were prepared for. That is, *If I let you in you might become so important to me that being with you might be truly and positively transformational and therefore, very risky.* This thought can be paralyzing, resulting in a hesitation or an inability to engage. It may feel like a state of endless procrastination. You may feel like you have no choice but to keep postponing interactions and take no action for resolving conflicts. In ambivalence you may think, I excuse my

3.   Esther Perel, *Mating in Captivity: Unlocking Erotic Intelligence* (New York: Harper, 2006), 25.

presence. I tell myself, something's wrong here. It's not you, it's me. I'm not here enough. I don't love you.

While becoming a better version of yourself might sound like a good idea, it comes with a downside: I might not recognize or like the new me. After all, there is nothing more frightening than going into something as a known quantity—I am me, I am exactly this self who I know and am familiar with—and, once there, being transformed in ways that are way beyond your control. Ambivalence then becomes the perfect defense against the immensity and uncertainty of the transformative process that love inevitably and inexorably is.

The Conflicts: What Are We Rupturing About?

We have identified twelve categories of conflicts within relationships. When the real-life aspects of these categories are going well, they inevitably make a relationship stronger. However, when there is an imbalance of power, a transition, an outside stressor, a secret unveiled, or even an internal conflict that becomes triggered within any of these categories, it can lead to a really powerful rupture. All of the following types of conflicts have the ability to manifest uncomfortable and vulnerable feelings, including some element of fear. In the recovery literature there's a saying: "There's only two fears: the first is that you won't get something you want. The second is that you'll lose something you have."[4]

Below is a list of major problem areas that couples state are responsible for not only ruptures, but when left unaddressed, can lead to the disintegration of the relationship. And while these are the most common reasons why people fight, don't worry if you don't see your issues on this list: there are plenty more. Relationships are formed as a voluntary unit; they can fall apart any time. And you can't get to the bottom line of insecurity and the accompanying fear and anxiety unless you are willing to address *your* contribution to both what *is* and what *is not* working in your relationship. This means that by acknowledging and making use of the two rules, you can figure out how you

---

4. *Twelve Steps and Twelve Traditions* (New York: Alcoholics Anonymous World Services, 1952), 76.

are contributing to the problems and conflict in your relationships, and then contribute to their resolution.

Money

Money—shocker!—is the number one stated reason couples give when asked, "Why did you divorce?" It's a tricky (that is, complicated) issue because, like the path to divorce itself, it is fraught with all of the confusing complexity that is par for the course in long-term love. Money is a primary source of security. It is the source of what we mean when we talk about socio-economic status (SES). Therefore, the problems that it can usher in are far-reaching, complex, and sometimes even contradictory.

The spectrum of money problems includes but is not limited to: too little money in the relationship, too much money in the relationship, one partner withholding money from the other, one partner spending more money than they have (or the other is comfortable spending), living above their lifestyle, living in too much austerity (or not enough), too much saving for the future, not enough saving for the future. Money is also a powerful tool for attaining and maintaining power—when we withhold money, we also withhold honesty, trust, and sense of security, we rupture the relationship.

Kelly and Jim have been married for five years. Jim lost a job about a year ago due to a company-wide layoff. Kelly felt anxious and fearful regarding her relatively new role as the family's solo earner. Immediately after the layoff, Kelly asked Jim to look for a new job. However, Jim didn't see the need to rush back to work since they had a significant amount of savings. Kelly saw the situation in a different light: for her it was not a fear of scarcity; she really appreciated when both of them were making money and contributing. Being the solo earner made her feel insecure and pressured. Jim could not understand Kelly's demand and thought she was being difficult.

Sex

Money and sex are often the two categories of conflicts that couples entering a relationship are totally unprepared to resolve because both are taboo subjects that parents do not communicate and model appropriate behavior directly to their children. It's as if we are walking into adulthood with an empty dictionary of what a discussion that includes these two most intimate topics should—or could—look like. When it comes to sex, everyone is making it up as they go—traversing into these anxiety-provoking areas of long-term love without a road map for doing so.

Sex problems can tap into core areas of emotional security (and lack thereof). These are internal conflicts that expose us to a risk of rejection. This can also include all the ways that sexual desire expresses itself in relationship that are both spoken and unspoken. The conscious expressions *what I want, how often I want it* are often fraught with histories of shame—societal, cultural, familial, and especially religious—that make it difficult, if not impossible, to actually articulate these desires.[5] This in and of itself can be a cause for a rupture. As sexuality educator, Emily Nagoski, says in her book *Come As You Are*, on the one hand, we police sex too much judging its "rightness" and its "wrongness," and expounding on how dangerous it is (pregnancy, STDs, crime—rape, etc.).[6] On the other, we get about zero useful education about actual sexual intimacy and achieving sexual pleasure.

Kim and Daniel have been together for ten years. Kim is in her mid-fifties, is five years older than Daniel, and recently started having pronounced menopausal symptoms that have not only made sex uncomfortable but also influences the way she feels about her own body. In short, Kim wasn't really feeling like having sex. However, Daniel felt rejected, despite Kim's explaining thoroughly about why she cannot bring herself to have sex with Daniel. Yet without the closeness that sex brought, Daniel began feeling distant from Kim, which led them to have more arguments and fights.

Many couples can sustain sexual intimacy over time, but some couples lose their sexual connection during the course of a long-term relationship. Some talk to each other and come to some understanding as to why they are not having sex like they used to. For example, men, as early as their fifties,

5. Suzanne Iasenza, *Transforming Sexual Narratives: A Relational Approach to Sex Therapy* (New York: Routledge, 2020), 47–67.
6. Emily Nagoski, *Come As You Are: The Surprising New Science That Will Transform Your Sex Life* (New York: Simon & Schuster, 2015), 16–17.

can develop erectile dysfunction (ED) and have other physical ailments that can limit their ability to achieve erections. According to the renowned sex therapist, Suzanne Iasenza, in a supportive relationship, the couple can discuss their physical limitations, seek appropriate medical treatment, and revise their sex menus so that they can resume and enjoy other forms of sexual intimacy.[7]

Two Worlds of Sex Collide

People in relationships experience sex—the very sex they are having with the same person over and over—differently. People can have differing levels of pleasure, different sense of closeness, intimacy, and emotional connection (vs. uncomfortable experience) that can result in someone wanting a lot of it and another who does not. If we're not communicating about sex, it is quite possible that the sex we're having with our partner is not the same sex they're having with us—as, without having an actual conversation, there is simply no way to know how sex is being experienced by our partner.

Infidelity

Some couples may stop having sex together for a variety of reasons: physical discomfort, waning libido, or because they are not getting along or not communicating. Some couples who got married to their high school sweethearts may never have had a chance to date other people. As a result, one partner may "outsource" their sexual desire, as one of our clients said, to another person outside of the marriage. Infidelity also comes in different forms, including emotional infidelity as well as sexual infidelity. Emotional infidelity is when one partner has a deep connection with someone outside their marriage, even if there is no sex involved.

---

7.   Suzanne Iasenza, *Transforming Sexual Narratives: A Relational Approach to Sex Therapy* (New York: Routledge, 2020), 60–77.

Jeff and Lisa had been married for a long time and, for many years, had drifted into a rather sex-free marriage. Whenever we broach the topic with them, each is convinced that "this is not our issue" because:

"Jeff doesn't need it, and I don't want it."

"Lisa hates it, and I can live without it."

However, upon further discussion, it became clear that Lisa could not bear to be sexual with Jeff after her second pregnancy (though neither of them easily recalled this), and Jeff could not bear to live without it and has been having numerous sexual and emotional trysts for years that were, finally (and this is why he initiated therapy) making him feel hatred—not for Lisa, but—for himself.

Parenting Styles

There are stereotypes that go along with what is considered good parenting and bad parenting, and these seem to shift according to which generation and culture we both belong to and are influenced by. A spectrum of parenting in the last generations runs from the current concern over so-called "helicopter parenting" all the way to the now largely outdated—and, for some, inconceivable—"latch-key kid" approach. Most parents fall somewhere in between these two extremes, but differences in parenting styles do not need to be wildly disparate to create immense, chronic and, at times, seemingly irreconcilable conflicts.

One of the reasons conflicts surrounding parenting can be so difficult is because our parents were, up to a certain point, our only role models of how parenting should be, and it either worked for us, or it didn't. Either way, we developed a model from how parenting should be, either in compliance or defiance of how good parents should act in addition to the cultural/generational trends in parenting. This being the case, it is easy for each person in a relationship to get stuck in a profound and convincing sense of being right (and righteous) about their parenting style. And, we will see throughout this book, there are few things more dangerous to successful conflict resolution than being right and especially righteousness.

Joe and Sam came to see us because they were constantly bickering over how to support each other when either one of them was "blowing their lid" at the kids. They both came from homes where loud, argumentative fighting was the status quo and had agreed that this behavior would be a "deal-breaker" in their relationship. They were aware of how their tumultuous upbringings could likely impact their parenting, so they agreed upon a plan for the moments when either one of them were escalating when it came to disciplining their kids. It seemed like a great idea: If you think that I'm losing it, you can tap in, suggest that I take a break, and take over for me until I can cool off.

We agreed, this seemed like a good idea. Yet it didn't work. During the first "intervention" everything seemed okay—Joe was losing it, Sam tapped in. Sam, being cool-headed at the time, was able to set limits with their older kid, implement what seemed like a fair consequence, and resume his day. But the next time when Sam lost it and Joe stepped in, Sam, without any clear or immediate understanding of what happened, felt "undercut" and "superseded"; he felt like he was being scolded and he attacked both Joe and the kid, who was now even more confused than before. In turn, Joe counterattacked, and it got ugly. In the end, it was their children who felt like they had to step in to try to calm their parents, which is a less than ideal position to put your kids in.

Work

Work has been put on the same level as love by psychoanalysis. Per Freud's own psychoanalytic theory, the most important and significant dynamic issues, patterns, and problems in our life are going to play themselves out in the vast realms of "work and love." So it shouldn't be shocking that we often find the same dynamics that are causing heartache at home (in "love") can be seen/ felt/experienced in our work lives. Issues related to employment, career, being an employee, being an employer, being self-employed, dealing with peers, colleagues, direct-reports, authority (and lack thereof) are all likely to occur throughout our lifelong relationship to, with, and in work.

All of these are one person's internal conflicts, not ruptures. However, the spectrum of work issues causing problems in relationship is equally vast. Too much, too little is the simplest way of stating the continuum, but within this spectrum exist all kinds of issues that tap into our feelings of self-esteem and efficacy, as well as social issues such as a sense of camaraderie, fellowship and community and, often supremely significant, issues of using work to avoid other anxiety-provoking experiences such as the intimacy of everyday life with our partner.

Kumiko worked in consulting for the last two decades and has finally achieved her career goal of becoming a partner at her firm. Yet the timing of this most anticipated promotion was a bit rough on her as she and her husband Jason—a freelance ad writer—have three young children. Kumiko has always struggled with "workaholism," and agreed to monitor her obsessive and compulsive behaviors regarding her new role, including leaving hours open in her schedule on the weekends to spend with her family. However, almost immediately after obtaining this role, Kumiko found herself in an abusive relationship with a senior member of the board of directors and quit.

Though now, Kumiko has "all the time in the world" to spend with her family, it has become apparent that she was using work to shore her up against her fear of being emotionally close to others. Kumiko's anxiety about spending "too much time" with her husband and kids started taking the form of incessant micromanagement. After all these years of caring for their kids as the primary caretaker, Jason was beginning to feel incompetent and, frankly, pissed off.

The In-Laws

Sometimes our clients are surprised when we tell them that the in-law issue is on the top five list of reasons people state when asked why they divorced. Yet we can see that in-law issues are similar to issues in parenting, in that it taps into our earlier experience of "environment," only this time—instead of a largely unconscious influence—the influence can be painfully and overwhelmingly direct. In-law issues are trickier than some of the other conflicts because they affect both the couple and their parents: you and/or/both your partner can be hurt or angry when an in-law conflict arises and so can the in-law themselves. And you and/or your partner can have trouble (dislike, even hate) with your partner's family members, *and* those family members can also "have trouble" with you. Couples who can agree where and when to draw boundaries with in-laws are the most successful. The conflict arises when this agreement cannot be met, especially when one partner takes the side of their parent over their mate.

Like other problem/conflict issues, the spectrum can stretch from too little (time, attention, involvement, connection) to too much, from my in-laws have moved in to take care of the kids, to my parents don't talk to my spouse. In-law issues often include in-laws not respecting the parents' wishes, boundaries, and rules. In-law issues often overlap with other issues, such as how in-laws believe their grandchildren should be raised; what race, economic status, and religion are acceptable; and other biased—and sometimes bigoted—values that are often insidiously perpetrated against the couple itself.

Many times, ruptures on the in-law front occur quite innocently. For instance, Josh and Tammy told us of a long-term agreement with the husband's parents to *never* discuss politics or religion. All went well for years until one morning Tammy brought up "blue zones," the places on the planet where numbers of people are living beyond 100 years. Her mother in-law said, "Well, that's not new, the Bible tells us of people—like Methuselah—who lived hundreds of years." Tammy, not being from a Christian background, had not heard this story before and giggled. In that moment, Josh could sense something in their marriage breaking apart. Sure enough, when he came out of the shower after dinner, his parents had cornered Tammy and were lecturing her with their thick book of Christian anthropology to back up their defense of Methuselah himself. Needless to say, this created a great rift between this couple and the husband's parents. This was an example of boundary breach.

Developing and maintaining relationships with in-laws takes time and effort from both people in a relationship. Having explicit agreements and understanding with your spouse helps immensely when you interact with your in-laws. For example, you and your partner can decide how many days comprise the right length of stay during holidays. With this agreement and understanding you can create good boundaries between your relationship and your in-laws.

Addiction (alcohol, drugs, porn, food, etc.)

Within the world of addiction treatment and recovery, it is taken as a truism that the opposite of addiction is connection—human, emotional connection. Addiction ushers in—whether we are consciously aware of it or not—a state of self-sufficiency in the addict that in turn results in both people within a couple feeling/being disconnected from each other and themselves. There are obvious and overtly destructive aspects of addiction about which libraries have been filled, but the more insidious ways that addiction builds walls against vulnerability, empathy, intimacy, and emotional investment are sometimes lost in less clearly destructive forms of habit, including obsessive and compulsive behaviors.

Many of the addictions that couples face as problems in their relationship are yay or nay addictions, as in, you do or do *not* do it (drink alcohol, use other drugs, smoke, etc.). But many others require a decision about what constitutes "sobriety" or "abstinence"—like food, sex, work, and ways of establishing boundaries in relationships. The continuum of behaviors and actions that are experienced as "sober" often become part of an implicit, or even explicit, agreement in a couple. Even the yays (I'm using) and the nays (I'm not) of addiction often become part of larger discussions that are not just about the addictive substance itself but also about personality characteristics and associated (destructive, distancing) behaviors. Therefore, ruptures that occur in addiction—which is often referred to as a family disease because of how it affects everyone involved—are sometimes shocking because they keep happening well after the substance abuser or addict has finally abstained from their addiction behavior. In fact, it is often the case that more destructive and emotionally distancing behaviors can begin to appear after the veil of addiction is lifted.

Though it drove him nuts for months, Don decided rather than to fight his teenage son's budding "gaming addiction," he would join him—with his wife's approval. *At first.* However, being someone who had been sober from alcohol and other drugs for a number of years might have been a tell-tale sign that such an "intervention" for their kid might not have been the most prudent decision and, in fact, might have been—as it turned out to be—a slippery slope. Unfortunately, this led them back to the kind of emotional disconnect that came so close to destroying their marriage when Don was actively involved with alcohol and other drugs and brought this couple right back to the same challenges they thought they'd recovered from some years before. Soon, it was unclear who was the bigger gaming addict: Don or their kid.

Quality Time/Emotional Intimacy

"Quality time" is a euphemism for a finite resource that is often highly conflicted. Many adults in relationships both want and don't want to spend time in each other's presence with the primary purpose being *me getting to know you, and you getting to know me.* The concomitant hope and dread are that as you get to know the "real me," you will find out what is "wrong" with me, with the silver lining that if you accept the real me then I will feel accepted as I actually am, warts and all. Avoiding spending quality time with each other is in fact a strategy by which we (often accidentally) protect ourselves from the intimacy we (think we) want and need from long-term love. On the end of the spectrum, focusing solely on spending quality time with each other can lead to a state of symbiosis, which can isolate us from establishing and maintaining a healthy social life and sense of self. Ironically, the fighting continues because there are no boundaries between you and your partner, and the risk of conflict is high.

Couples are also balancing their individual needs for both solitude and quality time together. We all need to make time for ourselves and our own interest as well as having time with our partners. However, the degree to which one wants solitude is unique to the individual. One partner can feel neglected when the other is spending too much time alone. One common complaint we hear is, "My partner loves to spend time streaming the *du jour* TV series! And not with me!"

The spectrum of conflicts here runs from spending too much time together—and making sure to plan this into our lives—to being so "busy" that we avoid each other (and the less attractive parts of ourselves) altogether. For instance, Haruna once worked with a couple who were struggling to find time for each other. Richard and Theresa first met and fell in love in New York City, but when Theresa became pregnant, they decided to move to Seattle to be closer to her large, Vietnamese family. The couple quickly became overwhelmed by the demands of their new life, which now was solely focused on Theresa's family as they didn't have a network of friends to rely on. A new baby also meant they didn't have lots of free time for each other. Theresa felt like her husband was not paying attention to her, while Richard thought his wife was becoming too involved with her extended family. Haruna was able to work with the couple to reveal that under these complaints, the real rupture was the loss of their old, pre-baby lives. Their move took them both away from the bond they had in New York and the dreams that brought them to New York in the first place.

Division of Labor (chores)

It has long been believed that there is a strong correlation between the sharing of chores and the frequency of sex in long-term romantic relationships—especially when these chores include childcare.[8] The spectrum here is relatively easy to detect as it often goes from shared somewhat to shared *not at all*, and rarely, shared *equally*. We still see the division of labor in the household is heavily skewed in the direction of women doing the heavy lifting when it comes to chores (such as dishes, laundry, and a variety of childcare responsibilities). And this construct remains true even when women are working—including when they are working full-time. So the spectrum of none, some, and equal is extremely relevant, and it makes sense that they highly influence, whether we are consciously aware of it or not, the willingness and desire to share other *intimate* areas of our lives together, such as sex. Yet if this rule was so obviously true, you would think that men would step up and help out. Perhaps if men were aware of this clear line they would be fighting to get a chance to do the dishes every night. A solid division of labor, where two people are sharing chores somewhat equally (at least they feel like they share the responsibility of their domestic chores/things), creates a sense of teamwork. And of course, it also leads to the overall feeling of *I don't have to figure this out on my own. I can*

---

8.   E. A. Harris, A. M. Gormezano, S. M. van Anders, "Gender Inequities in Household Labor Predict Lower Sexual Desire in Women Partnered with Men," *Archives of Sexual Behavior*, 2022 Nov. 51 (2022): 3847–870.

talk to my partner about this. This significantly helps to prevent one partner feeling overburdened or isolated.

For instance, Brad and Jolene never even thought about their division of labor during their wild and amazing (and extended—to nearly two years) "honeymoon" period. When Jolene became pregnant, she moved into Brad's apartment and although they weren't yet married, they were both equally thrilled at the prospect of sharing parenthood. That is, until Jolene faced the startling realization that, though she is a full-time nurse at a local hospital, Brad seems to have lost his ability to share in the chores of taking care of *his own* apartment. Not surprisingly, their sex life fell right off the cliff. Two years and many heated fights and frustrations later, their sex life had not resumed. While it was blamed initially on the pregnancy and then on the post-pregnancy period, Jolene's smoldering resentment seems to tell a more important tale about the division of labor.

Vacationing

When you are on vacation, you are in unfamiliar territory. So what you end up with is often an elevated level of anxiety and lots of transitions (you might transition to another time zone, language, location, and daily rhythm). For example, in the Caribbean islands, the pace of life is a lot slower than New York. When Alison and David went to Barbados with their two-year-old son, they spent the entire time fighting. Alison felt uneasy every time they had to drive on the "other" side of the road. David was cranky; he could not sleep well since the air conditioner in their room made loud noises and kept waking up him and their son.

And vacations are often burdened with that killer of human happiness: unrealistic expectations! The spectrum of issues/problems related to vacations run from "we don't have enough of them" (often because of finances, work conflicts, etc.) to "when we have them, we find out that they don't go so well." The don't-go-so-well vacation issues often relate, like issues related to retirement and quality time, to how effective we are at avoiding each other in our daily lives and how challenging it *actually* is to simply be *with* one another.

Katya and Melanie send message after message to each other with links to various vacation sites and activities available when they—with their two school kids—get to wherever it is that they are going to travel. They share every detail. They make sure that each agrees on all aspects of vacation planning. They put great efforts into doing so because their vacations often go haywire as soon as they land. And while it can seem like there is a sense of *mutuality* and *collaboration* to their planning, their vacations often result in periods of fighting, sulking, and refusals to participate by both of them.

Fluctuations in Power Dynamics

Power is among the dynamics in long-term love that does not *ever* resolve because power is constantly shifting in *all* relationships. Power dynamics can revolve around money: if one partner brings significantly more money into the household, they might feel entitled to make financial decisions (investment, saving, spending, vacationing, and education). They can also include emotional power dynamics. One partner can put the other "in their place" if they criticize their domestic life, and the recipient might end up feeling very small at home.

The spectrum of conflicts generally runs from one person who has what we call *felt, experienced, acknowledged,* and *ostensibly accepted superior power,* and the other not so much. That dynamic, however, is never stable and power plays tend to be constant. Subtle power moves—as minor as withholding a returned "I love you" when the other is walking out the door—can disrupt the security one experiences. So, the issues of greater power, no power, shared power, equal power, and many others are in a state of constant flux that, in and of itself, can cause all kind of problems, especially when the power dynamics are "supposed" to conform to stereotypes about our identities, roles, occupational status, incomes, etc.

Stan was laid off from his law firm just as his husband Roberto began to obtain more clients in his landscaping business. Roberto had been a self-proclaimed "house husband"—staying home to care for their child. But as the kid's school schedule began to leave more and more room for Roberto, he began taking his hobby, gardening, more seriously. A few years later, this hobby had become a business and Stan has "quite out of the blue" found himself envious, acting out his newfound sense of inferiority by withholding sex from his husband.

Cross-Cultural Miscommunication

The spectrum of problems that occurs in the realm of cross-cultural miscommunication is diverse and sprawling. Some include an awareness and acknowledgment of our various cultures' influences and effects, and a disavowal of said influence and impact. To make these conflicts more complicated, most of us have a less-than-clear awareness of how we are affected by the numerous cultural identifications—and ways that those are modeled and internalized—that we carry into our relationships.

For instance, Wendy grew up in New York City's Chinatown, the daughter of Chinese immigrants. Her parents encouraged her and her brother to assimilate as thoroughly as possible, which included abandoning her parents' Chinese language and her actual name: Jinting. When she met and fell in love with Juan (whose parents were originally from Puerto Rico) in high school, she was, to Juan and everyone else in her life, Wendy. But Jinting always hated the name Wendy, as it felt like a betrayal and abandonment of her culture. Some years into her marriage to Juan, she wanted—needed—to be referred to as Jinting.

Juan was struggling to understand and accept his wife's shift in thinking, even though he drew great pride in the fact that his own parents were committed to their cultural heritage—sharing their cultural identities (beginning with giving him a culturally consistent name) and language. When Jinting became pregnant and expressed the desire to give their baby a Chinese name, Juan was not on board. Needless to say, the collision of these two different cultures ended in conflict.

Conflicts related to cross-cultural issues happen not only between two apparent culture differences like above, but also within what seems to be a singular cultural experience. We have seen that no matter how similar we seem—and are—along lines of race, religion, socio-economic status, nationality, and even neighborhood (among others), we all grow up in different families. Linda grew up in a family where being frugal and saving money was the way to take care of oneself. Gabby grew up in the same town and the same religion and went to the same schools as Linda, but in her family the way to make money for the future was to invest. In this couple, there is a definite cross-cultural issue regarding how they spend and save. They argue because each of them learned a very different approach toward money.

Conflicts as Communication

The above-mentioned list are problems that are imperative areas for couples to be aware of, it is also crucial to know that conflicts themselves are not the only reasons why couples rupture. Some behaviors and communication styles are, without question, destructive to relationships. It is vital that we understand some common communication pitfalls that couples face *in real life*. According to Julie and John Gottman, "The Four Horsemen of the Apocalypse"[9] are behaviors that, if they occur regularly, are good predictors of either a failed or a terminally unhappy relationship.

1. **Criticism.** Criticism attacks the mate's character or personality. Here is an example of the difference between a complaint and criticism: *Complaint*: "There is no gas in the car. I'm aggravated that you didn't fill it up like you said you would." *Criticism*: "You never remember anything! You can't be counted on!"

2. **Contempt**. Contempt is a set of behaviors that communicate *disgust*. It includes sneering, sarcasm, name-calling, eye rolling, mockery, hostile humor, and condescension.

3. **Defensiveness**. These behaviors convey the message, *The problem is not me. It's you.* From this position you imply that because your partner threw the first stone, they are responsible for the entire conflict. You avoid taking responsibility for your own behavior by pointing to something they did *prior* to their complaint about you. You do not acknowledge that which is true in what they are saying about your behavior.

4. **Stonewalling**. In relationships where intense arguments break out suddenly, and where criticism and contempt lead to defensiveness, eventually one partner tunes out. This is the beginning of stonewalling. The stonewaller acts as if he (research indicates that 85 percent of stonewallers in marriages are husbands) couldn't care less about what the partner is saying or doing. He turns away from conflict

---

9.   John M. Gottman and Julie S. Gottman, "Gottman Couple Therapy." In A. S. Gurman, J. L. Lebow, and D. K. Snyder (Eds.), *Clinical Handbook of Couple Therapy* (New York: The Guilford Press, 2015), 129–57.

and from the relationship. According to the research conducted by the Gottman Institute, stonewalling can end a marriage if you do it consistently enough. When one partner stonewalls the other, it breaks the core nature of relationship, but also it makes it painful or impossible for the other to stay in the relationship. This is because relationships provide maximum homeostasis when inhabited by two not one. In the next chapter, you'll also learn that stonewalling is the same as a freeze-out, where two people in conflict just stops talking to the other as a punishment.

The Opportunity Ruptures Present: Repair

When we are in conflict, our relationships can be repaired. In fact, conflict resolution leads to the process of rupture and repair. The work that couples put into getting back on track is the key ingredient for empathy, reciprocity, and empowerment: the factors necessary for a successful, intimate relationship. It is the act of repair itself that is empowering—and allows couples to begin to develop trust that they can and will survive the vicissitudes of everyday life.

Every repair is a chance to develop a more secure attachment with each other and is an opportunity to develop a working faith that relationships that fall apart can be put back together—the whole process is, in fact, a *love-crash rehab*. This is often a shocking realization because so many of us have been taught and shown that conflict is unhealthy, destructive, and ought to be avoided at all costs. When in fact, conflict and its resolution is an essential ingredient for healthy relationships. Our model of conflict resolution is essentially *relationship health by a thousand repairs*.

Before our clients understand the process, they often look at their situation more pessimistically, with a rather high degree of criticism of themselves, their partners, and their relationship. They often tell us, "We rupture, but we don't repair." Our response is always the same: "If you're still with your partner, there's been some kind of repair. However, it's not terribly conscious or obvious because you aren't able to make use of the repair very well . . . yet. Or, you have other ruptures you have not been able to repair and feel stuck."

We tell our patients they cannot avoid ruptures and in fact, they need to welcome them if they are ever going to be able to experience true intimacy in their relationship. Many of our clients believe they want intimacy, only to discover that they have been working against this goal throughout their relationship and have been distancing themselves from their conflict and rupture. In the psychoanalytic model, the question about desire—*what do you want?*—is meant to uncover the psychological defenses against the anxiety associated with how unacceptable our true wants and needs can seem. Much of the original intention of psychoanalysis had to do with becoming aware of what we really want and gaining insight into the various ways we unintentionally protect ourselves from this awareness. These defenses include repression, suppression, dissociation, displacement, etc. The purpose of our psychological defense system is to protect us from being overwhelmed by our emotions (anxiety, especially). However, our psychological defenses do so by protecting us from our *awareness* of painful, scary, and uncomfortable feelings but not from the effects or influence of those emotions.

The new psychoanalytic question is *what's it for?* In our case, the "it" we're investigating is conflict. This new question helps us understand how we are in conflict in ways that may not be immediately clear to us. For instance, with or without realizing it, some couples might be using arguing to connect, but if they aren't aware of the defensive purpose of their actions, they can easily slip into the roles of enemies. In this case, they are using conflict to protect themselves from achieving a deeper intimacy with each other. You might use rupture as an opportunity to repair but end up criticizing your partner to make you feel superior or to make a point. In other words, this misuse of conflict is keeping you safe, but the outcome is that you are (unintentionally) isolated.

An attachment theory approach to repair is slightly different. Clinical psychologist Sue Johnson states that most conflicts are really protests over emotional disconnection.[10] If you are fighting to reconnect or reestablish your emotional connection with your partner, the conflict is not a sign that

---

10. Sue Johnson, *Hold Me Tight: Seven Conversations for a Lifetime of Love* (Boston: Little, Brown Spark, 2008), 45–47.

your relationship is in jeopardy. It is actually a healthy sign that you and your partner are both willing to protest against the disconnection.

Johnson believes the bond between two partners is intuitive and not always obvious. And the bond can become fragile and delicate at the time of conflict. For example, it is impossible to meet your partner's needs and wants all of the time. And there comes a time in every relationship when you need to say to your partner: "Honestly, I cannot." When this happens, both of you understand that one is disappointing and/or hurting the other, and that disappointments, rejections, and misunderstandings are inevitable in every relationship. And this is good news because every such incident and experience are opportunities to work together to accept and repair and also learn to negotiate with each other. In so doing, you are increasingly accepting your partner with all their imperfections. This for us is the path of true love.

The First Step to Repair: What's Already Working

Counterintuitively, we believe the first step to repair is to identify what is working in a relationship even before we show couples how to resolve their rupture. We're often so focused on our problems and are hyperaware about our issues that we can't see the real strengths we have already developed. Though our challenge throughout the book is to keep the focus on ourselves, once we get a sense of our contributions to what works in our relationship, it can become *safer* to affirm our partner's constructive contributions to the relationship. Our two rules, the conflict resolution, makes room for a shared sense of safety within so that we can more clearly see our partner's assets. Then, we can *safely* share what we like about each other, how we appreciate each other, or how we solve other problems together. In this way we can discover willingness, areas of self-esteem and empowerment as well as a deeper gratitude toward each other.

Asset mapping is a key component of constructive self-analysis. It identifies what's going on right and how we can use our best traits in the process of repair.

Exercise: List Your Attributes with Asset Mapping

Let's consider the many positive qualities you as individuals possess. Be generous as to how you are loving, caring, trustworthy, and even loveable. These personal and relationship assets will form the building blocks for all the work you will do in this book.

Partner A Example: I have a good sense of humor.

1. I _____

_____

2. I _____

_____

3. I _____

_____

Partner B Example: I am good at reaching out to my partner.

1. I _____

_____

2. I _____

_____

3. I _____

_____

Taking Inventory

In the recovery model, *taking inventory* is how one learns about, accepts, and eventually corrects behaviors that may not serve them. It's Step Four of the famous Twelve Steps: "Made a searching and fearless moral inventory of ourselves."

Inventory is where we account for our contribution to whatever problems, issues, or conflicts we are having so that we can cease the destructive behavior. It also involves seeing all the ways you are doing well in the world. Inventory asks you to look in the mirror, see how your positive attributes mitigate the less savory ones, and weigh for yourself the net results. The truth is, we are all more than the sum of our least attractive character attributes.

Exercise: Taking Inventory #1: Your Asset Inventory

Each partner can create an asset inventory. Record your own assets as they pertain to each category of relationship behaviors. Later, you will work together to see what assets you have as a couple that pertain to these questions.

Alliance: In what ways have I used my assets to be a better partner?
Example: I use my planning skills to organize events with my partner and children.

Partner A: _____

Partner B: _____

Commitment: How have I taken responsibility for my part in each conflict in this relationship?
Example: I take responsibility for my part in conflicts by admitting and apologizing.

Partner A: _____

Partner B: _____

Willingness to be Open and Honest: In what ways have I been willing—open, accurate, and honest—with my partner?
Example: We have a joint bank account: we are honest with each other when it comes to money.

Partner A: _____

Partner B: _____

Availability: How have I been available to my partner and sought to share an intimate connection?
Example: I am a good listener. I listen to my partner often.

Partner A: _____

Partner B: _____

Meeting Needs: In what ways do I let myself be nurtured by my partner? How do I contribute to my own health and well-being? Am I willing to ask for help and accept help?
Example: I ask my partner to give me a short back massage, periodically.

Partner A: _____

Partner B: _____

Decision-Making: What decisions have I made that take my partner's opinions into account?
Example: When our child asks for an extended curfew, I asked my partner for their opinion before I tell our child what we decided.

Partner A: _____

Partner B: _____

Emotional Openness: How and when am I able to share my feelings with my partner? How do I listen to my partner when they are sharing feelings?

Example: I listen to my partner half-heartedly. I talk to him when we are busy with our chores. No eye contact. No sitting down. I am usually at the kitchen getting dinner ready. My partner is also busy.

Partner A: _____

Partner B: _____

Following Through: What resources allow me to resolve unfinished business and follow through on commitments I've made with my partner? Example: I don't follow up on the issues that we discussed. So the same issues get resurfaced because I'm not changing my behavior.

Partner A: _____

Partner B: _____

What's Next

You will see how our PACER model can be used during rupture and repair as an opportunity to heal old wounds, including relationships with your family of origin, past romantic relationships, your community, and even your world.

First, we need to look at the ways you typically respond to ruptures and discover if your behaviors are serving you and your relationship. Now that you know conflicts will come up, remember that in order to get from rupture to repair you have to respond appropriately and not rely on old habits or reactionary modes.

CHAPTER TWO

The Unhelpful Choices in the Arsenal: The Armor of Aggression, Emotional Color-Blindness, and Mismatch

It's one thing to know that ruptures exist; it's another to know what to do when they occur. One significant problem we see with our couples clients is that they do not know how to appropriately respond to conflict. And that's probably because we were never taught the truth: conflicts are inevitable in any marriage or a long-term intimate relationship, and nobody talks about how to handle them when they arise.

Whether or not we actually admit it, most of us are carrying a barely repressed sense that "good" relationships are supposed to have a happily-ever-after quality. There is no scenario in the literary canon where the Princess and the Prince start fighting as they are getting ready for the ball, or worse, at a dinner party in front of others. So when we find ourselves in a conflict, we don't have the tools to get us out. That means we are all making it up as we go along. If you've been lucky or had great role models as parents, you and your partner have found a way to reconcile conflicts and move on. Unfortunately, most of us have not been so lucky.

It turns out that successfully navigating conflicts is the best ways to ensure a feeling of safety within a relationship. It sounds counterintuitive, but because we are so vulnerable when we are in a relationship, we need to ensure ourselves that we do have a sense of safety, which in turn, allows us to be more vulnerable. This is why each person's sense of safety develops through a process of coming to rely upon their partner and partnership: a willingness from each person to take the emotional risk of revealing the things about ourselves that we may not like or are difficult to accept (by ourselves), and the willingness of the other to accept us as we are, warts and all.

If the relationship lacks this tacit agreement, then each person in the relationship turns to themselves to provide that sense of safety. To do this, they put on their defensive armor, which is the way they will present themselves when they feel threatened. We don't always know for sure that we're feeling unsafe or threatened, so many respond to every situation wearing their armor. In this chapter, we're going to determine together what your defensive strategies during conflicts have been and begin to undo them so that you can embrace the feeling of safety and use conflicts as a tool to help move your relationship forward. First, let's determine what type of relationship you are currently in and how you are either consciously, or unconsciously, addressing ruptures.

What's Your Relationship Type?

In the seminal book, *The Marriage Clinic: A Scientifically Based Marital Therapy*, John Gottman talks about three types of relationships and how each deal with conflict.[1] The first is *a good enough relationship*, where a couple stays together and can work out ruptures productively because they each have a high tolerance for conflict. The second is *a relationship that doesn't work*, where conflicts expose the rifts, and the couple eventually breaks up/divorces. We do not consider this second type of relationship to be worst-case scenario because

1.   John Gottman, *The Marriage Clinic: A Scientifically Based Marital Therapy* (New York: W. W. Norton, 1999), 24.

some ruptures cannot be repaired. Some relationships will not always work out for all kinds of valid reasons. Surrendering to this reality can be—though it doesn't feel like it at the time—a realistic acceptance of a fit that is anything but, a la Goldilocks, "just right."

The third type of relationship is the most devastating: *when individuals suffer through ruptures that don't ever repair, yet they stay together as a couple.* This type of relationship often features lots of blaming and criticism of the other, including interpretations of particular events that are not always accurate. However, individuals stick with their set of facts rather than resolve conflicts because:

1) This may have been how conflicts were modeled during childhood.
2) The blame game assigns the role of the scapegoat and insures that the other is blame-free.
3) We may not feel safe to acknowledge and admit our part in the problem because we believe that it will be used as ammunition against us.
4) Sometimes we feel the need to protect the other. Instead of engaging in conflicts, we put a band-aid on the problem. Ironically, this method inadvertently protects us from the very things we want from romantic relationship, including safety, if we do it chronically.
5) We may not believe that people can change, so we avoid conflicts and just keep going.

Any of these interpretations are based on each person's perception of their history as a couple, including the mountain of conflicts they could not resolve together. No matter what the reason, these ideas keep individuals from seeing what is going on in real life, in the moment. Worse, they never get to repair. If you don't attempt to repair when you rupture, then you are on the royal road to isolation—shored up by the so-called "bone-crushing juggernaut of self-sufficiency."[2] When we are either all give, all take, withhold, or refuse to

---

2.   *Twelve Steps and Twelve Traditions,* (New York: AA World Services, Inc.), 37.

accept what the other has to offer during conflict, we cut off ourselves from each other, even when we are not intending to.

It is extraordinarily easy to slip into a relationship pattern that leaves us unaware of how isolated we are from each other. This is because love is a shock to the system, a left hook to our homeostasis! When conflict happens, it stings significantly more because your partner and your relationship matter more to you than any other relationship. Tapping into our psychological defenses is one way that allows us to survive the mayhem, the chaos, the insecurity and, yes, the rabid, manic joy that love unleashes. The primary task of our mind is to keep us safe from being overwhelmed by emotion. Because our psychological defense system is built to protect us against the awareness of anxiety, fear, and pain, we often "protect" ourselves against the awareness of the ways we put our hearts at risk when we love each other. As a result, misunderstandings, resentments, and isolation grow so that when we do fight, we often have a vast emotional distance to traverse if we are going to actually reach each other. By using our PACER model, you will learn how to use each new conflict as a "call for help" from yourself or your partner, so that you can break out of your defensive armor and return to connecting emotionally—with each other and with yourself.

Relational Dynamics That Do Not Resolve

A second relationship typing system was developed by psychoanalyst Shelly Goldklank.[3] She believes, as we do, that there are a series of dynamics always at play within any relationship that never fully resolve:

- **In-Out:** This dynamic relates to an imbalance in each person's attention and availability in the relationship. This in-out dynamic exists along a continuum where on one end we are not attentive and available at all (distancing), where one person is either leaving or has left, to the other extreme where one is paying such acute attention to the other—and wants that attention reciprocated—that they feel

3.   Shelley Goldklank, "The Shoop Shoop Song: A Guide to Psychoanalytic-Systemic Couple Therapy," *Contemporary Psychoanalysis*, 45 (2009): 3–25.

as if they cannot exist nor function without the other. This dynamic will be constantly shifting and is the most difficult for our clients to grasp because most of us believe we are *either* in *or* out, based on our relationship status: (i.e., I've been married for five years, ergo I am *in*). Yet when couples think about their daily interaction styles and patterns, they begin to recognize that their presence, availability, and responses to their partner's needs and desires indicates what can actually be subtle or drastic fluctuations in the reality of their in-ness or out-ness.

- **Up-Down:** The Up-Down dynamic is about power. While the idea of relational power gets a bad rap, the truth is a couple's power equilibrium is always present and shifting. In fact, power itself is neither good nor bad. Who gets to make the big decisions, control the money, define what constitutes proper family functioning, and make education choices for children are all possible contexts for power imbalance in a relationship. Within relationships, the challenge is what we do with our power. Are you aware of how power plays out and impacts your relationship? Do you know what power you and your partner have in your relationship? Do you make big decisions without your partner? Do you wield it against the other? Do you share it with your partner? Do you notice when power shifts and how you try to regain your power?

- **Near-Far:** The near-far dynamic is a shifting relational pattern of intimacy. Intimacy occurs when we are comfortable enough to reveal the deeper aspects, elements, and experiences of ourselves to someone who really matters. The dynamics of intimacy, the *getting-to-know-you* and *you-getting-to-know-me* is at play throughout the life course of all relationships. And much of this intimacy occurs by simply living shoulder-to-shoulder with each other and, therefore, showing each other what could be distasteful (and embarrassing) parts of ourselves without the least bit of intention to do so. The good parts and the bad parts are what becomes the foundation for the couple to get to know—and accept—our "us"-ness.

Handling the Emotions of Conflict

We meet too many clients who get to adulthood without ever exploring how to appropriately handle their feelings of anxiety and frustration and pain within their most intimate relationships. There are many reasons for this, but in more cases than not the reason is straightforward and simple: "No one showed me how to do this." Even if you grew up in a stable home, every relationship is unique and so are the conflicts that occur within them. It's easy to see how a lack of information could be mistranslated into "It cannot be done; this relationship cannot be fixed," and that stance is where many of us start after a rupture.

A second reason is that romantic relationships will generate feelings of vulnerability, including anxiety, fear, and insecurity, whether or not you are in a conflict. These feelings make us feel out of sorts, which then makes it difficult for us to embrace our emotions, listen to another, and be present for each other. It is hard for anyone to acknowledge the fact that they consciously or unconsciously hurt their partner. What's more, feelings of anxiety and pain can complicate our response to a conflict because these feelings create a state of *preparation*—a kind of bracing—for a threat that may or may not actually come. Think for a moment about whatever it is you are worrying about right now. How likely it is that the worst-case scenario is the most likely outcome? Yet when we are stuck in a period of conflict for long enough and preparing ourselves for some calamity, we are inadvertently putting ourselves into a deeper state of anxiety, pain, and fear that then influences how we engage with our partner when that worry actually materializes. Often, we use the same preparation tactics—which is our defensive armor—for whatever issue arises. And now we know, issues will absolutely arise.

Anxiety will also occur anytime we put ourselves (our hearts) at risk: it is actually a signal that tells us we are invested in the relationship. When conflict occurs, our anxiety is telling us that "something (or someone) is *wrong*." Our mind does not function well in the midst of anxiety and tension, and sometimes it tells us that the only way to get rid of the uncomfortable feeling is to *get rid of the person—or situation* (i.e., relationship). This reaction can lead to what we call the *blame game*, where each person scapegoats the other and believes the other person is the cause of their pain and anxiety.

50

Or when we are faced with the anxiety and pain that arises from conflict, we go back to our same preparation strategies in order to defend ourselves psychologically and quiet these emotions. These tactics effectively diminish our conscious awareness of anxiety—specifically, avoiding conflict altogether. This strategy is directly related to how we come to misunderstand our feelings and choose to deal with them by not dealing with them. Rather than revealing exactly how we feel to each other, we hide our anxieties and pain at great cost and use our armor to both protect us and separate us from the very things we want: vulnerability, empathy, intimacy, and emotional investment.

Our defensive armor can manifest itself through the innumerable ways we avoid, distract, and dissociate from both conflict and our feelings, as if both are unequivocally bad. Without the willingness and ability to listen to and navigate our feelings, we wind up thinking our way through much of our lives—and loves. Shunting our feelings, especially anxiety, can lead to obsessive thinking that blocks the conscious experience of emotion but leaves us still under their influence. The problem is that we *cannot outthink our feelings* and, though we might be unaware of the influence of emotion (especially love!), it is still going to impact our behavior. In fact, the psychoanalytic definition of *acting out* is when overwhelming emotion is shunted into our thinking and then expressed in actions or behaviors (an obsessive-compulsive routine). That is, the acted out behavior allows us to bypass an awareness of our emotions often with unintended and sometimes destructive results. In this case, it is not that we are *not* feeling; it is that we are unaware of what we are feeling. And, when all we have to interpret our feelings is our *thinking*, we wind up missing out on crucial information about what is going on inside us in response to what is going on in our lives—especially our relationships. For instance, some people cannot ask their partner, "I want you to do this task for me" because it makes them feel vulnerable to having their wishes rejected. So instead, they may choose not to bring up the request. Yet avoiding our desires leads to avoiding the acceptance and awareness of the very feelings we need to connect with our partner—and each other.

Acting out is a likely response to the partner who is scaring you, hurting you, and making you feel vulnerable. The acting out of these emotions can seem like taking old behavior patterns and playing them out with a partner, such as withdrawing emotionally or physically or pretending that everything is okay. However, these behaviors are up for interpretations and/or misinterpretations by another. For instance, we recently met with Mike and Tina, who are in a part-time punk band together. Tina owns a place where the band practices, and Mike is a restaurant owner. Money has never been a topic for discussion because it seemed like they always had plenty of it. Then, during the pandemic, their financial situation changed, but neither knew how the other was suffering. Mike started worrying because his restaurant had been closed for a significant amount of time, yet he still was committed to paying his staff. He was wracked with fear and anxiety about money but didn't reveal the situation to his wife. Ironically, Tina owns a three-million-dollar property that they had been using for band practice and was secretly thinking of selling it, but she was afraid to discuss this with Mike because the band itself was so important to him. They both thought they were doing the relationship a favor by not talking about money. They weren't trying to hide this from each other, they both had relatively good intentions, but it ended in a rupture they couldn't repair on their own. Each was avoiding their own anxiety and fear associated with money in order to "protect" the other, but their strategy—conscious and unconscious elements—backfired when the stress of financial insecurity created a rupture. As much as any overt actions of aggression, accumulations of avoidance can hurt the relationship. Luckily, both were thoughtful enough to know they needed some help, which is why they came to see us together.

A couples therapist like Haruna would view this situation as directly connected to concurrent stressful and traumatic situations outside the couple's relationship that overwhelmed partners' coping mechanism and abruptly changed the shape of their relationship as a couple. In this case, Mike and Tina's conflict was tied directly to the pandemic: an unprecedented global situation they never experienced before and could never control.

A psychoanalyst like Mark would refer to both Mike and Tina's avoidance as a *dissociated feeling*. It occurs when someone has a feeling that's too overwhelming to actually experience, so it gets expressed in an action, and in this case, the action began as avoidance but erupted into a full-on fight. With our help, each was able to see their part in the conflict and work diligently to get to repair.

You may be able to identify your own strategies for dealing with your emotions during conflicts, and that in itself can be off-putting, as in "Oh no, not this again. I'm back in the same place where I end every relationship." For instance, Heidi and Bruce have been married for about five years. Heidi had a few long-term boyfriends before she met Bruce. With each of these boyfriends, whenever she felt insecure, she withdrew from them yet kept a façade of "everything is okay" until the boyfriend broke up with her for not being engaged in the relationship. With Bruce, she is repeating this defensive, self-protecting behavior pattern. Whenever she feels insecure, she works long hours at the office and intentionally comes home late. Recently, Heidi was annoyed that Bruce did not invite her to his company's holiday party. Yet she can't seem to tell Bruce why she is keeping her distance.

The Three Reactive States of Perceived Threat

It turns out that we indeed have a choice in the ways we deal with conflict. Yet time after time we see that couples together, or the individuals within couples, engage in one of three dynamics. The problem is none of them really get to repair or work as an improvement tool for their relationship. When conflict is productive it can lead to a repair that actually progresses the relationship to the point where couples can be intimate, show empathy, feel emotionally invested, and allow themselves to be vulnerable with each other. But more often than not, conflict ends up in defensiveness where no one is listening to each other. Over time, these strategies create a relationship in which two people are physically together, yet they're emotionally isolated from each other.

The typical reactions to ruptures are often "too hot" or "too cold," defined by either fighting incessantly (destruction) or avoiding conflict completely (distance). When our feelings and our responses to them, run too hot, we go immediately to level eleven over a level two issue because we're dragging around the baggage from all the other ruptures that we haven't repaired. Yet too cold doesn't mean we are handling the rupture well, either.

The fight, flight, or freeze (and now we even have *fawn*) response are the well-known reactions to stress that occurs when hormones like cortisol are released in your body. This sympathetic nervous system response dates back to when our ancestors came face-to-face with danger. We also know that emotions like anxiety, fear, pain, and insecurity are typically expressed in these same reactive states that can be both defensive and offensive. They are the knee-jerk reactions we have to protect ourselves from danger—real and/ or imagined. The difference between a reaction and a response is simple: in reaction we act then think; in response we think then act.

These reactive states help us categorize how we deal with the danger that is the emotional disconnection occurring during a rupture. The problem is when we go into any of these reactive states, we take the focus off our self, see our partner as the cause of the problem, and engage in the blame game. When we perceive our partner as the enemy, we tend to believe our relationship is also problematic. What's more, being in one of these reactive states prevents us from taking the opportunity to use the rupture for repair. The only way we can get to repair is if we focus on ourselves without judgment and with compassion.

You probably have a fairly good sense of which reactive state is your standard behavior, as well as your partner's. However, you may not realize why you react the way you do. You can move from one reactive state to another, and you can rapidly fluctuate between them. You can also wind up in a particular reactive state, depending on the conflict, without the least intention to do so. These reactive states will be profoundly affected by whatever state of safety you have achieved through internalization of your history of successfully (or not) navigating conflicts.

Fight/Overt Aggression

The fight response typically looks like overt aggression and is the most obvious reaction to a rupture: it's an attack and can run the gamut from yelling to physicality. When one lashes out at another, they are in effect putting on their hard armor of anger and aggression, covering up their feelings of vulnerability while sticking to their version of the blame game. If a conflict exists that is so overwhelming that both partners attack each other, the incident that caused them to fight in the first place gets buried and the situations morphs into a full-blown war, when all they can think about is winning the fight. "You are hurting me; I'm going to hurt you. I'm not leaving room for you to respond; I'm coming at you because you are coming at me."

Clinical psychologist Sue Johnson believes that we all have strong needs for attachment, starting with our family of origin and then ultimately transferring that attachment need to our intimate partner.[4] But when we are disconnected from our partner, we feel less safe, and we blame our partner for the disconnected, abandoned feelings we experience. The fighting itself is then symbolic of each person's experience of feeling disconnected, as each person is protesting against the loss of their secure attachment.

For some people, fighting with their partner comes naturally: they may have seen this behavior as something their parents did. Others may have had parents who existed within different reactive states and choose fighting in direct opposition to a cold distance they witnessed when their parents were in conflict.

One reactive state is certainly not better than another. All the reactive states are equally destructive, but at least when there is fighting, it is an easily recognizable call for help. But just because it's a call for help doesn't mean that either partner in a relationship can hear it.

Fight and Flight/Mismatch

The second pattern occurs when both partners are in different reactive states, and the conflict shuts down without any resolution. This ends in the flight response: when it becomes emotionally unbearable for both partners to continue the argument in their own reactive state, they each retreat—fly—by creating, and sustaining, a mismatch. On the surface, the temperature goes down and cools the friction generated from the conflict. However, underneath the seemingly cooled surface of the relationship, resentments continue to accumulate. In this reactive state, painful and scary emotions are dissociated, acted-out as distance and disconnection. They become checked out, involved in a distracting or distancing behavior, and they are not in the right mindset for repair. The pain remains hot, the fear intact—both acted out in elaborate

---

4. Sue Johnson, *Hold Me Tight: Seven Conversations for a Lifetime of Love* (Boston, MA: Little, Brown Spark, 2008), 113.

distancing maneuvers designed to avoid any emotional interaction regarding the issues that caused conflict.

This type of conflict is also referred to as *cat or mouse cycle* fighting. If one person wants to "talk it out" (fight), but the other avoids (flight), the second person may feel like they are being chased and forced to resolve the fight. This is equally frustrating and upsetting for both partners. Instead, our PACER model will help you avoid this mismatch. You will learn how to "bring the conflict with us" and explore the rupture and use it in a way that does not devalue your partner and/or relationship so that you can get to repair.

The Gottman's have found that partners who *turn toward* each other and do not flee have better marriages. That's a good reason to notice when you are in the reactive state of cat and mouse, cool down, and then change your behavior: bring your willingness, pay attention to your partner, affirm your relationship, or show affection or create another positive connection. Using our tools, it will become possible to end the running away or chasing, to slow down and stop, to *turn toward* each other and meet upon the common ground of peace, understanding, and love. The road through conflict can lead there; but we will not make it by side-stepping and avoiding the conflict—and each other.

Freeze/Emotional Color-Blindness

The third reactive state is at the opposite extreme of aggression. We find ourselves there when the only way to deal with our anxieties and pain is to check out from real life conflict. Though this might seem like a state of flight, freeze is an emotional shutdown designed to protect and avoid the fear, pain, and sense of vulnerability that comes not just from conflict but with the *threat of intimacy*—what happens when we come to know each other as we actually are. In this sense, when we are so afraid of the risks of intimacy that come from confronting and repairing conflict, we hide our emotions: in effect, we shut them down. The stronger the feelings, the more effort we put into avoiding them.

Where flight is an active state of "running from" experienced emotion, freeze is a stonewall, a shutdown, a full stop. It could be a dissociated state that can exist for years without the slightest bit of recognition that "anything is *really* wrong."[5] Or, it can be an intentional decision to knowingly postpone conflict. We live in a world that promotes perfectionism and pathologizes conflict, so either reason for the freeze response can be viewed as moving through life under cruise control.

By freezing out our emotions and each other, any potential conflict exists without vibrancy, and in this "blah" we do not have the motivation to fix—or even address—the rupture. This is why we refer to this state as *emotional color blindness*: we whitewash everything with non-emotion. In the extreme, emotional color blindness can look like depression. And at the far end of color blindness is a complete isolation from each other. When this state is exposed, the temperature underneath the cool surface of the relationship might remain hot with pain, resentment, and sadness.

Exercise: Identifying Emotional Color-Blindness

Think about a recent conflict:
- Identify exchanges that sound like avoidance as opposed to honest sharing. Avoidance can also manifest as communicating without honesty and openness.
- Identify implicit or explicit messages you think you were giving each other.
- Now, what style of conflict is your natural response when you engage with your partner? What changes you would like to make? How do you think you would do that?

Understanding the Vulnerability Cycle

Renown couple therapists and researchers Michelle Scheinkman and Mona Dekoven Fishbane have created a model that encapsulates what many couples go through during conflicts. They believe, as we do, that couples can get themselves

---

5.   Dissociation, from an interpersonal perspective, can manifest as depression—and can be counted among those "things" that can alleviate our conscious experience of anxiety (Bose, 1995, 1998).

stuck in a relationship impasse. These impasses are characterized by intense reactivity and escalation during a conflict, where each partner holds onto rigid positions and irrational beliefs based on their past histories. When they are stuck in a reactive cycle, each partner ends up feeling hurt, frustrated, and upset.

Yet these impasses are more than what they seem to be on the surface. In essence, all three reactive states of aggression, mismatch, and emotional color blindness are masking vulnerability, confusion, and personal wishes. When vulnerabilities are triggered, the individual tends to perceive risk and anticipate pain. They then react to the actual or perceived hurtful behavior of the other person in an automatic, self-protective way, as if the present situation is the same as a stressful situation experienced in the past or in a context outside the relationship. Their survival strategies—which are the same as the reactive states—held in reserve, are automatically activated, and partners begin to act from them: they put on their armor to create a sense of safety and control.

While survival strategies may be self-protective, they are often counterproductive solutions for the relationship. They tend to stimulate in the other person the very behaviors the individual is trying to avoid. When acting from survival strategies, persons often behave in self-referential and defensive ways and this insensitivity to the other triggers the partner's own vulnerabilities and their automatic, self-protective responses.

The end result is what is referred to as a *vulnerability cycle,* where each partner's survival strategies is triggering the other in a never-ending, defensive, and self-preserving battle. And because this cycle can potentially go on indefinitely, that's what makes any impasse so heated, confusing, and intense.[6]

As you'll learn, the PACER model is one effective way to break the cycle. You will be able to learn to speak from a place of vulnerability, instead of falling back on your armor of survival strategies. Only then will you be able to see the views, needs, vulnerabilities, and strengths of your partner.

---

6.   Michele Scheinkman and Mona D. Fishbane, "The Vulnerability Cycle: Working with Impasses in Couple Therapy," *Family Process* 43(3) (2004): 279–99.

Jen and Tom and the Underground War

"We *fight* like wasps," Jen told us when we first met her and Tom.

"We don't fight; it's more like we *fly* away," Tom said, explaining that for most of their marriage they each retreated in silence whenever there was a conflict.

"Last year we didn't even celebrate our tenth anniversary—and that was an indication to me that we were at war." Jen acknowledged that years of avoidance had left them both in a state of *flight*—and running away from conflict.

"For so long," Tom admitted, "I wanted to be the husband, the father, and the provider I thought you needed me to be. Yet despite my best efforts, I drove our finances into the toilet."

"And" added Jen, "all I wanted from you was partnership—a partnership that was becoming increasingly impossible to have as long as you, and you solely, were running the show."

By avoiding acknowledgment of the challenges that come along with long-term love, Jen and Tom had, at first, felt grateful to be in what seemed like a conflict-free relationship, but the truth was that they had both pushed all of their anxieties, insecurities, and vulnerabilities underground, and silently engaged in a cold war that neither of them was able to recognize until Tom admitted that his "running of the show," financially had led to ruin.

When they came to us in year eleven, Jen and Tom were facing a true financial catastrophe. Tom's impulsive overspending, and Jen's mindlessly signing off on it, finally brought them out of their color-blinded reactive states and directly into aggression. Shockingly to both of them, they were even fighting in the waiting room. Their screaming seemed to release months of anger and resentment that unearthed years of fear, sadness, and isolation.

Both were completely terrified of the fighting. However, as we brought them into the office, we explained that even a full-on battle doesn't just go away, it can also permutate and be submerged underground as a lingering threat. This threat then operates as a mutual destruction agreement—an unconscious pact that ensures they will continue to rupture.

It took some time—months of fighting in the office, innumerable repairs to match the ruptures that had been unaddressed—before Jen and Tom began to internalize the safety and healing associated with the process and start to experiment with dealing with conflicts at home. In our office, we worked on uncovering Jen and Tom's underlying financial issues. As we unpacked them, they were able to use each rupture as an opportunity for healing the fear and pain that was driving their flights from conflict. "Never talking about money," said Jen, "was an agreement that we never agreed on."

They were able to see that each time they argued it brought up deep shame and humiliation for both of them. So, over the years, they each decided—on their own—to put themselves into positions where they could act out their delusions of self-sufficiency (because in fact there were many, many ways in which these two did rely upon each other), numb/protect themselves to/from their anxieties and insecurities and pretend like everything was always okay. Once everyone's feelings were brought out, Jen and Tom found themselves to be a far better team in dealing with real-life problems than either of them had been when trying to resolve their crises—especially financial—alone.

"It's just amazing, looking back, that I thought my money issues could be contained to, well, money."

"Or" added Jen, "that your money issues were *your* money issues, and not *ours*."

"And so the war erupted."

"And we learned to fall apart."

"And we learned to work together to put ourselves back together again."

Exercise: Identifying Your Defensive and Destructive Behaviors

Being in a reactive state can manifest as specific behaviors—and behavior patterns—that express our uncomfortable emotions. Yet this process only suppresses our *awareness* of these emotions and not the emotions themselves. This is why the disturbing impact of these behaviors affects our partners, even without us knowing it.

The following chart explains how reactive states become behaviors that block our awareness of anxiety and hurt, shows the behavior in real life, and its outcomes.

Defensive Behavior (Reactive State)	Who Used the Behavior and Why	The Destructive Impact of the Behavior
Example A Criticizing each other by comparing their relationship to another, seemingly more ideal couple, claiming to be "helpful" (by using the other couple as a "role model"), breaking into conflict. (Flight)	Both partners. It helped the couple, but it created insecurity, a sense of feeling criticized, and feelings of not being good enough.	Devaluing the relationship by creating a one-sided negative feeling that ended up distancing each partner from the other and became a proxy for addressing other underlying issues.
Example B Frequent drug use: one partner pretended to be unaware, leading to denial, or may be frustrated and disappointed leading to emotional distancing. (Freeze)	The couple came to an unspoken agreement that the drug abusing partner was "only" using drugs "recreationally," but it got worse as the partners avoided the issue, which then became a model for avoiding all other issues.	Both partners pretended the compulsive and destructive behavior was normal and everything was okay. Yet, there were lots of issues in their relationship. Bills were not paid and both of them were using credits cards to pay for basic expenses.

Now, using the above samples as a reference, write down two or three examples of your own reactive states and associated defensive behaviors.

Defensive Behavior (Reactive State)	Who Used the Behavior and Why	The Destructive Impact of the Behavior

Now, answer the following questions:
- Why am I using defensive behaviors?
- Do you recognize the way these behaviors affect your partner? What is it doing to you and your partner?
- What do you see as the gain of such behavior? For instance, does it keep your partner away when you are overwhelmed? Has it helped you navigate a difficult relationship?
- Does your defensive behavior nurture intimacy in this relationship? Does it protect your vulnerability and shore up your defensive position? Does it interfere with the intimacy between you and your partner?

- How rigid are the attitudes and actions that go with your defensive and distancing behavior? How long do you end up keeping your defensive and distancing behavior?
- Is it possible that defensive and reactive states are your default strategies for dealing with others? Do you end up upsetting yourself and your partner by being defensive and reactive?
- How malleable might these interaction patterns be?
- How stuck do you feel by repeating the interaction pattern?
- Who taught you to protect and defend yourself in these ways? What was the context in which this person was teaching you to defend themselves?
- Can you see any familiarity/connection between how your defensive and reactive behaviors have manifested in your relationships in past and present? Might the transformation you seek come from changing the relationship dynamic between you and your partner? What might that look like?
- How do you want to respond to your partner instead of reacting defensively?

Exercise: Forging a New Relationship with Our Reactive States

Identify one or two ongoing issues in your relationship. Using what you've learned about your reactive states, let's use these issues to better understand where (what reactive state) you "land" when these issues arise.

Individually, write brief descriptions of the two issues. Then under each item, write down how you experience your reactive state. From this perspective, write about, in detail, what you see as your role in that issue. If either partner doesn't want to write about their role or is unsure what their part is, note that as well.

Next, share what you've written with your partner. If areas of disagreement about the issues arise, write those down, too.

From the list, agree on one item to work on together. It's best not to use an issue that you're at an uncomfortable stalemate or that is creating resentment. Instead, choose something you can talk about honestly without creating bad feelings between you.

Next, discuss the following questions together:

1. What do you think this conflict is *really* about? (For example, is your reaction due to the fact that you don't believe there is a reason your partner refuses to participate in household chores, other than that they simply don't like doing it?).
2. Once you better understand your reactive state, can you see that there are underlying or undiscussed feelings or attitudes involved?
3. Why is this a problem that you both believe needs to be addressed, rather than allowing it to "ride" (i.e., picking—or *not* picking—this as a "battle")?
4. What impact, direct or indirect, has this "use" of your defensive and reactive state(s) had on other aspects of your relationship? On your family, your household, and beyond?
5. What benefit does your reactive state produce from staying stuck in a reactive state rather than working to actually resolve this issue?
6. When you are hurt during conflict, what do you do to regroup?
7. How could you begin to resolve the issue? Is it possible to break it up into smaller or more manageable parts?
8. How does open discussion of reactive states change your perception of the issue and affect your willingness to work on it?

CHAPTER THREE

As the Honeymoon Subsides, Real Life Comes A-Knocking

During the beginning stage of your relationship, what is typically called *the honeymoon period*, everything your partner does is just perfection. It's a vibrant state where you want to be with each other as much as you can. It's also a time filled with intense emotions that can glue two individuals together and help them become lifelong partners. In essence, it is the experience of falling in love.

Our honeymoon period started on our first date and kept going for the next eighteen months. It began on a stormy winter night at a dark, quiet Italian restaurant in New York's East Village. Mark recalls that it was love at first sight, and he couldn't help but attempt to bridge the unfathomable distance that seemed to exist between the first and second dates (two days later) with a kiss, before watching Haruna descend into the subway. He vividly remembers Haruna showing up to the restaurant in a *marigold* turtleneck sweater. Haruna didn't mention until years later, after hearing their origin story from Mark's point of view a thousand times, that she never owned a marigold turtleneck sweater or anything resembling that. We now agree that what Mark was remembering was that she was glowing, and that part was (and still is) true.

Haruna remembers that meeting Mark was almost transformational. She felt completely drawn to Mark: during dinner they could not stop talking. After their first date there were daily emails and texts. Haruna felt that whenever she saw Mark it was like walking on clouds: magical and light as feathers.

Sometimes, the honeymoon period can feel like the relationship is almost another entity that is out of our control; this was the case for us. It was a visceral experience of quickly becoming an "us." We both recall being inseparable, spending lots of time together almost every day, talking, planning trips, making love, and becoming immediately unable to imagine life without the other. Biological anthropologist Helen Fisher, describes our "symptoms" of falling in love as *euphoria*, which often includes daydreaming about the other, as well as physical changes including a loss of appetite and increased overall energy.[1]

Yet there were also times during our blissed-out honeymoon, that, while magical, were also filled with the terror and insecurity of *not being good enough*. Mark remembers thinking, Will I come to count on you, only to be thoroughly disappointed as I have been in every other relationship up to this point? His anxieties and insecurities during the honeymoon period were overwhelming, flooding him with memories of past loves, both attempted and lost, and the pain from dashed dreams. But still, at that point, Mark said to himself whenever these anxieties surfaced, Haruna and I are in love, and nothing's going to stand in the way of that.

Haruna remembers the honeymoon period as a time of feeling very scared and simultaneously very much in love. The more she was drawn to Mark, the more scared she felt, terrified that the relationship could potentially end. Haruna would dwell on her own personality traits and insecurities, and think, How can Mark accept these parts of me? What if he finds out? Haruna needed lots of support from her friends to get through the insecurity of the honeymoon period. Every time she talked about her fears with her friends, they would remind her that all she needed to do was to show up and have fun.

The honeymoon stage typically refers to the first few months of a relationship, and the feelings we develop during this stage can last forever, even when they are mingled with the realities of everyday life. In fact, the feelings and memories from the honeymoon period are foundational to the entire relationship and influence your willingness to navigate your way together

---

1.   Helen E. Fisher, *Anatomy of Love*, Second Edition (New York: WW Norton, 2016).

into the more intimate experiences of long-term love. We call on these feelings during times of crisis as we remember that we are in love, and these feelings will be the ones that help us maintain our relationship when things go wrong.

And while love continues throughout a relationship, there will be an end to the honeymoon stage proper. How long this stage actually lasts will vary for every couple. Over time, as you keep building your relationship with your partner, the honeymoon period fades and a *real-life relationship*—which we refer to as IRL (in real life)—starts to form. Yet between the honeymoon and IRL comes a period of great challenge where rather than simply adjusting to real life, couples often experience a gamut of psychological defenses that can potentially transform the relationship as well as the individuals. This transformation can powerfully bind two people together for life. Or it can send the relationship on a path of destruction and distancing.

Your Brain in Love

Romantic relationships can be assigned into three central aspects: lust, attraction, and attachment. Lust is the hormone-driven phase where we first experience sexual desire for another person. The honeymoon phase describes relationships heavily focused on attraction. The pleasure center of the brain is activated, and we feel an overwhelming fixation with our partner. This fixation can be correlated to changes in brain chemistry, which is scientifically defined as *limerence*.

Limerence is a mental state of profound romantic infatuation that creates a "high" similar to drug use.[2] During this time, the pituitary gland releases neurochemicals that increase feelings of sexual attraction, euphoria, excitement, and mental fixation.[3] For both men and women, there is a short-term hormonal fluctuation: cortisol levels are significantly higher when we recently fall in love, and testosterone levels decrease for

2.   Helen E. Fisher, Xiaomeng Xu, Arthur Aron, and Lucy L. Brown, "Intense, Passionate, Romantic Love: A Natural Addiction? How the Fields That Investigate Romance and Substance Abuse Can Inform Each Other," *Frontiers in Psychology*, 7, (2016): 687–97.
3.   Lisa Holmes, "Here's Why the Honeymoon Phase Is So Intoxicating," *Science*, 2021. https://keeplerapp.com/honeymoon-phase/ (downloaded on 7/16/2023).

men and increase for women.[4] The brain becomes flooded with dopamine and norepinephrine—two neurotransmitters responsible for that giddy, euphoric feeling you get when you are motivated to seek a reward, which in this case is the company of the person you love. Norepinephrine increases heart rate, keeps you up at night thinking about the person you love, and makes you preoccupied with your partner. Falling in love can also lower the brain chemical serotonin. Low serotonin levels are common in people with obsessive-compulsive disorders. Like Ulysses tied to the mast, this is the likely culprit as to why you can feel almost obsessed with your partner—and why you can't stop thinking about them no matter how hard you try.

During the honeymoon stage, these thoughts and corresponding behaviors can be similar to an addiction.[5] In fact, the same regions in the brain light up when you're attracted to someone as when a drug addict takes cocaine. When you fall in love, areas of the brain called the *caudate nucleus* and the *ventral tegmental area* are more active.[6] The caudate nucleus is thought to integrate your "rush" of romantic passion with your complex emotions and thoughts about your beloved.

Because the chemical changes in the body and brain during the honeymoon phase can be exhausting and distracting, most romantic relationships become centered on attachment instead of attraction within about two years once the body develops a tolerance to the pleasure stimulants. From a biological perspective, this is when the honeymoon period ends. Attachment, promoted by the neurochemicals oxytocin and vasopressin, is a calmer kind of love—a feeling of being good friends, companions who have chosen one another for the long haul.[7] These hormones create an overall sense of well-being and security that is conducive to a lasting relationship.

4.   Donatella Marazitti and Domenico Canale, "Hormonal Changes When Falling in Love." *Psychoneuroendocrinology* 29(7) (2004): 931–36.
5.   Helen Fisher, *Anatomy of Love: A Natural History of Mating, Marriage, and Why We Stray* (New York: W. W. Norton, 2016).
6.   Lucy L. Brown and Helen E Fisher, "The Anatomy of Love" Know Thy Brain, Know Thy Self, Know Thy Partner." https://theanatomyoflove.com (downloaded on 4/29/2023).
7.   Helen E. Fisher, "Cupid in Quarantine: What Brain Science Can Teach Us about Love," *New York Times* (April 13, 2020).

The Universal Truth: Every Honeymoon Ends

Our culture has clearly made the point that intimate relationships are supposed to be a wonderful experience. We have been led to believe the ultimate love narrative, where Cinderella and the Prince always live happily ever after. But in real life, Cinderella and the Prince actually talk to each other, and sometimes they fight. This oppositional truth may be the reason why many of our clients complain that real life is the ultimate bait-and-switch—they are shocked to find out that the perfect person they fell in love with turns out to be just another flawed human being. For these couples, the transformation of seeing their partner *as they actually are*—flawed—is just too much. Disappointment threatens to become the silver bullet that can kill the great dream of what had previously felt like some kind of salvation.

The honeymoon period morphs into IRL when each person starts to feel the inevitable inklings of disappointment in their partner. Sometimes, the honeymoon period wanes slowly. Sometimes, there's an abrupt shift. It could be accompanied by a change in relationship dynamics (in/out, up/down, near/far), a transitional rupture (a move, death in the family, etc.) or something as simple as an everyday conflict. Whatever the cause, we begin to see that our partner is no longer perfect in every way. For instance, Mark recalls slowly feeling the gut-punch of disappointment when Haruna proved herself to be merely human after all. Haruna remembers feeling confused, sad, and angry when there was a buildup of small disappointments in their relationship.

These feelings do not signal a falling out of love. In fact, as you integrate your relationship into IRL, couples are often very much in love and still exploring each other. What changes is that you begin to notice the rest of the world around you, especially when challenges arise. The question becomes how each of you are going to navigate the inevitable conflicts that come up in a real-life relationship. Can you learn to argue and apologize after hurting each other's feelings? Can you accept that there may be some negotiations you need to carry out with each other?

For many couples facing their first ruptures, there is definitely a mix of feelings ranging from relief to dread, and some couples transition into a real-life relationship a lot smoother than others. There is often a common sense of dread and doom, when individuals worry, What if we can't talk things out and come out of the argument together?

If both partners can talk about, recover, and repair from their very first arguments, there can be a sense of relief: the relationship can weather the storms of disappointment and conflicts. Even the most difficult fights can ultimately form the bedrock of a successful, intimate relationship. In fact, we have seen in case after case over numerous years that it is the skill of working together to repair that will provide the foundation for a strong relationship. While each subsequent argument strips away the veil of honeymoon, when they are successfully navigated, they can provide each person with an increased capacity to deal with real life issues. What's more, these first few conflicts can open up couples to the risks and rewards that come along with being vulnerable, empathetic, intimate and, ultimately, invested in each other and the relationship.

From Mark's psychoanalytic perspective, long-term love is going to change us and our sense of self. Whether we are consciously aware of it or not, this change is where we each begin to transform from an "I" to both an "I" and an "us." Ever since our initial honeymoon period, neither of us has been—or will ever be—the same version of ourselves who walked into an Italian restaurant on that cold winter night in the East Village.

Haruna's couple therapy training teaches that long-term love is transformational but in different ways. Her perspective is that each relationship will heal the wounds from past relationships, nourish the partners, and help them grow in a way that one may never predict. When there is long-term love in the relationship, it can become a place where couples get to keep learning about themselves, reinventing themselves, and grow in a wholesome way.[8]

For example, Haruna was not aware of how impatient she could be. Using the PACER model, she learned that Mark needed her to be patient with him. Mark recalls that before his relationship with Haruna he was unable and unwilling to turn to other people for help, especially in romantic relationships. This led to a kind of self-sufficiency that resulted in him feeling alone in most

---

8.   Stephen M. Drigotas, Caryl E. Rusbult, Jennifer Wieselquist, Sarah W. Whitton, "Close Partner as Sculptor of the Ideal Self: Behavioral Affirmation and the Michelangelo Phenomenon," *Journal of Personality and Social Psychology* 1999 Aug. 77(2): 293–323.

of his previous relationships. Haruna also recalls not being able to rely on a romantic partner and felt isolated in other romantic relationships before meeting Mark. Through our transformation into an "us"—the third entity that is the relationship itself—we have become people who are able and willing to take in what the other partner offers, to allow it to affect us, to nourish us, and to rely on each other.

When Mark was in jump school at Fort Benning, the instructor said, "Falling out of an airplane never killed anyone—it's the sudden stop!" Likewise, those first fights can be such bad news for the couple and can even take down the entire relationship. These are couples who find it difficult to transition out of the honeymoon and into real-life. In the beginning stages of a romantic relationship, many people believe that this person, and/or relationship, is going to rescue them, and some simply cannot bear the reality that this other person/relationship is not going to save them. This news is a killer for those who do not realize how thoroughly they were holding onto that Cinderella fantasy, and often, their relationships can't survive the crash.

Our transition from the honeymoon to IRL was an intense tumble. We were so thoroughly blissed-out for the first eighteen months of wild, wild love. We had a mind-blowingly romantic and love-filled wedding in our favorite place, Tompkins Square Park (East Village, NYC) and a reception at the same restaurant where we first met. We took a honeymoon road-trip throughout Eastern Europe. We had a baby we were just mad about, a cozy (and, yes, tiny) love-nest in Manhattan. Then suddenly—wham—a series of catastrophes hit that would wipe us out completely and continue to do so for the next couple of years. Haruna's pregnancy and cancer diagnosis, Mark's extreme financial pressures, selling an apartment and moving. Even though we were head over heels in love with each other, we were so deep in rupture that we both thought our marriage wouldn't make it.

For other couples who don't have the obvious catastrophes we experienced, they are left scratching their heads when IRL comes knocking on their door. So what really happened? What was the honeymoon period all about? Why does it have to end? And why does it end so badly for so many couples? We've found that the answer lies in the series of psychological defenses that characterize the beginning and the end of the honeymoon period.

Honeymoons Start with Idealization

The honeymoon phase is often characterized as a time when our search for perfection is realized, whether it's the perfect partner or the perfect relationship. And though we all experience it in our own way, the need to maintain this perfect image of our partner and/or the relationship refers to the psychological defense called *idealization.* In this state we see all the wonderful aspects of somebody or something, to the point where their less-than-fabulous traits, or sometimes the rest of the world's dramas, fall deep into the background of our lives.

Idealization sounds wonderful, and in some senses, it is. However, the reason we do it is complicated. It is a necessary bonding process of two people, both a chemical reaction and a strategy for relating to each other. And it is a form of psychological protection against the massive insecurity of putting ourselves in terrible risk.

We use idealization to lessen our disappointments with ourselves. It is a psychological defense against our own anxiety: we create a haze over our perception or experience so we see what we want to see in the other to make up for the shortcomings we see in ourselves. We idealize our partner as the greatest thing that ever happened to us, as in "This person and this relationship are going to save my life and will rescue me from the horrible fate of being single, lonely, and isolated." Whether the honeymoon lasts for six months, nine months, a year, a year and a half, we live with this belief. And we expect a reciprocity of feelings that the other person is having similar feelings about us. In fact, gathering evidence that our partner is sharing similar feelings—especially through professing undying love, time spent together, lovemaking, etc.—is sometimes all that keeps us from falling apart under the pressure of the anxiety that can come with the great emotional investment we are making in our partner and relationship. As we've learned about internal conflict, overwhelming anxiety can come from ironically believing that we've finally got what we've been after yet worry that once we come to rely on it, it will be taken away from us.

Exercise: Remembering the First Encounter

During the honeymoon stage, there is a clear reciprocity: you love your partner very dearly, want your partner to do things for you, and your partner wants to show you love as well. But when you are fighting, it's easy for partners to distance themselves emotionally and relationally and to forget the fact that they were and have been attracted to each other in many ways. These exercises will remind you of your honeymoon period and why you are together in the first place. These questions can help you grab hold of the foundational elements and positive memories of love so that you can use them with the PACER model.

Let's go back to the beginning: how did your relationship start? What was it about your partner that was so intriguing? Did the coupling happen fast, or did it take time? Did you have any reservations, or did it seem like you were a perfect fit?

You can answer these same questions alone and/or with your partner:
1. Where did you meet? How did your meeting come about?
2. What was it that attracted you?
3. Was there anything about meeting each other that felt special? If yes, how did you feel about that?
4. How old were you and what was going on in your life?
5. What do you recall about the first meeting? What stood out—and still stands out? And, what made you want to have a next date?

Write down anything else about your first meeting(s) that stand out in your mind—especially feelings or behaviors. Avoid censoring yourself. Write down your feelings and thoughts. Then, share your answers with each other, being especially mindful of what it was that brought you together in the first place.

Exercise: There Was Something About Us

This collective "story" is the beginning of what we refer to as your sense of "us-ness." So, let's drill down even further into what happened on your first meeting. Answer these questions individually.

1. What traits do you remember as first catching your attention?
    a. Physical traits or overall appearance.
    b. Particular emotional or other nonverbal signals.
    c. The way they conversed or shared ideas.
2. Instant, magnetic sexual attraction. Unable to put into words? If so, try to do so now.
3. Next, write a detailed description of what made your partner exciting to you.
    a. Was it something emotional, intellectual, physical, spiritual?
    b. Did you like their sense of humor?
    c. Did they make you feel safe?
    d. If you felt only sexual attraction at first, discuss that and describe how that changed or didn't change.
4. Now share your responses with each other. Discuss similarities and differences.
    a. How does it feel *right now* to be doing this exercise with each other?
    b. Did either of you intentionally leave out anything important? Do you know why you did?
    c. Are you aware *right now* of feelings you had about or for each other when you first met? What is it like to recall them?
    d. Do you remember particular activities that brought you and your partner joy and excitement when you first met? Do you and your partner still get to do activities that bring you joy and excitement? If you stopped doing them, write down why.

Is Conflict a Symbol of Exiting the Honeymoon?

Some couples fight more frequently, and even run into conflicts, as their honeymoon period is ending. We believe they do so because they are grieving the loss of the intense connection and rosy honeymoon period. You may have thought you and your partner were the perfect unit that could tackle anything and everything. But if real life issues take center stage, you may mourn the loss of the honeymoon. Upon analysis we can now see—and admit—that this was what happened to us (sigh).

This is another reason why we believe conflict is not a sign that your relationship isn't working: it can be a signal of yearning for reconnection. What will make or break a relationship isn't the conflict, the collision, but how you choose to resolve it.

When the Honeymoon Ends with Devaluation

There are, in general, two ways a couple can come out of an idealized dynamic. Either your partner remains the best thing that ever happened to you (as in, They might not be perfect but they are still the best thing that ever happened to me) or they are, for at least a period of time, quite emphatically *not*. When your partner becomes the "less than" in this equation, we call this shift in feelings *devaluation*.

The transition from idealization to devaluation can be swift. In fact, devaluation can occur almost simultaneously with the process of coming to terms with real life. As partners, we become devalued when the idealization defense against our own insecurity crashes into the wall of real-life, when we realize that our partners aren't 100 percent the best, so they aren't going to save us from our own insecurities and existential isolation. With this realization, we then shore up our own defenses by trying to disinvest from the partner and/or the relationship as completely as possible. In order to do so, we have to make up a reason: a new certainty that whatever is going wrong in the relationship is categorically the other partner's fault.

In so doing, we flip idealization on its head. Instead of believing that our partner is the absolute best, we defend ourselves by finding all the ways that they are the worst. The immense insecurity and anxiety associated with the early stages of relationship triggers this defensive reaction to protect us from being overwhelmed by the anxiety connected to the risk of allowing someone who—like all people, is not so perfect and rather flawed—to matter so much. When we devalue our "perfect" partner, we immediately reduce the risk of putting our heart in such great peril.

And, just like the idealization defense, the devaluing response protects us from being overwhelmed, as it also put us into a state where we are not in touch with our emotions. We can get stunned and confused by the devaluation defense. In this psychological state we are blocking our emotions and lose the overall perspective of what is happening in our relationship, and we microfocus on what is not ideal about the partner. Rather than allowing ourselves to acclimate to an emotional environment where we have put ourselves at risk by our increasing investment in a person and relationship that is not within our ability to control, we can easily lose our awareness of how important the other person—and our relationship itself—is.

We believe devaluation is an internal resistance to creating the new entity that is "us," especially once it becomes clear that the partner who initially seemed perfect is rather flawed (just like we all are), regardless of how transformational love has been and is. This transformation includes a gnawing awareness that with love comes the challenge of accepting ourselves and our partners as we actually are (what we call *the intimacy of everyday life*). As I am transforming from a "me" to an "us," I am also becoming *dependent* upon another person in ways that are immensely anxiety-provoking because, let's face it, it's really scary to rely on someone else. Much of the conflict that comes right after the honeymoon stage may be a last-ditch effort to hold onto that version of yourself that you walked into the relationship with, only to realize, that version of you is long, long gone. In fact, we believe this "us" is at the core of who/what we are treating in couples therapy: the alliance you and I form when we are we.

Love and being in a relationship present an ongoing challenge to our sense of security. Most of us are filled with the intense anxiety about being in an ongoing process of transformation, which we have little control over the outcome. A great deal of our sense of security comes from having a sense of "who I have been, am, and will be." In a relationship, we are never in control of the "us" that we are becoming. And there is an extra layer of insecurity coming from the fact that we are also not in control of how our partner will change and evolve.

Devaluation protects us from all of these changes but stopping them in their tracks. While idealization tends to be a pretty extreme phenomenon, devaluation doesn't have to be, but it often is. A number of outcomes can happen next:

- Devaluation can easily become a relationship killer and why it is possible that some of us don't survive the transition from the honeymoon into IRL. In this scenario, we convince ourselves that our partner or the relationship has no value, and we end it.
- As we begin to see our partner in a less than idealized state, we compartmentalize their devalued traits, keeping them separate from the rest of the relationship. Compartmentalizing our partner's faults allows couples to continue to enjoy their relationship by focusing on the parts of our partner that we like. This strategy works for maintaining a relationship, but it puts each person in a position to miss out on certain facets of intimacy: if we are only seeing the likeable parts of our partners, we are not accepting them as they are.
- When the relationship gets impinged upon by arguments and fights, the partners start feeling defeated and distant. We then use devaluation to check-out, not completely exiting the relationship, but no longer fully "showing up" (especially emotionally) the way we had before (during the honeymoon). This is an example of what we referred to in Chapter Two as *emotional color-blindness*.
- We can pause, look at our history of using devaluation as a defense, ride the bumpy waves of our own less-than-perfect reactions to our partner's imperfection, and begin to see this is an opportunity for a more realistic acceptance of our partner/relationship—as is.

The devaluation dynamic can be so powerful that you might actually believe your partner no longer has any value (bullet-point #1), and that's when we get an irreparable result. Yet sometimes, devaluation is used when your partner hasn't "changed" at all. Instead, you may have the realization that they might have too much value, and they are threatening to matter so much that you won't be able to live without them. If we stay in this reactive state, we can easily side-step the actual intimacy that comes from accepting each other, the relationship, and real life, as is. When this happens, you inadvertently are protecting yourself from experiencing the scarier, although rewarding aspects of love where your heart is at risk (and this can happen with either bullet point #2 or #3).

In our relationship, we went from a highly idealized place to a low and mutual devaluation. We had so many catastrophic, transitional IRL issues at the beginning of our marriage that we went straight from idealizing each other and our relationship to us both believing it was over. We both mourned the honeymoon period, which was filled with idealization and then devalued each other when IRL hit us hard. We saw each other's imperfect traits and resisted to create an "us" with the imperfect other. At the end of this devaluation period, each of us was thoroughly convinced that the other was completely at fault, threatening to leave the marriage if the other would not "take full responsibility" for our ongoing state of failure and "FIX IT" (that is, fix you)! Profound threats, ultimatums, combined with strong "suggestions" about where the other "must go" (for instance, therapy, a twelve-step program, back home to Japan or California) were a daily conversation for us during this period.

The late Australian therapist, Michael White was famous for saying, "The problem is the problem. The person is not the problem."[9] He means the problems couples face can never be resolved by determining *who is at fault*. It is *how* each couple reacts to the problem that determines how they will resolve it and allows them to form an alliance to do so.[10]

9.   Michael White, *Maps of Narrative Practice* (New York: W. W. Norton, 2007).
10. Michael White and David Epson, *Narrative Means to Therapeutic Ends* (New York: W. W. Norton, 1990).

It is easy to connect a problem with a person. It is much harder to separate the problem from the person with whom you are having difficulty. This is why it was so easy for us to believe the problems we were facing in our marriage were because of the other, even when the problems were completely out of anyone's control, such as a cancer diagnosis.

Roommates, Friends, and Lovers

Romantic relationships occur on three levels. One of Haruna's supervisors at the Ackerman Family Institute, Miguel Torres, believes every romantic relationship occurs on three levels: lovers, friends, and roommates. The first level begins during the honeymoon period, where a couple connects with each other as lovers. You may be having lots of sex, taking great vacations, or talking incessantly with each other.

In a real-life relationship, couples are juggling these three roles all at once. One minute you're lovers, and the next minute you're friends, and the next minute you're roommates. For instance, when you have a baby, both of you have to work extra hard to take care of your newborn, and the level of lovers might be put to backburner for a little while.

This shifting isn't a sign that the relationship is in trouble. In fact, we think it's a natural phenomenon in a long-term, committed relationship. Each level is just as important as the others. In fact, they feed on each other. Being a roommate requires having a basic level of courtesy for each other. Friends share intimate thoughts and their inner lives. And lovers share the physical and sexual connection that's beyond what you would do with a friend, which also opens you up to another level of vulnerability.

The Difference between Devaluation and Disappointment

Sometimes ruptures expose disappointments in either your partner or your relationship. For instance, you may come to realize that your partner isn't as easygoing as you expected. Or they might not be chill at all. Disappointment is the stuff of everyday life, and we have to be able to tolerate it. It's a great skill to be able to be disappointed and to think, I'm disappointed in your attitude. But you didn't kill me. You didn't stab me in the heart. You disappointed me.

You can't be successful as an IRL couple if you cannot tolerate being disappointed. If your psychological defense system pushes you so far past disappointment that instead of being disappointed legitimately, you've got to drain your partner of all value, then you're devaluing, and it is going to be difficult for you to accept anyone—including yourself—as they are in real life. An overreaction to this same disappointment might look like devaluation, You're not what I bargained for. You're no longer any good for me. We're no good.

Disappointments are often derived from our own emotional blind spots to recognizing and articulating our wants and needs, and our desire for our partner to know something about ourselves that we don't even know. For example, you may have a set of expectations of your partner that are based on what you may think is ideal behavior. Your expectations are grounded in how you view the world. Some of these expectations may be related to gender roles, life goals, or cultural/societal/generational values. Sometimes you discover your expectations of your partner were wrong: they don't want the same things that you do. And that's how you end up feeling disappointed, hurt, and angry.

Allowing yourself to be disappointed is a key to accepting your partner, and yourself, as you both are. By recognizing the feelings of disappointment, you have the opportunity to reexamine your expectations and come to understand your partner better. If you can stay with your disappointment without going to devaluation, you can get to repair. Just because your partner disappoints you doesn't mean that the relationship is over.

Ava and Ethan: High on Hopes and Expectations

People who protect themselves from intimacy with idealization tend to do so believing they are seeking—and doing—just the opposite. They use love to protect themselves from the anxiety of intimacy and continue to believe what they are doing together is the act of intimacy. Yet these high hopes and expectations are often the unconscious driving force that initially signals the end of the honeymoon stage.

"There I was," said Ava, "with everything I ever wanted in a relationship."

"Don't you mean '*There we were*'"? asked Ethan.

"No," countered Ava, "and that was the problem. When I looked around at all we've created together, all we've built, I had this terrible sense that the price I'd paid was a sense of being increasingly estranged from you. As long as we could both simply enjoy all of the milestones that adult relationships typically hit and accept that as the reason we were together then everything was—and would be—fine. Why not? Why couldn't conflict-free mean *fine*—really fine?"

"Yes," said Ethan, "and now that very sense that everything is fine is what's not fine?"

Ava told us: "Whenever either one of us answers the stereotypical New York question, 'Howyadoin'?' with anything like 'okay,' we are both on alert to check in with each other about what's really going on, because 'okay' means there is some disappointment lurking in the background."

It is unlikely that anyone is actually jumping for joy when a relationship hits the skids, when we wake up after years of long-term partnership to find ourselves estranged. However, avoiding intimacy is not necessarily the same thing as the absence of love. It is, more often, a blockage to our awareness of natural insecurities and conscious experience of love. Love has to have been a threat in the first place in order for us to block our awareness of it.

The end of the honeymoon is fraught with anxiety specific to the threat and hope of deep intimacy. Like so many people who after having weathered a storm of crisis and conflict together feel a closeness that could be achieved in no other way, people who develop, maintain, and then work through letting go of the idealizations of the honeymoon are often in a position to be open and experience an even deeper sense of love and intimacy.

When we get to the other side of the honeymoon together, we have a greater capacity to access our entire emotional range: joy, sadness, fear, frustration, disappointment, forgiveness, and love—the true real life of love. "What this looks like," says Ethan, " is that I know when I am hurt and I know when I am afraid, and I am willing to say so before escaping into the distance that nearly killed us."

Exercise: Where Are the Disappointments?

There will always be things about a partner that one doesn't like or agree with, but we have to reconcile our expectations with the reality of who they are in order to live with—and in—the kind of acceptance successful relationships thrive in.

Answer the following questions as honestly as you can.
- What is a real-life situation/scenario that lead to your feelings of disappointment?
- Did your disappointment lead to devaluation and catastrophized thinking?
- Is it possible that you contributed to some of this disappointment?
- Now that you know that disappointments are a part of the development of IRL relationship, Can you remember and accept that there have been and will be disappointments as well as love in this relationship?

Exercise: Understanding Expectations and How They Lead to Disappointments

As we've seen, expectations can be the weeds that have grown into our conscious or unconscious resentments. They can grow to the point where they can suffocate our other emotions, turning our natural disappointments into lethal weapons. Understanding them and how they block our experiences of acceptance and even gratitude for our partner and our relationship is crucial. Let's see if the following exercise can help you do so.

Part One
- List what you love or appreciate about your partner.
- What are your expectations of your partner?
- Why are these expectations important to you?

Here's an example:
- I love my partner because of how involved they are in the care of our kids.
- I need my partner to have a full-time job since I don't feel comfortable being the sole breadwinner.
- It is for my sense of financial security. My family showed me that two partners having a full-time job was important.

Part Two

It is nearly impossible for your partner to meet all your expectations. And if you have so many expectations, you will be disappointed and upset every time your partner does not meet them. If you have many expectations of your partner, which ones can you let go of?

Rank your expectations as follows:
- The top three are the ones you need your partner to respect. List them here. Then, see if you can figure out a work-around to this expectation. Not all expectations are negotiable.
- If you have more expectations, write them down, and circle the ones you think you can let go of.

Here's an example:
1. I need my partner to clean and organize our apartment once a week with me. I can let this go since we can hire a cleaning person.
2. I need my partner to be a gym buddy. I can let this go because I can go to the gym alone or with my friends.
3. I need my partner to be ambitious in their career. I am ambitious so I can't let this go.

Part Three

Have you had conversations about your expectations with your partner? Or do they only come up when you fight? Which is true for your top three expectations? Keep in mind that when couples go through a transition such as having a baby, their expectations of each other can change, temporarily or permanently.

For example:
1. I want to take maternity leave after having a baby. How long should I go without working?
2. I want my partner to take paternity leave. How long can we both go without working?
3. I want to move out of an apartment and into a house in the suburbs after working at my current company for the next three years.
4. I want us to do somewhat equal amount of chores.

The Path to IRL Relationship Happiness

We've been told to look for someone who loves us unconditionally, no matter how we behave. However, that's an illusion and a myth. The truth is it is unreasonable to search for an unconditional love because there is no such thing.

We've been told the closest one might come to subjectively describing and experiencing a truly unconditional love is that between a parent and a child. But what if we've got it all wrong? What if that remains a distant second to the truest of true love: the *love* experienced by a growing child for their parent. It is the child, after all, who, all throughout development, is challenged to accept and tolerate their parents as they *actually are*.

In no way, at no time, does a parent genuinely accept the child in their care as they *really* are. That would be antithetical to the primary task of parenting: to mold and shape the maturing human being to fit in with culture and society. It is not a parent's job to accept the growing human as is; instead, it is the developing child's challenge to accept and care for the parent by doing their best to be exactly the kind of creature the parent needs them to be in order to feel that the job of parenting has been accomplished in a good enough manner.

To love unconditionally is therefore the most basic survival skill. We must learn to perform in ways that convince the world (our parents) of our value. We have all, therefore, loved unconditionally and developed behavioral and relational patterns/routines designed to keep us alive. How well we accomplished it will tell much about how we allow ourselves to accept and take in what the rest of the world—other people—have to offer.

In the best of all possible outcomes, children are able to join their parents in an ascending synergy of reciprocal care that is experienced as unconditional love. Children idealize their parents, experiencing them as "the world" and needing to believe the world is "just" so as to survive the vicissitudes of growing up.[11] Lerner and Simmons (1966) *just-world hypothesis* or *just-world fallacy* is the assumption that a person's actions always bring morally fair and fitting consequences to that person so that all noble actions are eventually rewarded and all evil actions are eventually punished. In other words, the just-world hypothesis is the tendency to attribute consequences to—or expect consequences as the result of—a universal force that restores moral balance. The fallacy is that this implies (often unintentionally) the existence of cosmic justice, destiny, divine providence, stability, or order and often serves to rationalize people's misfortune on the grounds that "they deserve it." We believe this fallacy often results in the case that the world—as represented by our parents—must be "just" in the mind of a child if they are to survive. For example, in the mind of the child, the parent's most errant behavior, including abuse, is experienced as the *fault* of the child—not the offending parent. Throughout the course of our upbringing, we either can or cannot, will or will not, come to accept that our parents are really just people who are (hopefully) doing their best to care for us. Regardless of how well or poorly they do this job of raising us, it is up to us to either accept or reject life—and everyone and all things in it—as they actually are.

Your successes and failures of coming to terms with real-life with your parents will translate into how you accept real love with a partner. The truth is, we don't need unconditional love; we need to feel like we are contributing to a healthy, loving, intimate, reciprocal relationship. This entity—the relationship—can nourish you and your partner as you both work toward developing and maintaining a real-life relationship. Full acceptance is not unconditional love. Instead, it is a process of getting to know each other and to experience ourselves and each other as we actually are in the living of our

---

11. Melvin J. Lerner and Carolyn H. Simmons, "Observer's Reaction to the 'Innocent Victim': Compassion or Rejection?" *Journal of Personality and Social Psychology*, 4, no. 2 (1966): 203–10.

lives together every day—the intimacy of everyday life. What's more, each relationship is built on *reciprocity,* which here means discussing and negotiating each other's needs and is a requirement of intimacy. We should be in a balance of both unconditionally giving to our partners and meeting our own needs.

The transition from honeymoon to real-life—the initial repairs of the early ruptures—can lead to the special ingredients of both love and ongoing personal growth: vulnerability, empathy, intimacy, and emotional investment. These experiences—what we call the four pillars of true love—are also transformational in and of themselves. If you are consciously or subconsciously anxious about any of these experiences, you may believe that you have a *fear of intimacy.* However, we believe it is not simply intimacy that you fear but the whole process of loving and being loved—and its transformational elements.

In the brilliant book, *Sapiens,* Yuval Noah Harari writes, "Happiness does not really depend on objective conditions of either wealth, health, or even community. Rather, it depends on the correlation between objective conditions and subjective expectations."[12] Another way of saying this is *happiness is a balance of expectations up against outcomes,* and the same is true for happiness when it comes to relationships. Idealization allows us to hold onto unrealistic expectations. Devaluation is a reaction that does not allow an acceptance of each other as we are in real life. Happiness, in this sense, is therefore not just an acceptance of who and what we are (as individuals and as a couple), but an understanding of ourselves and each other.

We hope the exercises in this chapter have allowed you to experience some sense of the security that you have already earned by staying the course in your relationship. We believe this sense of security, along with a genuine sense of the investment you each have in each other and your relationship, will be crucial when you go further in repairing the ruptures, current and past, that have made it difficult to access the four pillars of love.

Perhaps, as you explore your conflict history and patterns, you'll see that you are revisiting the same issues without coming up with solutions. Maybe your solutions conflict so much so that the other's suggestions cannot be perceived as logical answers to the problem. Stumbling into a stalemate might

12. Yuval N. Harari, *Sapiens: A Brief History of Humankind* (New York: Harper, 2011), 428.

make you less likely to want to work together. In fact, the idea of working together might actually feed your anxiety. All of these reactions are quite normal when you are facing the challenges of real-life love.

When your mind is stuck in a loop, you can interrupt it by getting up and moving around or doing a different task or activity. In some ways, that's what you have been doing together as you work on the exercises in this chapter. Agreeing to hear your partner's perspectives is the first step in helping each other in a reciprocal way.

CHAPTER FOUR

Welcoming the Unwelcome Parts of Yourself

While other relationship experts explore how to cope with the partner you have, we believe a better strategy is to keep the focus on ourselves. The truth is no one else is ever going to be able to change on your timeline, and you can't get your partner to change at all unless your partner *wants* to change. If you want to make real improvements to your relationship, you might as well do the work on yourself first.

Our philosophy may be familiar to those in recovery who have heard the phrase "If I'm not the problem, there is no solution." In recovery, this quote refers to the process of empowerment and healing through "making amends" for ways in which the recovering person has harmed others. In this amend-making, you can honestly and realistically assess what drove/ compelled your destructive action, account for the underlying feelings and motivations, and, armed with this awareness, commit to ceasing the harmful behavior. In relationship ruptures, the same statement is equally accurate. If there is anything universally true about conflict, it is that it *takes two to tango,* which means there is always an opportunity to see your role in any conflict.

Keeping the focus on yourself is not just about claiming what you have done wrong. It's also the best way to recognize exactly how you are contributing to what's good about your relationship, which is what the exercises in Chapter One uncovered. By now, you may feel that you know yourself a little better. In this chapter, we will dig a little deeper, uncover the motivations and feelings that lie underneath some of your conscious and unconscious behaviors. With this knowledge, you can begin to put down your defensive armor as you learn how to accept yourself as you are right now, not the person you used to be before the relationship, and not the person you ideally see yourself as being. Only then will you and your partner be able to manage each of your contributions to conflicts as they arise. Each time we rupture, keeping the focus on ourselves gives us the power to join in on the repair.

First, let's see where and how your past experiences are affecting your current relationship. We'll start by learning to recognize the aspects of ourselves that we really don't like. We call this the *unwelcome parts of yourself.*

The quiet question we asked other kids on the playground when we were in kindergarten—"Do you like me?"—haunts all of our relationships. And this is most especially true in a relationship that matters at the life-or-death level that most of us wind up in when we fall in love. So we protect ourselves through the development of powerful psychological defenses that keep us from knowing how deeply our heart is at risk when we fall in love.

These defenses result in our *unwelcome parts*: they are our over-reactions to our vulnerabilities that manifest because our heart is constantly at risk in a love relationship. They are the emotions we cover up because we can't tolerate them and do not feel safe enough to have them exposed to someone as important to us as our partner. We develop behaviors and elaborate routines to stabilize our relationship and cover up our vulnerabilities yet, in the process, we lose our connection to what it means to be *sensitive:* to know what it is that scares and hurts us.

When we overprotect ourselves from these risks, we, ironically, face much greater chances of losing our relationship because of the very reactions we use to defend against the risk we are in. These behaviors are in the arsenal of your psychological defense system and they are designed to protect you from being overwhelmed by anxiety, fear, and pain. Therefore, when we don't understand our most vulnerable feelings, they are transformed into acted out and coping behaviors, which are often misunderstood and sometimes even destructive.

Ultimately, these behaviors make it more difficult for us and our partners to acknowledge, much less accept, each other as we are.

The psychoanalytic perspective teaches that these feelings were developed early, and the ways you've chosen to deal with them or avoid them, can result in specific habitual and often impulsive behaviors. Renowned couples therapist Michelle Scheinkman teaches that in the course of life we all experience vulnerabilities in close relationships and develop core defensive armors to navigate these vulnerabilities. These defensive armors can become adaptive to new situations.

For instance, our patient Len was so addicted to pornography that he couldn't bear to share his shame about his behavior with his wife, Shane. Len thought his addiction was the cause of their frequent conflicts. While it may have played a part, we explained to him that his pornography addiction was an acting out behavior, like a tantrum a child throws when they are frustrated or angry. The behavior was actually a signal that Shane picked up on but didn't know what to do with it.

We explained that the porn wasn't Len's dirty secret or unwelcome part; the feelings the porn use was eliciting, namely shame and guilt, was what he needed to unpack. We first acknowledged that being honest about excessive pornography use with his wife is hard to do, because any discussion of sex is usually taboo. Then we needed to work with him to show him how these feelings, and how he chose to deal with them, were affecting his marriage. Len, like many men, was not encouraged to talk about his feelings throughout his upbringing. Family therapist and author of *How Can I Get Through to You,*[1] Terrence Real states that compared to women, men typically lack the verbal skills needed to clearly communicate the vulnerable feelings such as guilt, shame, and fear, all of which were difficult for Len to share with Shane. Instead, they avoided sex all together, which led to Len and Shane being locked in a virtual cold war. The end result was that Len was having a sexual relationship with himself—and his computer—that was full of shame and guilt. If he didn't

---

1. Terrence Real, *How Can I Get Through to You: Closing the Intimacy Gap between Men and Women* (New York: Scribner, 2001), 201–05.

get a handle on his unwelcome parts and find a way to express them, he would be forever stuck behind a proverbial wall with them as his only company.

Behaviors that are protecting us from our unwelcome parts can be so effective that they can take on a life of their own. In fact, some of these behaviors become a part of our overall sense of self. Len viewed himself as "a guy who couldn't get his sex drive under control." But the truth is, his behavior surrounding porn is not a full reflection of his character. Instead, it is a reaction to underlying—and generally blocked—feelings of shame and inferiority (interfering with his willingness to ask for what he wants sexually), which did influence the way Shane felt about him and their relationship.

The problem is that emotions build on themselves and, over time, become more intense, and the behaviors associated with them become habitualized, even when it's not called for. Here's another example: have you ever thought your partner has a "fear of intimacy" and accused them of being "cold," "distant," "unemotional," or "hard to reach"? What you are seeing is their consistent reactions to their most vulnerable emotions that are uncomfortable for them to access, experience, tolerate, and make use of. What we experience as our sense of self is a very complicated experience that you cannot nail down to any one emotion, thought, or behavior.

Unfortunately, these acting out behaviors don't release, ease, mitigate, or cancel out the emotions we are protecting ourselves from; they only block our awareness of them. The technical term for this blocking process is *dissociation*, and it is highly associated with the ways the mind protects us from being overwhelmed by anxiety—especially when it reaches traumatic levels. The world-renowned traumatologist Bessel van der Kolk asserts in his book, *The Body Keeps the Score*, that "dissociation prevents trauma from becoming integrated within the conglomerated, ever-shifting stores of autobiographical memory."[2] In other words, when we are overwhelmed by anxiety, the way we think of ourselves, and the emotions we are feeling, are profoundly cut off from our experience, affecting what we know and recognize as "me."[3] In their

2.   Bessel van der Kolk, *The Body Keeps the Score: Brain, Mind, and Body in the Healing of Trauma* (New York: Penguin, 2014), 182.
3.   Harry Stack Sullivan (1953) theory of dissociation and *not-me* experience is summarized by Feist and Feist (2008) as follows: "During mid-infancy a child acquires

place, the dissociated experiences that we cannot acknowledge are acted out. In relationships this acting out behavior is referred to as *enacted*.[4]

For our purposes, "enacted" describes any behavior played out in a relationship dynamic that allows an intolerable emotion to bypass our conscious awareness. But we do not eradicate the intolerable emotions, only our *awareness* of such feelings. This means the bad feels that we have about ourselves remain intact, even when our behaviors work effectively to get rid

---

three me personifications (bad-me, good-me, and not-me) that form the building blocks of the self-personification. Each is related to the evolving conception of me or my body. The *bad-me personification* is fashioned from experiences of punishment and disapproval that infants receive from their mothering one. The resulting anxiety is strong enough to teach infants that they are bad, but it is not so severe as to cause the experience to be dissociated or *selectively unattended*. Like all personifications, the bad-me is shaped out of the interpersonal situation; that is, infants can learn that they are bad only from someone else, ordinarily the bad-mother. The *good-me personification* results from infants' experiences with reward and approval. Infants feel good about themselves when they perceive their mother's expressions of tenderness. Such experiences diminish anxiety and foster the good-me personification. Sudden severe anxiety, however, may cause an infant to form the *not-me personification* and to dissociate experiences related to that anxiety" (pp. 222–23).

4.   A psychoanalytic term for acting out unconscious feelings relationally—that is, co-acting out, or playing out, our feelings in interaction rather than consciously experiencing—or being aware of—them. In relational psychoanalysis the term *enactment* is used to describe the nonreflecting playing out of a mental scenario, rather than verbally describing the associated thoughts and feelings. The term enactment was first introduced by Theodore Jacobs (1986) to describe the re-actualization of unsymbolized and unconscious emotional experiences involved in the relationship between the patient and the therapist. More precisely, Jacobs refers to the countertransference enactment, thus highlighting the implications of the personality characteristics, affective frame, representations and analyst's conflicts for the patient and the interactional behavior. Currently, the concept of enactment is usually used to explain the re-experience of a role assumed during childhood, which is recited on the stage of the therapist's consulting room: the analyst is given a specific role to play; both the patient and the analyst lose in this context their sense of distance, interacting with each other verbally and nonverbally, leading to intrapsychic dynamics in the form of interactions within the therapeutic setting (Aon, 1996). In the perspective of relational psychoanalysis, the central aspect of therapeutic change is given by the liberation of the patient and the analyst from the repetitive unconscious patterns due to the reflective awareness' acquisition of the relational interchange and the contribution of both parties. Traumatized patients, especially, tend to bond with their therapists not so much through words as through enactments, expressing unconsciously—by the action—the dissociated aspects of the self and the object representation (Bromberg, 1996, 1998, 2011).

of our conscious awareness of them. And, because we do not get rid of the actual feelings, only our awareness of them, the behaviors that work to rid ourselves of unacceptable and intolerable awareness are, ironically, fueled by an impossible goal: To get rid of the bad feelings I have about myself. But this is a vicious circle. The more I dislike myself the more I act out in ways to eradicate that feeling by acting in ways that cause other people close to me to treat me like an unlikeable person. A person who even *I don't like.*

Acting out behaviors begin as an emotion that is difficult and intolerable to you—*Me? I'm not so good* (so, *You won't/don't like me*)—and that you certainly don't want your partner to see (for example, feeling hurt or abandoned). Instead of being expressed directly, this emotion becomes an obsessive thought, as in *Why won't my wife have sex with me? Something must be wrong with her, and something is wrong with me.* Because it does not feel safe enough to express these feelings directly, you express them as a behavior (for Len, it was masturbation; for others it could be pouting, brooding, avoidance). In this process, you lose touch with your unwelcome parts (the underlying vulnerable emotion that has been, because a threat to our sense of self and sense of safety, dissociated) and yet because you haven't expressed them directly, they remain unwelcome. In fact, it is not the unwelcome parts themselves, but the miscommunicated and misunderstood behavioral manifestation of them that are standing in your way from getting what you want from long-term love.

History or Where Are These Behaviors Coming From

The ability to be vulnerable so that we can access the other "pillars of true love" is not easy to achieve. It is highly associated with our history of feeling safe—or not. In fact, our psychological defense system itself could be said to be founded upon how safe we are able to feel as we moved through our world, one relationship at a time.

Vulnerable feelings from our past can make our current relationship feel unsafe. And yet, taking risks in the realm of vulnerability, challenging our relationship to accept the things about ourselves that feel unsafe to reveal is actually the only way to build a sense of safety into our relationship. Surprisingly, one of the ways we take such risks is getting into conflict with

94

someone we love. In conflict, those parts of ourselves we'd rather not see reveal themselves. With each rupture, the building of safety that we achieve is challenged. Therefore, it is important to recognize that when you are defending yourself against accepting your partner and your relationship as they actually are, it is often a last-ditch effort against showing those unwelcome parts to someone we're not sure will (or can) accept them.

To be fair, so many of us simply don't know what accepting ourselves and each other means. We might think it means, I've fallen in love and each of the following will be true forever:

- My partner is going to accept questionable parts of me.
- If someone loves me that means that my partner won't see (a la idealization) those hard-to-tolerate parts of me.
- Love has cured me of the unacceptable parts of me.

However, these thoughts are fantasies or wishful thinking and continue to assist you in avoiding your unwelcome parts. To really accept and be accepted "as is" means that you are not just accepting your partner *as they are*, but you are agreeing to take the risk that your partner is going to see the warts-and-all version of you, and they might not like it.

Most of us have had plenty experiences of bringing our *worst self* to the table. However, we often are surprised when it happens. This is because the process of living in close proximity with someone who matters so much triggers our "unwelcome parts," and they often slip out to protect us without our awareness—or permission! Then comes the real challenge of whether or not we can communicate about our "worst self" slipping out, make amends, and accept each other as we really are.

Our unwelcome parts can also protect us from wounds that have happened in the past so that they do not happen again. Some of these wounds are deep and still quite open, and some are shallow and almost ready to heal themselves. In romantic relationships, your partner might open an old wound without knowing it. Your current relationship can stir up the most salient—and often repressed, suppressed, and/or dissociated—memories from your past (distant and near). From a psychoanalytic perspective, these are feelings you might have internalized from your early home environment. As these memories surface, the feelings are re-experienced, and old and unresolved hurts that you might have had defensive reactions and responses to earlier come back.

These vulnerable feelings can also bubble up from wounds from previous relationships. The difference is we may be well aware of these types of wounds compared to the wounds of our childhood. For example, you may have experienced the sense of dread and hope at the beginning of a new relationship, as in "I hope this is going to work and not end up like my previous relationship." Sometimes this fear is so significant that you end up reacting to your partner even if you are aware of your own particular fear and worries. Inside a reaction, there is little thinking and lots of acting in order to defend/protect yourself.

Your current relationship can also make you feel vulnerable, isolated, and unsafe at times. It legitimately hurts when our partners consistently miss or don't respond to our requests and wishes. When people say, "I hate my relationship" or "I hate my partner," what they are actually hating is not their partner, but the vicious verbal and behavioral communication dynamics between them after having their needs and wants dismissed. After the fight, even if they could not resolve the fight, some couples engage in "make-up sex." And while this can become a helpful tool to recover from a fight because they know they can connect with each other in this physically/sexually intimate way and feel loved and cared for by the other, leaving the issue of unwelcome parts unresolved can become problematic over time. In fact, couples who use sex to mitigate and avoid their unwelcome parts often unintentionally create a build-up of unresolved emotions and issues and can end up becoming distant from each other.

Getting to those feelings together requires a kind of communication that is increasingly both a direct and legitimate expression of:

- What is going on in the relationship.
- What that "going on" is bringing up from your own history and into the present relationship.
- How you are going to work to welcome a fuller version/experience of each of you into the relationship.

This is the process of cocreating *safety* (a hospitable environment for honesty and vulnerability) and one of the highlights of our PACER model. We cannot create a hospitable environment for our unwelcome parts if it is not safe enough. When those parts of ourselves appear it can be terrifying, it can take us back to moments in this or other relationships where it was not safe enough to be ourselves and express vulnerable emotion. Most psychoanalytic theories propose that the relationships from our past become internalized and are a powerful source of repeating these same dynamics in our current relationships (enactment). This is especially true for dynamics that occurred during conflicts that were left unresolved. In a sense, then, when conflicts occur, it is not just one partner battling the other, but one internalized other who is also battling another internalized other.

Kathy and Miguel: Old Wounds and New Armor

Our clients Kathy and Miguel have been married for two years. Kathy was married before and in the previous marriage she was unable to communicate with her ex-husband James when he went on a business trip, which made her feel lonely and afraid. His job would take him away from home for at least a week at a time, and Kathy really wanted James to call her once a day to check in. James thought that her request was "controlling," and eventually the marriage fell apart.

A few years later, Kathy met Miguel and got remarried. Yet every time that Miguel has to go on a business trip Kathy gets angry, and while he's away sends him combative text messages. Miguel feels perplexed and criticized and doesn't respond to them. As he told us, "Why should I send her a message since she is being so nasty?"

In this conflict, Kathy's defenses are covering her unwelcome fear and separation anxiety, which were open wounds from her previous marriage. It is not easy to acknowledge in front of your partner how you reacted when you are feeling so vulnerable. Yet, because your partner is the one who is the closest to you, it is important to recognize that you caused pain. We helped facilitate and open dialogue where Kathy had a chance to let Miguel know that she gets insecure when he goes away, which is why she wants him to call her once a day. Miguel was able to acknowledge his reaction, and let Kathy know that he wants her to tell him what she needs without criticism and angry demands.

As we create safety together—one rupture, one repair at a time—we can begin to let our guard down and drop our defensive weapons so that we can have a shared experience of the risks we are navigating together. And, in so doing, decrease the likelihood that we will act them out. Sharing vulnerable emotions, it turns out, is the exact opposite of acting them out.

The Unwelcome Parts as "Baggage"

No one sees any of our warts-and-all stuff through the idealized honeymoon stage. But, as we learned in the last chapter, when the honeymoon's over and the rose-colored glasses lose their hue, we are faced to accept real life. And that's when your baggage finally arrives. Your baggage is the set of unresolved feelings and behaviors that show up from your history as your unwelcome parts.

Your baggage can be the beliefs that are influenced by familial values, cultural values, gender roles, societal values, and generational values. While it is normal to have ingrained beliefs, when we hold onto these beliefs too rigidly, it can create distance between you and your partner and blind you from seeing what is happening in the relationship. For example, Haruna had to let go of her need to always be right when she married Mark. In her upbringing, she saw that her parents' marriage, whoever was right had more power, and she saw in her own relationship that whoever was wrong got criticized. Her unwelcome part was believing that she always had to be right, which made her blame Mark and criticize him for being wrong.

You may be able to repress, deny, block, inhibit all your baggage, but doing so means that you've literally left yourself outside the door, and you'll never feel at home in your relationship. You'll always be on guard; you'll always be performing or pretending, contorting yourself through the proverbial hoops that might only exist because you brought them with you from the unresolved conflicts in your history. Avoiding your baggage means that you deeply believe no one will accept you as you *really* are.

> However, the baggage always arrives. Trips down memory lane—this all-important relationship jogging loose memories, dynamics, habits, and patterns you learned throughout your life thus far—are inevitable. Leaving your baggage—your past, unwelcome parts—behind is never really an option.

Gordon and Derrick: Avoiding the Unwelcome Parts

There are some situations where people are so afraid and defended against intimacy—or the anxiety associated with it—that they choose relationships that allow no room for those within to express who they really are. In this case, the only thing worse than the baggage arriving is the baggage *not* arriving. Take Gordon and Derrick, who were set up, each by a friend who "just knew" they'd be a perfect match. And, as it was true that for as long as they were perfect, they were a match.

"In reality, our relationship felt like a performance," said Derrick, "and I believe that Gordon, although his was more about setting the hoops out to be jumped through rather than jumping through them himself, felt the same way. Yet to everyone else, we looked just perfect."

Being constricted to a role creates a rigid structure that makes it difficult, if not impossible, for us to be—and to feel like—ourselves. When we are avoiding the unwelcome parts, that's the goal: to be anyone other than that version of ourselves who seems so infinitely rejectable. Most of the time the behavior that came with the repressed feelings is destructive. In Derrick's case, his good behavior was in fact, what was "bad."

Derrick went on, "We never ever fought, we never argued, in fact, we could never say what we were actually feeling toward each other. In fact, we barely spoke to each other when we were on our own. Yet to everyone else, we looked great. We were the envy of others and, when the Marriage Equality Act went through, it was practically a given that we'd get married. And that's exactly when the wake-up call rang for me. I realized I was trapped in a perfect prison. I had contorted myself into the expectations that I needed to believe Gordon had imposed."

Yet many of us believe that whatever the relationship prison looks like, it tends to be co-constructed. So we weren't surprised when Derrick continued to say, "When the problems began, it was easy to blame Gordon because he was so willing to put his needs up front, to tell me how important it was that we 'behave' in a very prescribed way. His guidelines did make us look good, and they also protected each of us from any real threat of honesty because we were always on our best behavior."

The strict maintenance of our idealizations is the trap we fall into when we turn to acting out behaviors to avoid being overwhelmed by insecurity. In doing so, we wind up avoiding who and what we really are, which is another behavior that defends ourselves against the experience of honesty that leads to intimacy. Without that, relationships are not able to develop the muscles necessary to endure, manage, and navigate the vicissitudes of everyday life.

"We had no way to drop our guard as manifested via our 'perfect couple' routine and be ourselves. And, after some time, I felt suffocated and lonely. And then, one day while Gordon was away on a business trip, I impulsively packed up my stuff and moved out. Amazingly enough, he did not dispute it, never asked me why, and went out of his way to maintain an amicable relationship while it was ending. Why not? Neither of us had any real sense of what—or who—we were losing anyway."

Derrick and Malik: Welcoming the Unwelcome Parts

It wasn't until Derrick was in a new relationship with Malik that he was able to see his role in the breakup, and that role was not accepting his unwelcome parts.

"Even though my relationship with Gordon felt like a tyranny," said Derrick, "I can see that Gordon's need to be in control was a perfect—perfectly oppressive—fit with my fear that were anyone to really *know me* he'd go running for the hills. So, that tyranny, that oppression, was really something that I had in me to keep me safe. Gordon just helped ensure that I'd comply with the limits of my own fear—of being accepted and loved as I really am."

"It's not so much that I was ready," said Malik, "but when I met Derrick I, too, had been sick of hiding out in relationships where the real me was feeling left out. Like I was there, but *whoever* that was, was not me."

"Falling in love is one thing," noted Derrick, "believing that my lover is trustworthy and will accept me as I am, is another. And this is especially true when one is gun-shy and wanting to do anything to ensure that he is not merely repeating past mistakes—mistakes like sidelining essential parts of myself, as I did with Gordon, in the desperate hope that someone—now Malik—will like me and not dump my ass."

"It would have been nice if I'd known that that's what Derrick was doing," admitted Malik, "as sometimes it just seemed like he was being purposefully difficult . . ."

"Without Gordon patrolling my behavior, I wound up being just like him. I didn't even know I had it in me, but I wound up inspecting Malik every time he walked out the door, seeing if what he was wearing was okay, worried that he looked disheveled and poorly taken care of just like Gordon—and my own mother—used to say to me. I was doing all that I could to control Malik."

Malik added, "Which started to push me away."

"I guess," said Derrick "that was part of the point. But all that insecurity and awkwardness that I needed to leave out of my relationship with Gordon could just no longer be repressed."

"Indeed."

"And" added Derrick, "thank goodness, right?"

"Well," agreed Malik, "right. But it certainly wasn't easy. In fact, there were plenty of times I didn't think we were going to make it."

"I wasn't sure either," admitted Derrick, "but it was almost impossible to communicate to you in all that madness how relieved I was that whatever it was we were doing—yes, I was acting very badly, being a real asshole, punishing you when I thought you were not representing us well to the world, withholding sex, scared to talk or tell you what was going on—we were not hiding. I swore I'd never ever agree to *that* again."

Dull thud (as the ending of the Gordon-Derrick relationship had been) or not, terminating a long-term love relationship is painful for many reasons regardless of how desirous and necessary it is. In fact, in Derrick's case, one of the things that made it so painful is that it was just another in a long series of failed relationships. The difference was (is) that this time Derrick felt a desperate need—and, more clearly, a "desperate willingness"—to be honest with himself and "break the pattern of leaving myself out of the relationship."

According to Derrick: "That meant taking risks I'd never taken, facing fears I quite simply didn't even know I had. And this freaked me out and made me act like a controlling lunatic."

"And" chimed in Malik, "though I'd like to simply agree and say, 'Yeah, Derrick acted like a control freak,' what really happened was that when one of us landed in lunacy, the other was, more often than not, more than willing to jump right into the mayhem."

Derrick added, "That was oddly the very first time I felt myself breaking out of the isolation that had always haunted me in every relationship as soon as the honeymoon's over. But now I realize that a deep relationship is based on results, not wishes."

Identify Feelings: Getting Underneath Behaviors

Now that you are beginning to understand how your behaviors can be stand-ins or defenses for your unwelcome emotions, let's see where these emotions are coming from. The truth is that some people don't understand their own emotions or they are afraid of them. So, as we learned in Chapter Two, they immediately put on the armor of aggression in order to hide their confusing and vulnerable feelings.

We all have a mixture of feelings about our partners, especially during a rupture. For instance, you might be feeling disappointed in your partner, but if you take a step back, you need to uncover what's causing that feeling. It might be one of several more vulnerable feelings, such as hurt, scared, or sadness.

These vulnerable feelings are referred to as *primary feelings*. American psychologist Dr. Robert Plutchik proposed that there are eight primary and oppositional emotions that act as the foundation for all other emotions. They are the pairs joy and sadness, acceptance and disgust, fear and anger, and surprise and anticipation. He arranged them in an emotion wheel that looks like this:[5]

5.   Robert Plutchik, "A General Psychoevolutionary Theory of Emotion," in Robert Plutchik and Henry Kellerman (Eds.), *Emotion: Theory, Research and Experience, Theories of Emotion*, vol. 1 (New York: Academic Press, 1980), 3–33.

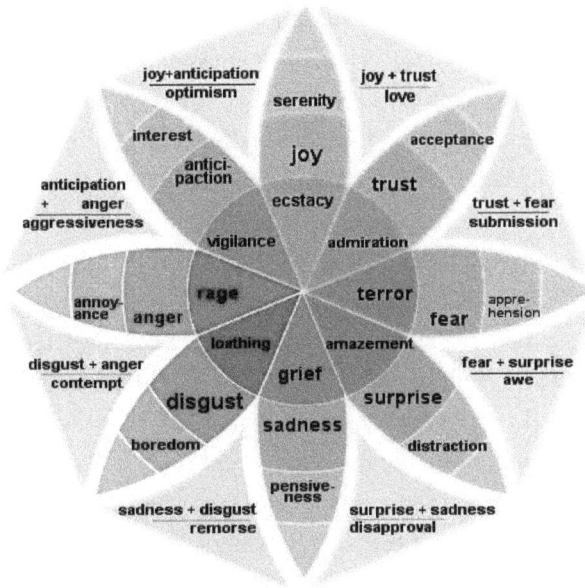

An emotion wheel helps us to work our way backward from the combination of acting out behavior and putting on the armor of aggression to find its root cause. The center circle contains our most intense emotions. The first ring outside the center contains our primary feelings, and their opposites are listed across from each other. As the rings pull away from the center, each petal contains the related, albeit less intense emotion. The emotions that appear between the petals are a combination of the two primary emotions that surround them.

Use the wheel to examine how you are feeling in any given moment. The goal is to articulate your emotions in a healthy, productive, and constructive way, not a reactive one. Once you've identified your emotion, think about what events or interactions activated it. This ability alone may empower you to express how you feel in ways that are in your control.

There will be times when our behaviors toward our partners are not ideal. We may act in ways that are out of proportion, embarrassing, and shameful. When your emotions are roiling, step back and regroup with the emotion wheel: stop, identify your emotion, and find out what's driving it. As you look at the words in the center circle and move toward the outer circles, you may find it's actually the softer, more vulnerable emotions that are driving your behavior. You don't necessarily act out loneliness in the same way you act out in rage, but the rage may be the extension of the loneliness—unexpressed, unarticulated, unprocessed, and misunderstood. The emotion wheel offers an easy way into a conversation to show your partner how you are feeling, discuss what happened, apologize, and move forward.

Don't be surprised if your partner shares that their underlying emotion is anger. We've found that anger is probably the emotion that people in rupture are dealing with, because it is so thoroughly effective at protecting us from the more vulnerable feelings that often lie underneath. In fact, we find if one hits pause and takes a step back from what seems like the initial reaction (anger), they often can find the more vulnerable emotions—especially hurt and fear—that the anger is covering up. An emotion wheel could help them see their anger, and if they (or you) are using anger as an armor to protect them from the feelings of vulnerability.

Armor and Crutches

Armor is our defensive, unwelcome parts. But that is not all we have in our arsenal when we are in conflict. We also have crutches, which are our private thoughts that protect us from relational injuries. Armors are very obvious behaviors, while crutches are secret defensive thoughts that aren't apparent. It is human to have these defenses at the ready, and we need both armor and crutches to get through difficult experiences when we feel attacked and betrayed.

For instance, you may respond to your partner's criticism with armor and say, "Screw you!" Or you can respond with a crutch and say aloud, "Yes. You are right," but in your mind you say to yourself, Nobody can tell me what to do!

Exercise: Identify Your Feelings

Use the emotion wheel to accurately identify your feelings.
- Recall a recent argument you had with your partner and write down as accurately as you can what each party said.
- What emotions came up most often for you, and what was happening when they did? Distinguish between feelings you showed and didn't show. For example, I felt hurt when my partner rejected my sexual advances. I felt rejected but my behavior looked like I was apathetic and I didn't really care. I began paying attention to other people to make her feel uncomfortable.
- What is your impression of the feelings that your partner had during the disagreement, simultaneously or not. How did your interpretation of their feelings affect the argument?

Focusing on Feelings of Anger

The primary emotions that underlie anger are the ones that usually leave us feeling vulnerable, such as fear, pain, and sadness. Yet many people are so detached from their anxieties that they don't know what their anger is protecting them from. Becoming aware of your defenses and what emotions are underneath can help you get in touch with your specific vulnerability. You created this defense for a reason: because something in your life wasn't safe. So you put up your wall to protect yourself.

Fear and hurt are often unwelcome emotions in a relationship. First, our culture at large certainly does not accept displays of vulnerability. It is equally unlikely that there are many circumstances where leading off with fear and pain are considered attractive. And so, by the time most people are experiencing the fear of vulnerability in a relationship, this feeling has already been covered up by behaviors that communicate the exact opposite. In fact, the fear of abandonment, rejection, and the pain of loneliness (if we're lucky enough to actually feel these things as the raw emotions that they actually are) often show up as our most unwelcome parts, instead of more accurately representing our vulnerability.

Exercise: The Anger Conversion Chart

People are not aware of their vulnerability, but strike instead, stopping an argument with anger and force. So how do you deal with your vulnerable feelings more effectively so that you do not have to put up your armor of anger? The Anger Conversion Chart can help you acknowledge the feelings that live underneath your anger because anger is covering up for vulnerability. In many schools of psychology, anger is considered a secondary emotion to the emotions related to vulnerability. Which is why underneath anger, there can be anxiety, fear, insecurity, pain, rejection, and sadness.

Anger can look like:	Anger can cover up these vulnerabilities:
Attack	Fear
Criticism	Feeling put down and attacked
Dismissal	Feeling unwanted
Judgment	Insecurity
Making fun of	Pain
Stonewalling	Rejection
Withdrawal	Sadness

- What does your anger look like?
- What's hidden underneath your anger? What's your vulnerability?
- What would it take for you to share your vulnerability instead of in the form of anger?
- Would a different expression of anger make your partner more aware of how you are actually feeling? Instead of stonewalling, you say to your partner, "I have felt hurt and rejected."

Taking Inventory Again: Pinpointing Your Unwelcome Parts

The fact that you're reading this book tells us that your unwelcome parts have made themselves known, not because you're so enlightened and know yourself so well (although that may be true), but more likely that your partner has brought them to your attention. The truth is your most unwelcome parts are always on display. The problem is you don't see them as anything but less-than-ideal-yet-irreversible parts of your character.

We use the word *character* to refer to the sum total of our psychological defenses: it's the armor we use to defend ourselves from being overwhelmed by emotion[6]. There are many, many ways we defend ourselves against being hurt, against being scared, and, as we have seen, against being aware that we are being hurt and/or scared. Character is then our habitual way of being in the world, in which we develop certain routines and rituals that protect us from being overwhelmed by emotion so that we can function effectively. Our character can change depending on our environment. Character is then the tool that allows for dissociation.

Your character only becomes problematic when you overuse it and if you make it the only way to deal with conflict, over-protecting and defending yourself (usually quite unintentionally) from the things that you want, especially from your partner. Each time we use these defenses, your partner sees that you are being defensive, and in return, interacts with you from their defensive position. When defense invites another defense, it can result in frustration, distance, and destruction.

For instance, Mark acknowledges that part of his character is that he often goofs around during serious conversations. He knows he does it, and he's not proud of it, but when Haruna first brought it to his attention he believed that it was "just part of who I am." Mark was always the class clown, and people responded enthusiastically to his antics when he was growing up. Yet on reflections, he remembers that his silliness drove every other person he ever dated nuts. By using the PACER model, Mark was able to realize that his underlying feelings when acting provocatively aren't simply goofy, but that

6. Mark B. Borg, Jr., "Venturing Beyond the Consulting Room: Psychoanalysis in Community Crisis Intervention," *Contemporary Psychoanalysis*, 40 no. 2 (2004): 147–74.

this aspect of his character breaks through whenever he is uncomfortable with his own vulnerability—especially when Haruna is being genuinely loving and vulnerable herself. When he stopped justifying and rationalizing this defensive behavior and started to see that it was not Haruna who pushed him toward this behavior, he was more able to take in the love she offers.

Identifying the defenses that inform your character doesn't mean you are being critical of yourself. We're not asking you to strip down and walk the streets in shame, but to open the door to a realm where you can discover things about yourself that merit acceptance. Vulnerability is the glue that binds partners, while defenses pull partners away. We all make mistakes in life. And we make mistakes in relationships, too.

The best way we've found to really dig deep into the why of your behavior is by *taking inventory*. We can't tell you how many times our patients are taking their inventory and having their mind blown. Week after week, our patients say some version of "Whoa, now I can see how I interact with my partner." It's like we are helping them flick on the light bulb in their mind. Time and time again we tell our patients that "the best defense against taking someone else's inventory is to take our own." When the inventory-taker is willing to reveal their own vulnerabilities, the other person will drop their defenses and do the same. Ultimately, inventory can help you establish a cornerstone for a genuinely cocreated sense of safety.

Taking inventory is less about our overt behavior and more about what it covers up. For instance, Mark came out of the Army with not only the GI Bill, which allowed him to pay for college but also with a drill sergeant's mentality about timeliness. And while it seemed like this is nothing but a "mature, adult" attitude toward punctuality, the need for timeliness became a weapon he could use to justify two of his unwelcome parts: self-righteousness and righteous indignation.

The insight into the anxiety that drove Mark's time sensibility was only uncovered when he began to take inventory of his time-management behavior, as well as the behaviors that came with it (criticism, harassment, etc.). In inventory, Mark discovered that the idea of being late made him feel like he was losing control and brought him back to a time in his life when his parents' marriage was falling apart, and he constantly wondered who, if anyone, would be home when he got home from school. Uncovering this connection allowed both Mark and Haruna to better understand Mark's reaction to time-management *and* motivate them to take on new responsibilities for time-management together. This meant Haruna would commit to being more mindful of how the management of time affects Mark, and Mark would commit to retiring from the job of "time cop" and let others be responsible for getting everywhere on time (also, tinkering with what "on time" means, i.e., not necessarily thirty minutes early).

You may find that you cannot take an inventory of what you did to contribute to a fight due to your own self-criticism, which may be masking a fear of being criticized by others. When you live in terror of being seen as flawed, unlikeable, or unlovable, it often results in the knee-jerk taking of other people's inventory. The spiral begins: taking your partner's inventory enforces your belief that it's all your partner's fault after all, which may then mean to you that you made a bad choice in a partner, and all that you can do now is hope that they'll change. These thoughts leave us feeling isolated, reeling from the sense of making such a bad decision *and* having not a clue what to do about it.

"No inventory taking" is the slang in the twelve-step community for keeping our own judgments and criticism off our partner.[7] Sometimes, this feels like an impossible task. We've found, though, that the best prevention against taking someone else's inventory is to start by taking your own. Taking your partner's inventory is a weapon; taking your own is the rough draft of a cease-fire agreement.

Exercise: Taking Inventory #2

You've already done the first step of inventory-taking in Chapter One by identifying your assets. The second step involves examining your part in a conflict; later, we will use the PACER model to take inventory of

---

7.   Many of us attempt to light-touch and rationalize our criticism with the term "positive feedback," but extensive research in business development tells us that "In 38 percent of cases, feedback not only did not improve performance, it actively makes it worse." (Kluger & DeNisi, 1996), 281.

your relationship. For now, choose a recurring issue that has historically justified a specific behavior.

The Behavior _____

Who was hurt, and what was the nature of this conflict/harm done to others or to myself?	How I defended myself. How I justified/ rationalized the defensive behavior.	What vulnerable feelings were underneath and/or were expressed through my defensive behavior?	What have I learned about myself through this assessment? What can I do differently next time by taking my own inventory?

Outside of taking inventory, conflict provides another opportunity to identify your defenses. Conflict tends to be, at least initially, the acting out of the secondary feelings to our most vulnerable primary feelings. The moments when we feel most vulnerable are the moments we attack or create ruptures or conflicts because we don't want people to know that we're vulnerable.

Conflict is an opportunity to get at what is really going on because the likelihood is if you are fighting with someone you really love, the fight itself is an acting out of a protection against something much more vulnerable to you. In this case, it's likely that you don't want your partner to see your vulnerability because you have already been hurt and do not feel safe enough in this interaction to actually express this feeling. So instead of expressing the hurt, you cover it up with defensive or an acting out behavior that leads to another rupture.

Exercise: Welcoming the Unwelcome Parts of Yourself

Here is a tool to help you understand how your unwelcome parts show up in conflicts. When you discover your vulnerabilities and the feelings that surround your unwelcome parts, you will be able to express them better during a rupture and then get to a repair.

We are using money as an example of conflict because it is the number one reason why people divorce. You can substitute whatever is your most sensitive issue in your relationship:

1. Write down the answer to: what is my relationship to money and what kind of security issues —and/or insecurity—arise related to money? (For example, I want my partner to adhere to how I relate to—"handle"—our financial affairs.)
2. If you feel righteous about the ways you deal with—and relate to—money, do you have any emotional room to listen to the way your partner relates to money? In reality, how you relate to money—and associated security/insecurity issues—is likely to invite your partner to see some of your most intimate unwelcome parts.
3. If you don't have the emotional room to listen to the way your partner relates to money, think about why?
4. If you want your partner to adhere to—and have respect and compassion for—your relationship to money, then you are looking for your partner to validate your point of view. First, let's compassionately validate the way you take care of money by welcoming the unwelcome parts of yourself. The truth is, it is

extremely difficult for people to have a conversation about money with anyone, including their partner. Your unwelcome parts may have come from a deep sense of insecurity, so much so that you avoid the topic of money altogether (how many times have you ever asked anyone "What's in your wallet?"). Think how your unwelcome parts show up when you are having a conversation about money with your partner:

- What was my defense/armor (raising my voice, keep interrupting, criticizing, etc.)?
- Could you forgive yourself for this behavior?
- What emotion was underneath my defense/armor? Fear, worries, insecurity, shame, emotional pain, righteousness? Be compassionate with yourself as you uncover your raw, vulnerable feelings that are attached to money: this line of questioning is in fact a courageous action.
- Could you let your partner know that underneath your defense (raising my voice, keep interrupting, and criticizing) was the emotion _____. If you can't put your finger on your underlying emotion yet, can you say, "I really don't know how to talk about money collaboratively. But I want us to figure this out together."
- Can you make your talk about money more of an ongoing activity? Money is an ongoing discussion you will have with your partner. Think of it as something you are practicing as you live your life with your partner in real life.

CHAPTER FIVE

History Repeats Itself through Unresolved Conflicts

An idea often associated with Freudian psychoanalysis (and popular culture) is that we marry our opposite-sex parent. However, we believe that it's not so much a parent who we marry, but that love relationships offer the opportunity to heal old wounds and resolve conflicts from our family of origin. The difference is significant.

Psychoanalysis focuses on the tendency to repeat a familiar dynamic, a well-grooved pattern of interaction. When it comes to love relationships, conventional wisdom suggests that you are attracted to your opposite-sex parent and then bring that parent's role from your old family conflicts into your new relationship. Sometimes, partners exhibit a particular behavior that reminds the other of one of their parents, like being indulgent or withholding affection. Or it can be an unconscious process where you experience old feelings and then "invite" a partner to engage in your familial patterns. Either way, you can find yourself in a full-on repetition of family dynamics that you enjoyed in the past or hoped to avoid. And this is less about the role and/or behavior of any particular family member, and more the repetition of dynamics (and associated defenses) within which the whole family was embroiled in.

When I find a familiar *you*, I have also found the familiar *me*. The partner provides the relational context for repeating dynamics that are familiar and allows me to feel like myself, a self that is familiar, comfortable, and well-defended against overwhelming anxiety. In this relational context I am defended against acknowledging and owning the parts of myself that I've split off from my consciousness in order to survive. In the realm of relationship dynamics, this corresponds with what Freud called the *repetition compulsion*.[1] It can be compared to the definition of insanity popular in twelve-step programs: repeating the same thing over and over, expecting different results. In a repetition compulsion, a person repeats a traumatic event or its circumstances. This includes either reenacting the event or putting oneself in situations where the event is likely to occur again.

This pattern was described by Sigmund Freud in his 1920 essay "Beyond the Pleasure Principle."[2] He observed a child throwing his favorite toy from his crib, becoming upset at the loss, then reeling the toy back in, only to replay this action repetitively. Such behavior is often observed in children when they throw a toy out of reach, then cry for it to be retrieved. Freud theorized that children are attempting to master the sensation of loss, possibly using the toy as a surrogate for their mothers who cannot always be physically present.

Freud believed there were two ways the past can be relived: 1) through memories or 2) through actions, such as in repetition compulsion. Schools of thought vary on how they view the concept of repetition; for example, the passive type, in which a person consistently chooses familiar experiences as a means of dealing with problems from the past, such as staying in a situation of pain and chaos instead of risking possible traumatic new experiences. Another might balk at new experiences for fear they will be more painful than their present situation.

Another school of thought suggests a participatory form of repetition in which a person actively engages in behavior that mimics an earlier stressor, either deliberately or unconsciously. In such cases, terrifying childhood experiences may become sources of attraction in adulthood. For instance, a person who was spanked as a child may incorporate this into their adult sexual practices,

1. Sigmund Freud, "Remembering, Repeating and Working Through." In *The Standard Edition of the Complete Psychological Works of Sigmund Freud, Vol. 12*, translated and edited by James Strachey, 145–56. (London: The Hogarth Press, 1914), 150.
2. Sigmund Freud, "Beyond the Pleasure Principle." In *Standard Edition of the Complete Works of Sigmund Freud, Vol. 18*, 3–64 (London: The Hogarth Press, 1920).

or a victim of sexual abuse may attempt to seduce a person in authority in their life, such as a boss or therapist. Psychoanalysts describe this as an attempt at mastery of their feelings and experience, in the sense that they unconsciously want to go through the same situation, but with a different outcome than was experienced in the past. This view is based on the notion that behavior may be due to "psychodynamic factors" driven by motivations and emotional states we are not aware of. What drives us "crazy" is that we often *repeat* the dynamics so effectively that we often include, in the completion of the repetitive cycle, the less-than-optimal outcome. In the case of the childhood spanking, the feelings of being hurt and humiliated get "repeated" in adult interactions, which result in crazy-making patterns in adult relationships.[3]

Our PACER model leaves room for the possibility that repetition is not just about making ourselves—and each other—insane, but, instead, a purposeful attempt to resolve an old conflict. We agree with the renowned theorist and psychotherapist Harville Hendrix who suggests that "the fundamental drive of the unconscious mind [is to be] safe, is to be healed, and to be whole."[4]

We agree that much of what we know about ourselves in relationship— and, even more of what we don't—has been influenced by the environment in which we were raised. The way you internalized the unresolved conflicts of your parents and the relationships you had with your parents will influence how you are in relationships now.

Behavioral probability statistics uses the term *regression to the mean* to show how behaviors and patterns of interaction specifically return to our most expected way of functioning. This regression to the familiar may be why we are drawn to reenact our most salient and familiar pattern of interaction in

3.   Trauma theories provide complements and alternatives to the unconscious motivation model; however, this may be a form of fundamental attribution error therapists ironically use with patients, "blaming the victim" by postulating a "need" to engage in self-harm. Sometimes these behaviors are driven by masochism and mastery, but they are often the result of early traumatic conditioning, protective mechanisms wired in during childhood that persist into adulthood without any primary meaning or intent. Distinguishing habit from motivated behavior is critical, as well as understanding the relationships between the two in adult life. (Borg, Brenner, and Barry, 2022).
4.   Harville Hendrix, *Getting the Love You Want: A Guide for Couples* (New York: Henry Holt & Company, 2008), 88.

our current relationships. And the closer the relationship the more powerful the drive to recreate the familiar dynamic. In this exact sense, we really do marry into our old family conflicts.

Internalizing the unresolved conflicts of your parents, or even previous relationships, is how we bring the "baggage" we discussed in the Chapter Four into a relationship. Our baggage can include conflicts from our environment that we were involved in, whether or not they were spoken about. In fact, the spoken and unspoken rules you make between yourself and your partner are often not only between the two of you but actually between your past self and the "environment" (i.e., parents, family unit). In this sense, you are *transferring* your old conflicts onto your contemporary relationships.

For example, if your last relationship ended because your partner had an affair, you might fear that your current partner will have an affair. Even though you realize you are in a new relationship with a new partner, you can't help feeling suspicious every time your current partner talks to someone other than you. In this way your past issues can have a "glass ceiling effect" on your relationship, limiting how much you are trusting the new relationship, willing to be vulnerable, or allowing the relationship to succeed.

We then *enact*, or play out, these old dynamics with our partner because we are behaving in the most familiar way we know. It only becomes enactment when our partner joins us, playing out their own historical family dynamics. This is particularly true when we face complicated challenges because the way we play out these dynamics in love relationships tend to unconsciously invite others to respond (and/or react) in ways that often relate to and repeat the patterns we bring with us. This is why most therapists believe we do not wind up with each other—our most intimate partners—by accident. With each new relationship, we unconsciously wish to repair our past with our current partner.

Projecting Unresolved Conflicts

One common psychological defense allows us to take the qualities we dislike about ourselves and, rather than deal with them, perceive those same intolerable aspects in others. Therapists from a number of different schools of thought call this *projecting*. As a result, we impose feelings about those parts of ourselves that we don't like onto other people. When you are projecting these qualities and associated feelings onto your partner, disappointments can grow from molehills to mountains.

Matilda brought her unresolved family conflict into love relationships in the past without knowing it and had a difficult time separating her family history from her present experiences. She told us, "Do the guys I go out with all have something in common, or do I just keep making lousy choices? All my relationships start out the same. At first, I'm excited—one might say obsessed. And if the guy puts me off, I go after him even harder. Yet the instant a guy lets me know he's really interested in me, I start having second thoughts: out of nowhere, I start seeing things about him that I don't like. And before long, whatever that 'flaw' is becomes my excuse for calling the whole thing off."

We could see that Matilda was apprehensive about letting *any* relationship become important. She then shared that her parents had a terrible marriage. "The whole time I was a kid, I worried about whether or not my parents were going to leave me. One of them was always saying they'd had enough or yelling 'get out' at the other. It scared me so much! I was afraid they'd just leave and I'd be left alone."

We showed Matilda that her actions toward her boyfriends were a preemptive strike: she was projecting her fear that any man who came across as stable would eventually leave her, so she made sure she left first. Then a few weeks into therapy Matilda came into our office beaming. She had met Jorge, who had come from a similar family dynamic. By this time Matilda had the confidence to share her frightening feelings with him, and she was able to *take back her projections* (meaning she could begin to discern the frightening and painful ideas she had about relationships from the behaviors she was seeing in Jorge); she put down her hard armor of defenses. This was the beginning of creating a new homeostasis not built around fear of closeness to others but around honesty about her vulnerability.

Scars and Armor

Meditation teacher Jeff Warren suggests that we respect the scary and painful remnants of our history and see these as scars that remind us of where we've been, who we've been, what we've been through, and the lessons we've learned. Sometimes these scars will throb, reminding us that they are still present and a part of who we are. Even though they hurt sometimes, we can live with them, as they are part of what has allowed us to love each other—and ourselves—as we are.

Owning your history can also help you look at each type of armor you have collected so that you can see what you may need to keep and what can be let go. You are holding onto some types of armor because they are knee-jerk, ready-to go rescue tools. However, in the context of your current relationship, this same armor can be destructive or useless.

Enactments Result in Agreements That Turn into Mottos

Human beings, like all living things, tend toward homeostasis, which is a fancy way of saying that our biological systems are programmed to maintain equilibrium and to return to a set equilibrium if disturbed. This need also plays out in our social configurations—families, social and work relationships, even our larger social and political systems. In fact, social scientists—such as social theorists and eminent family therapist Don Jackson[5]—tell us that seeking out and staying in stable systems is natural to our humanity.[6]

It's no surprise that for every couple, each partner brings their unresolved family conflicts into the new relationship. Ultimately, all of these conflicts

5. Don D. Jackson, "The Question of Family Homeostasis," *International Journal of Family Therapy,* 3(1) (1981): 5–15.
6. *Homeostasis* refers to how a person under conflicting stresses and motivations can maintain a stable psychological condition. Social homeostasis refers to the ability of an individual to detect the quantity and quality of social contact, compare it to an established set-point in a command center, and adjust the effort expended to seek social contact through an effector system. (Matthews and Tye, 2019)

affect how you and your partner become an "us." This is why we believe every relationship revolves around the dynamic of the relationship itself, the "us" we create, instead of how one partner behaves toward another.

Sometimes, you and your partner will make implicit and/or explicit agreements with each other as a way of addressing these unresolved conflicts. These can include expectations/new joint mottos like:

- We're never going to talk about our feelings.
- We're never going to talk about our past relationships.
- Let's leave all the influences of our dating history outside of this relationship.

For instance, our client Robin comes from an upper middle-class family whose motto was "be careful how you spend your money." Will grew up in public housing, and his family motto was "when you have extra money you can treat yourself," even though there were very few occasions that Will's family had extra money. The way that Will and Robin enact these incompatible mottos became a stalemate when they were trying to buy a home. There was never a house good enough for Robin to let go of her savings, which made Will feel angry, frustrated, deprived, and a little manipulated as they missed opportunity after opportunity to get the one thing they both really wanted, which was a larger living space.

What we enact is often difficult for us to see because it threatens to put us in touch with the scary and painful parts of our past vulnerability and pain. Our behaviors are knee-jerk reactions to pain and emotional open wounds. They are also an expression of experiences that we blocked—or dissociated from. Problematic behaviors surface when you are trying to resolve old unresolved conflicts in the brand-new relationship. However, each time we develop new ways of relating to the world—especially romantic partners—our behaviors can remain influenced by our past, forming a wall between the things we need to love and to be loved.

For example, when Trish was growing up, her parents demanded that she quietly sit at the dinner table. The second she started talking she was told to go to her room. There were many other occasions that Trish was criticized and harshly disciplined in her family. From this experience, she made it a goal to anticipate what her girlfriend Sophia wanted from her and acted quickly on it. Yet through this enactment, Trish was leaving her deepest self and wishes out of the relationship for fear of being criticized and rejected.

While we're busy playing out old dynamics, we're also hoping against hope that we'll break free from these same destructive patterns—you know, the ones you said you'd "never repeat." So it's no surprise that we feel super betrayed when old dynamics show up in our current love relationship because, as one of our clients said to her wife, "You were supposed to cure me of the wounds that I received from my family!"

By recognizing how we are enacting old conflicts, we can begin to see how they affect our current relationship and how they contribute to ruptures. If we are conscious about what we're playing out, then we don't have to be imprisoned by the ways we are influenced by our past. We get to create our own new script.

Loving, Kind Behaviors

Not only do we marry our unresolved conflicts, but we also marry warm and kind family dynamics and then create behavior patterns based on the loving aspects of our upbringing. Sometimes we remember an idealized state of our upbringing. One such motto is: "The environment I grew up in is the environment I'm going to continue to inhabit throughout my life, especially my love life."

The fact that you are in a relationship means that you can draw on some loving aspects of your past and enact them with your partner. And, despite your current conflicts and/or frequent ruptures, it is possible you remember a time when you felt loved and cared for by your partner. It is helpful to acknowledge that even when you are having a rupture in your relationship, it doesn't mean every part of the relationship has failed. But it might mean that you are ready to look at your previous unresolved conflicts and the way you are bringing those conflicts to the present.

It might be tempting to avoid each other when such scary and painful feelings resurface. But if you do so repeatedly, you will miss the opportunity for repairing the current rupture and resolving the conflicts you brought with you. You also miss the opportunity for connection, and you may end up distanced from and misunderstood by your partner. The reality is that your capacity to love, and the history and current practice of loving each other—what we call your *love tank*—isn't empty. Spending time together and working out your conflicts via the PACER model will allow you to refill your love tank.

When Mottos Are Problematic

Mottos can be problematic when they are rigid and create unrealistic expectations. And when they do not apply to what is actually happening in the present moment, the mottos themselves create conflict. Mottos tend to be reflective of the person, or people, who initially uttered and stood by them. They come to represent the (family) system itself, but much like the psychological defense system itself, they tend to leave out the whole truth and focus on some "positive" attribute that covers up what we perceive as our flaws (insecurities, sensitivities, etc.). In other words, mottos tend to be statements coming from an idealized version of our upbringing, a way of covering up truths about how things *really* were. For instance, a family motto like, "We always stick together," can be an indication that sticking together was an impossible and unreachable goal, yet we bring it into our contemporary life as a means of disavowing previous family conflicts or hoping that it can happen now. Consider where you are getting your mottos and what these mottos say about what you consider to be the ideal relationship for which you are attempting—or getting your partner to—conform with. For most of us, following these mottos is a recipe for disaster, leading to a strange fantasy state where we find ourselves missing things we never had.

Exercise: The Impact of Family Mottos

Some coping strategies are set in place at the time of family distress and become a knee-jerk reaction to a conflict/fight. Becoming aware of them is the first step toward disarming them. In this exercise, you will list examples of how your old family routines became inflexible family agreements that turned into mottos. Then describe how this affected you—and how they play out in your current relationship. Some examples are listed in the table.

Family Motto	This Motto Came Out of Routines Enacted With	This Motto's Impact on Me
Example: Don't show your feelings.	Dad	When family arguments broke out, I'd leave the room, so nobody would know how afraid I was. I was left in isolation with my fear.
Example: Always be on your best behavior inside and outside the house so nobody suspects anything is wrong with our family.	Mom	Since I could never just be myself, I made almost no friends in school.
Write Your Answer Here:		

Next, list the mottos of your current relationship and describe how they affect both you and your partner. You may start to see how your defining family mottos can impact your relationship with your partner.

Reflect on how you feel about yourself and your partner after acting in accordance with your family mottos.

Motto	How I Interpret the Motto	How the Motto Affects Our Relationship
Example: Deny everything.	Instead of openly discussing troubling issues with my partner, I ignore problems and pretend everything's fine.	We mutually agree to ignore troubling issues, which leaves both of us feeling disconnected and alone.
Example: Blame others.	I tell my partner we have money problems because she can't get a decent paying job.	I used my salary as justification for humiliating my wife, who already feels bad about how little she makes. I do it so that she can't say anything back to me.
Write Your Answer Here:		

Being Right Is a Failed Strategy for Resolving Conflicts

Not all defining family mottos are bad, yet sometimes even the acceptable ones don't belong in your new relationship. Even if they worked in your family of origin, they may leave you feeling scared, angry, vindictive, or righteous when you unintentionally use them to protect yourself from the more vulnerable challenges of long-term love, or blindly insert them into situations where they don't belong.

The enactments (influenced by family mottos) where we might "see" problematic behaviors in our partners and want to force, "fix," avoid, or attack them is the exact opposite of showing empathy—in fact, it actively gets in the way of doing so. Pummeling others with insights, suggestions, criticism, and even overly intense care (no matter how well justified) makes it impossible for them to offer anything in return. This strategy is instead a defense that—whether avoiding conflict or actively engaged in it—results in distance and relationship destruction.

Sometimes we judge our partner based on our personal mottos, even if we do not verbalize them to our partners. When they fail to live up to our expectations, we immediately go to right/wrong, good/bad thinking, as in, I am right and they are wrong. Then we come up with a behavior in which we're always in the right. Yet "rightness" is actually what's been screwing us up when it comes to resolving conflicts. Rightness is exactly what prevents us from contributing to a solution to the problem. The reason is that feeling right blinds us from seeing what is happening and prevents us from hearing our partner's perspectives. And there is no hope of resolving conflicts if we cannot find our part in them. Because enactment is a process where we play out painful and frightening aspects of our own histories; it is very hard to see—much less own—our part on the problem. Luckily, the PACER model helps to get us out of this mode.

Internal Agreements Create Both Peace and Defensive Strategies

Internal agreements are the ones we have with ourselves: the rules of the road that we set up, based on our past experiences. They typically develop over time in your formative years and become a natural part of your character. If character is the sum total of your psychological defenses, each of our understandings of "me" is our most contemporary, up-to-date record of everything we've been through and everything that's been done to us. It's our reaction to all the people who have hurt, scared, loved, and cared for us. These internal agreements have been developing for years, they are stable, sturdy, and not at all easy to change: they act like a compass that helps us navigate our relationship life. However, sometimes this compass can be applied to a present situation even when it is no longer helpful. Your sense of safety and peace, which comes from your internal agreements are essential to our experience of ourselves, so giving up an internal agreement, even if it no longer serves you, is a big ask.

Some unacceptable behaviors can result from internal agreements. When this happens, the responses tend to be anticipatory, like a life hack to deal with dread over future events and are reasoned by if/then statements (if you do this then I'm allowed to do that) or ultimatums (I'll end things if I don't get my way). This is a highly defensive state of being in the world; we believe we're proactively protecting ourselves from being mistreated.

Externalizing internal agreements through your behaviors can put a couple in a battle of tit for tat. In this way, the motto of one who justifies and rationalizes destructive, distancing, and provocative behavior can be "The best defense is a good offense."

For instance:

- If my partner forgot to send me a text message about a teacher-parent conference, then I am not going to attend it.
- If my partner did not participate in the chores this week, then I will not show up for his soccer game, this week or ever.
- If my girlfriend tells me what to wear for the wedding we are attending, I am going to wear something that is definitely not her choice.

Internal agreements are exceptionally hard to recognize in ourselves or do anything about. We've likely seen them in action with other people in everyday life: destructive and distancing responses, sour facial expressions, and rude treatment from those around us. But we don't notice when we implement those behaviors ourselves because one of the ways that the mind "helps" us is to block out—*selectively inattend*[7]—information about ourselves

7.   Harry Stack Sullivan, *The Interpersonal Theory of Psychiatry* (New York: W. W. Norton, 1953), 158–70.

that could make us anxious or unattractive and downright unlikable to others. And because our internal agreements have a built-in morality that helps us navigate confusing, chaotic situations and relationships, it can blind us from seeing how we need to adjust our compass in a present relationship.

However, our reactions are actually placing a target on our forehead. When you walk around with a scowl on your face you are inviting other people to respond in kind, which then becomes a defensiveness that's hard to get rid of.

Exercise: Recognizing Internal Agreements

Your task in this exercise is to understand your existing internal agreements. We believe understanding your internal agreements will give you a better chance to make conscious choices and change both your agreements and the behaviors based on the agreements, so that you can create a new way to relate to your partner. You may have developed new coping mechanisms in order to create different dynamics with your partner than how you related to your parents. It will help to understand what those are now and to see whether or not you are accomplishing that goal.

Internal Agreement	How this agreement plays out in my relationship	The long-term impact on how I relate to my partner
Example A: Since I'm the only one who provides decent care in the relationship, I won't allow others to contribute to my well-being.	One of us feels burdened and resentful while the other feels rejected and devalued.	No one I'm involved with seems invested in dealing with any problems that arise, so I act out to avoid trusting others and getting close with others.

Internal Agreement	How this agreement plays out in my relationship	The long-term impact on how I relate to my partner
Example B: I accept whatever others offer me, whether it's what I really want or not but then stew in resentment and feel ignored and hurt.	I feel misunderstood and cannot imagine staying with my partner long-term, though for some reason I've been unable to leave.	I sense my partner doesn't value me, so I quietly resist accepting what he does for me, just like he refuses everything I offer him.
Write Your Examples Example 1:		
Example 2:		

Now, think about the following:

- What do your agreements suggest about how you use attitudes and actions to guard against your partner?

- Did you force your partner to comply with your moral standard?
- How rigid are your agreements, and the attitudes and actions that go with them?
- Is it possible that your agreements have put you in a position to be hurt?
- How malleable might these agreements be?

Can your relationship change now that you can see what your agreements have been between you and the world? What might that look like?

When Agreements Fail

Some conflicts begin when you or your partner start to enact the internal agreements that you brought from your history without realizing. Or the agreements you thought you explicitly made didn't really exist or if you did make them known, were in fact doomed to fail.

For example, we had an agreement that each thought was explicit but turned out to be implicit. That agreement was, *I'm not going to repeat my parents' relationship; you're not going to repeat yours.* For Haruna, this meant, *I am not going to repeat my father's command and following rage.* Mark thought, *I am not going to repeat my mother's provocation.* Unfortunately, these were a flawed set of agreements because, as you've just learned, we're most likely going to repeat certain elements of family dynamics . In fact, we can only repair from the ruptures that these dynamics created when we *do* bring them with us, acknowledge and own them, and then get to work addressing them!

Exercise: Roles and Rules

Roles I Play in Our Relationship	How and Where My Role Originated	Effects of My Role on Us	What Would Happen if I Didn't Take On This Role?
I often remain passive or pretend that I have no opinion in major decision-making.	It's how my father responded to my mother's domineering behavior to keep the peace.	I keep my real needs hidden from my partner for fear of disturbing the peace and end up feeling neglected and abandoned.	I think I would participate more in decision-making. I might be able to confront my fear of disturbing the peace.
I stick to a bystander role when anything goes wrong in our relationship.	When I was a kid, we lived with my father's parents. They constantly criticized my mom, but my father never stood up for her.	When my partner has problems with others, I silently look for ways to blame him for it.	I would feel more confident in speaking up and supporting my partner.
Your Answer:			

Revisit the above exercises you have already completed, identifying ways that you act out roles and rules that you remember from the household in which you grew up. After identifying your roles, use the examples in the previous page to help you draw out how your part in the routine(s) originated and how they play out in your relationships.

Letting Go

Identifying the unresolved conflict and the behaviors you have attached to them is actually the easy part: the harder part is letting go. The truth is that the behavior served you at some point and that's why you kept going with it. However, it's not serving your relationship or your partner. Instead, you unintentionally distance yourself from the person who wants to care for you.

You are not going to resolve the conflicts you had with your parents by enacting them in your current relationship. But you can start to recognize these patterns, and consciously choose new ways of relating to yourself and each other. In this way, you can make peace with the past and stop taking the past into the present. The key is focusing on the here and now.

Some people who were abused or neglected by their parents believe they cannot create a healthy, stable relationship with their partners because they don't have a good model. They come into that relationship insecure, and in a way, powerless. Yet this doesn't have to be the case. We believe that each relationship is a unique creation, and you and your partner can construct it with love, openness, understanding, and trust. Abuse survivors can build a loving relationship that is completely different from their upbringing. Often, relationships that are less threatening, like friendships, can serve as bridges—and healing experiences—as you move toward more intimate relationships. Focus on the here and now because you are already creating a different environment and dynamics with your partner.

Relationships grow and change, and you can always initiate this process of growth. Each time you rupture and each time you come back and repair, you're already in a different relationship. Each time you do this you're distinguishing yourself from your old patterns that you brought in, and you're distinguishing yourself from your family of origin. You're really becoming a novel kind of "us" each time you repair.

CHAPTER SIX

Cultural Factors Can Cause Conflict

Cultural factors exist in every relationship; the mystery is how they will play out. You and your partner's perspectives are framed by each of your cultures and backgrounds: it is likely your partner does not think about the world in ways that are similar—if not exactly the same—to the ways you do. The agreements you have created together and alone are also laden with implicit and explicit cultural factors that may not fully register until they make themselves known within the setting of a conflict.

Culture is defined as the shared characteristics of a group of people, which encompasses place of birth, religion, language, socioeconomic status, social behaviors, art, literature, geography, education, and more. Culture includes these overt identity markers as well as the hidden, covert aspects of our sense of self, which could be influenced by your families' history and experiences. For instance, there are many cultural experiences, some of them traumatic—such as those having to do with abuse and bigotry—that can be intergenerationally transmitted.[1]

Within biracial or bicultural couples, like ours, everyday life is often unknowingly lived through cultural factors that can get misinterpreted or miscommunicated causing ruptures large and small. For instance, Haruna

1.   Pratyusha Tummala-Narra, "Cultural Identity in the Context of Trauma and Immigration from a Psychoanalytic Perspective," *Psychoanalytic Psychology*, 31(3) (2014): 396–409.

grew up in a traditional Japanese family where saying "I love you" or "I want you" to a spouse or partner simply does not happen. In Japanese culture, couples often confirm their love as a behavioral expression of taking care of one another. However, Mark's Southern California family was very expressive in terms of affection. It wasn't until after our honeymoon period was over that we realized we had a conflicting set of needs to repeat certain aspects of our cultural experiences. Mark longed for the in-your-face expressions of 1970s hippie-love and acceptance his family embraced; Haruna was comfortable with the emotional and physical spacious parameters of her childhood. Haruna was conflicted because she felt simultaneously desired and uncomfortable by Mark's affection; Mark was challenged to accept what he felt was a less all-encompassing way of being loved. This disconnect in expectations of what love should look like left both of us feeling confused, frustrated, and distant, and these states lead to conflict. It wasn't until we took the time to uncover all our cultural differences that we could fully understand and fulfill each other's expectations of what our unique type of love could look like.

Interestingly, the more overt your differences are the easier they are to acknowledge and perhaps even bridge. However, when couples appear to be culturally similar is when the real trouble might occur. For instance, Hari and Prisha grew up in the same neighborhood in a tight-knit, Southeast Asian, Indian community in New Jersey. When they fell in love in high school, they felt like they already knew each other very well because they shared so many cultural similarities (race, ethnicity, socioeconomic status, religion, customs, family, friends) and had always attended the same schools. They separated geographically when each went to college, married soon after, and started a family. After a few years of marriage, they came to see us. As Prisha said, "The only thing that seems similar between us now is that we both feel misunderstood and suffocated."

What happened? Over the years, Hari and Prisha had made lots of assumptions about the other, each believing that because they were from such similar backgrounds and had been together for so long that the other would automatically think, behave, and want the same as they did. As a result, they dismissed each other's unique qualities or opinions. In short, they did not know how to appreciate each other's differences. Hari told us, "When I wanted an apple, I assumed that Prisha wanted an apple. But what she wanted was an orange. I got upset every time she wanted something else."

Even when two people seem "exactly the same"—as Hari and Prisha did—they can still bring into a relationship their own cultural factors they are not even aware of. Yet when these aspects show up (ironically, because of the increased sense of security that comes with intimacy and letting our guard down with or without consciously intending to do so), they can reveal parts of ourselves we may not have been prepared to see. Ultimately, facing these aspects leads to an evolving sense of intimacy with each other, including a greater acceptance of all parts of ourselves.

Exercise: Identifying Culture(s)

The Rule of Two and keeping the focus on yourself applies to understanding your culture. Using the following definitions and descriptions, let's begin to explore your culture.

- **Culture:** The shared values, norms, traditions, customs, art, history, folklore, and institutions of a group of people.
- **Cultural Group:** We each belong to many different cultural groups. We belong to groups based on our ethnicity or race, gender, politics, marital status, religion, age, or even the region of the country we are from. Cultural groups also include sexual orientation, socioeconomic status, physical abilities, and profession.
- **Cultural Identity:** The many different group affiliations we hold come together to create a unique, multifaceted cultural identity. Because of this complexity, we believe every stereotype is a wasted opportunity: we are all more than the sum of our different cultural parts.
- **Cultural Filter:** Our cultural identity creates a filter through which we experience each day and each other. Cultural filters create the norms and expectations and contribute to our "agreements"—those shared, not shared, and sometimes unknown, even to us. How we think, feel, and react to the world around us is directly influenced by our cultural filter.

Cultural Groups

- Many people have never thought of themselves as having a culture, let alone more than one! Some of these are overt and easy to identify, such as race, nationality, and gender. Other affiliations develop as we grow up and expand our sense of self. Without identifying your particular cultural groups, you're missing an opportunity to fully know yourself and each other.

Think about the following culture groups, and see how each has influenced your sense of self (add more categories if necessary):

- Career: _____
- Education: _____
- Family makeup: (birth order, gender of parents, sexual orientation of parents and siblings): _____
- Generation categorization/age/developmental milestone: _____
- Income/Socioeconomic status: _____
- Language of origin/dialect/proficiency of common language: _____
- Mental health status: _____
- National origin: _____
- Physical ability: _____
- Political belief: _____
- Race/ethnicity: _____
- Religion: _____
- Other: _____
- Other: _____

Cultural Identities

When asked to define a "cultural group," many of us find that it is not so much a cultural group that comes to mind, but an amalgam of group affiliations that make up our identity. How different culture groups intersect and interact inside of us—and manifest in our intimate relationships—is not always clear, and their importance often appears only after we have developed a sense of safety to be ourselves within a long-term relationship.

In fact, when Suki and Rima began dating, Rima had distanced herself from her middle-class Muslim-Lebanese family because of how angrily they reacted to her being gay. Suki maintained that her parents—from mainland China—avoided recognition of her sexuality and instead focused primarily on raising her to succeed academically. Rima became increasingly conflicted about her cultural roots, and intentionally eschewed all things related to her parents. And though in this way she consciously disavowed some important elements of her culture, she and Suki found themselves arguing fiercely over parenting styles. Ironically, each of them wanted to raise their new daughter based largely on their own respective cultural values.

Thinking about this example, ask yourself the following questions:
- Now that you have identified your culture groups, did you discover a new way of looking at your cultural identity?
- How might your cultural identity shape your perspective on how you relate to each other and yourself in the context of your relationship?
- Which of your partner's cultural factors do you have difficulty accepting? For example, if one partner comes from a wealthy family, and you believe she spends money unnecessarily.
- How do you think sharing elements of your identity in a different cultural context could affect how your partner interacts with you? For example, certain cultures may be sensitive to specific religions or nationalities and may react in a particular way—be it positively or negatively—if they learn about this part of your identity.

- How does your cultural identity shape your expectations for how you and your partner *should* interact with each other? Can you see ways that these expectations form the agreements you have brought with you—but not necessarily consciously shared—with your partner? What kinds of consequences or interactions have you seen from this practice? How might this understanding contribute to repairing ruptures now that you have this insight?
- How did your cultural background teach you to resolve conflict? Do you think you and your partner share the same style of resolving conflict? Sometimes, disagreements about how to resolve ruptures can cause distance and disconnection between two partners. These disagreements can have a cultural component: some cultures do not encourage open discussion or confrontation about anything, including disagreements.
- Can a more extensive understanding of the cultural aspects of your own and your partner's cultural identity help you understand the ruptures—especially the typical ones that repeat and have become patterns—in your relationship?
- Can you each share the ways that a new understanding of your culture(s) can contribute to more effective processes of repair? Instead of using your way of resolving a conflict, can you consider trying to resolve conflict using the way your partner knows?

Emotional Investment Factors

Your emotional investments are the aspects of your culture that you accept, like, and love, and that influences how you relate to and experience yourself and others. We have a conscious awareness of some of these emotional investments, and others arise more profoundly as we build a life in relationship. For instance, as Rebecca and Luke grew closer, they grew increasingly distant from their own religious upbringings: hers Jewish and his born-again Christian. They knew these differences would cause conflict for both of their families of origin but were surprised to find that even after they felt they had distanced themselves from their religion, they both found themselves to be highly invested in their own religious holidays. This couple realized their cultural factors were much more important to them than either had imagined, and they'd have to make room for all of them if their relationship was going to be a success.

List some of the ways your culture enhances your behavior and the ways you interact with your partner:

1. _____

2. _____

3. _____

4. _____

Cultural Discomforts

Some affiliations of cultural identity can cause discomfort and embarrassment. They may even be at odds with other cultural groups with which you identify. There may be aspects of your culture that you are conflicted about and don't want to accept as part of your identity. Or you may be defensive about the ways other people stereotype your culture. For instance, Carmen grew up in a family and neighborhood where they were predominantly Democrats, and she acknowledged that her family had an overt and serious distrust of Conservatives. She had always felt embarrassed about this, but it became intolerable when she fell in love with Wharton, whose family is mostly Republicans.

The most uncomfortable aspects of your culture that you are afraid of bringing into your relationship are:

1. _____

2. _____

3. _____

4. _____

Now that you are aware of these cultural challenges, can you make room for your partner's culture or cultural choices, especially if they are different from yours?

Cultural Filters

Cultural filters work like *filters* on a camera lens: they are the expectations, biases, and ideology that can affect what people see, how they feel, and how they interact with others (especially those with differing cultural backgrounds). Tim and Sandy had been together for quite some time and it wasn't until they quit their jobs and started a business that Sandy began "seeing" Tim as an entitled, controlling, elitist—which is the filter through which she "saw" members of his nationality, race, gender, and socioeconomic status.

List some ways your culture has created a filter that influences how you experience yourself and your partner, when you are getting along and when you are having conflicts: does your filter change depending on how you are interacting with your partner? If so, why?

1. _____

2. _____

3. _____

4. _____

Do My Cultural Assumptions Serve My Relationship?

Now that you have identified the many cultures you are influenced by, let's take a look at which behaviors, cultural values, or customs you are holding onto and why. In the psychoanalytic model that Mark subscribes to, some behaviors are defenses meant to protect us from anxiety. Mark also spent many years as a community psychologist exploring the ways psychoanalytic concepts and practices can inform community crisis intervention. He found that communities—and, by extension, cultures—can develop character defenses in the form of rituals, expectations, and taboos that set guidelines (explicit and implicit) for ways that members "should" behave in order to maintain a shared sense of security. He believes these behavioral expectations can influence the ways each person within a couple keeps themselves "safe" from the anxieties associated with the very things they want from relationship: vulnerability, empathy, intimacy, emotional investment (the "four pillars of love"). Therefore, our various cultural identities influence, and are influenced by, our openness to the scarier parts of long-term love.[2]

Haruna believes culture is an influential factor that can define what aspects of romantic relationships are ideal, and what are not, and is in agreement with family therapist Celia J. Falicov, who describes the way people behave toward one another is heavily influenced by their cultural values.[3] For example, in a collectivistic culture that prioritizes the group over any individual, like Haruna's Japanese upbringing, direct, assertive conversations are not considered the ideal way to resolve conflict. Her

2.   Harry Stack Sullivan believed that people's interactions with others, especially their significant others, determine their sense of security and sense of self, which, in turn, motivates their behavior. He developed a concept called the "self-system," which is a set of security operations—a thoroughly culturally influenced way of experiencing ourselves—that operates through understanding, accepting and adopting cultural norms and then using them to navigate life. When we are in compliance with those norms we feel secure and accepted; when we find ourselves unable to do so, we can experience extreme anxiety—anxieties that might relate to our sense of self and our continuing value as members of a particular group.

3.   Celia J. Falicov, "The Cultural Meaning of Family Triangles," in M. McGoldrick and R. J. Green, (Eds) *Revisioning Culture in Family Therapy* (New York: Guilford Press, 1998), 37–49.

cultural upbringing contrasts with a more individualistic culture, which is the norm in the US. To her, keeping one's thoughts and feeling to yourself is ideal; for Mark, the opposite was true.

By exploring your cultural factors, ask yourself, What is this cultural behavior for? And are these assumptions still serving me in this relationship and serving my relationship? Once we take a deeper look at where our values come from, we can reevaluate them in the context of the present moment: if a particular value does not help the relationship, we can challenge it. We can ask ourselves if our values represent *actual needs*, or are they values that got filtered into our psyche in a way that now has control and influence that we no longer want or need.

For instance, Tamar grew up in a household where everyone watched television together. She has fond memories that TV was one way she could connect to her parents, yet her husband, Peter complains that having the TV on all the time doesn't leave room for conversation. When Tamar dug into the "what was it for" question in the context of her current relationship with her husband, she realized that watching TV was considered family time but was often used as a way of checking out and not having to talk to each other. We asked Tamar, "Now that you know that Peter wants to talk to you at dinner, does television watching serve your relationship?" It didn't take long for her to see that TV is less alluring than having a conversation with Peter.

The more we understand the influences we've had, the more likely we get to choose what we actually want. For Tamar, she was able to tell us, "You know, so much television watching was a part of my culture that it took a while to realize that it was actually destructive and was standing in the way of building something loving with Peter. It worked for my family but it does not work for me and Peter."

Culture, Conflicts, and Power Dynamics

When couples fall into conflict, it is easy for each of them to believe that one of them is right and one of them is wrong. But each person embodies their own "rightness" in a way that is highly influenced by their own cultural upbringing (and influences). This question, therefore, can become deadlocked as each partner struggles to claim, own, and express their own truth and rightness. And when there is a "right" there is inevitably a "wrong." So the question of who is right and who is wrong is essentially a way in which the struggle for power enters a relationship. And this struggle is not only about who is right or wrong, but also about whose perspective is dominant.

We have lost count of how often we hear, at the beginning of a couples therapy, that everything would be fine in the relationship if only they would accept that they are right and the other is wrong. In fact, most couples enter therapy not to process feelings, hurts, and pain, but instead to receive a judgment as to which of the two is "right." It gets even more complicated when there are two different cultural backgrounds that inform each party, whether or not they are aware of it as well as what qualities and characteristics define right and wrong.

Yet, the goal of couples therapy isn't to find the answer to who is right about any particular situation. The goal instead is to make room for all perspectives and cultural influences, and help partners accept each other, despite their differences, so that both parties can collaboratively make an informed decision, understand each other's perspective, and negotiate with each other when needed. This is how decision-making power can be shared.

Real power comes when you keep the focus on yourself, and then take responsibility for how you contribute to the conflicts in your relationship as well as what is going well. When you recognize your part of the problem, the strength and courage it takes becomes *empowering* to break free from the idea that there is a winner and a loser.

Power struggles also involve the dynamics of synergy versus scarcity. Scarcity is a power model that says, "The more you have, the less I have." The synergy model says, "The more power you have, the more power I have. We both have more power when we work together."

Synergy is empowering in that it allows us to let go of the need to be right or to be dominating. In synergy, we can each be right. We can also both be flexible and accepting because it is becoming safer to explore new experiences, ideas, and ways of relating.

Hiromi and Andy Struggle with Culture and Power Dynamics

The first thing Hiromi told us when she walked into our office was "I want to divorce my husband."

Then she told us that she was originally from Japan. She met her husband, Andy, in New York City: he is first generation Korean American. Hiromi is fed up with being an equal income earner who is also expected to take care of all of the cooking and cleaning. In her culture, as well as Andy's, the wife is typically responsible for cooking and cleaning, which is a culturally expected role for a wife. However, since both started working from home, the added responsibility for cooking lunch and cleaning up afterward was more than she could handle.

One day Hiromi had to rush out of their lunch together to make a Zoom meeting, and she didn't have time to do the dishes. Andy was annoyed when he came back to the kitchen later that day and found dirty dishes in the sink. That's when Hiromi reached her breaking point and said, "You do the dishes, I made lunch."

Andy immediately started complaining about having to do the dishes, which prompted Hiromi to say, "Why are you acting like a f—ing dick?"

Which is when Andy said, "F you. F this house. F this mess," and threw the dirty dishes at the wall.

In our office, Hiromi told us, "I don't know how I can stay married to him. He refused to clean up and put me in danger. I want to move out immediately. What he did was absolutely outrageous."

Listening to Hiromi, we could clearly see the role Andy played in the conflict: he was certainly the aggressor. But what role did Hiromi think she played? Her answer at first was "nothing." She was simply the receiver of the aggression.

We gently reminded her that was probably not the case. Haruna asked, "What do you think about when you called him a f—ing dick? I can imagine that he felt hurt and angry." Then we explained that when you only focus on what your partner did, you are doing a disservice to the relationship. Hiromi did not tell Andy how she felt when she cursed at him. She covered up her needs and pain by calling him names, using hurtful language. The truth is disappointments often get amplified when one partner focuses their anger on the other. Hiromi felt justified because she was doing a ton of work in and out of the home, yet Andy refused to clean the dishes and threw the dishes at the wall.

Keeping the focus on your partner also makes it harder for you to find your part in the conflict, and the harder it will be to repair the rupture. Without seeing your role in the conflict, you will not be able to contribute to the solution. All you can do is hope and pray that your partner will change, and then everything will be all better. This strategy is another way of saying that you have no power.

We then helped Hiromi sit with the idea of acknowledging her accountability. She realized where she contributed to her own amplified disappointments, and told us, "Early in our marriage I took on all these homemaking tasks because that is what my mother did. And then, in a way, if I'm really honest with myself, I set myself up for being horribly resentful because I didn't let Andy do any housework. I was so caught up with the idea of being a good wife like my mother and aunts all strived to be. It didn't matter that I have a graduate degree equal to Andy's, and that we both work fifty to sixty hours a week. I wanted to be the perfect wife I know he expected."

Hiromi realized that she shouldn't have called Andy names and was able to see the conflict: her disappointment was her expectations of her marriage and not her husband. She realized that if she focused solely on Andy, she would be in a self-justification state. Yet by focusing on herself, she was able to identify her need to be the good wife her culture defined. She then worked on letting go of this strong attachment to the role.

Then Haruna said to Hiromi, "Could you think about having a conversation with Andy about what happened. He owes you an apology, and you owe him an apology. Can you talk about setting up new roles now that you are working from home together, something like where you make lunch, and he does the dishes."

Hiromi realized she needs to let go of her perfectionism and let Andy be a more active partner at home. With this new awareness, she could talk to her husband about sharing the division of labor, starting with doing dishes.

Creating a Culture of Two

Regardless of your individual cultural affiliations, every single relationship creates its own culture with its own values and customs made in the form of agreements. We refer to this as a *culture of two,* which is the ultimate goal of a successful relationship.

Without any conscious volitional choice, we bring our culture with us. The rules and regulations we bring from our culture into a relationship will undoubtedly collide with what our partners bring with them. Therefore, the formation of each *culture of two* is likely to be confusing, challenging, and will most likely be central to some of the themes and patterns of conflict. Yet, when you work together, you are in fact expanding your cultural norms, allowing for new perspectives and broadening your tolerance for accepting the other, which can be quite lovely and healing.

A culture of two begins with a psychoanalytic concept called *chumship.* According to Harry Stack Sullivan, a child's first high-stakes friendship is typically formed in preadolescence with a friend of the same sex, a "chum," and is crucial to personality growth.[4] In this relationship, the other person's interest and security become as important as one's own. The preadolescent who successfully enters a chumship finds someone with whom they can share their innermost thoughts and feelings in an atmosphere of acceptance. Successful chumships offer an opportunity to see and experience significant differences in each other that comes through the cultural filter of one's own family, to work through disagreements and learn to compromise, and lays the groundwork for later relationships.

We believe every love relationship is a form of chumship, which is why the more we know about cultural factors and their influence over ourselves and our partners, the better. Then, we can take all the positive aspects of each other's culture and figure out a way to incorporate them so that we're both aware of them in daily practice, which then solidifies the third identity that is your relationship.

4.   Harry Stack Sullivan, *The Interpersonal Theory of Psychiatry* (New York: W. W. Norton, 1953), 73.

Your culture of two develops in its own unique way and is constantly being shaped by your differences, similarities, conflicts, and how you as a couple handle them together (avoid, destruct, discuss, negotiate, or repair). It is forming a third entity, the foundation for your lived experience as an "us." When couples come to therapy with us, what we are really "treating" is this third entity.

Elsa and Bryan Develop a Culture of Two

Elsa's cultural values and behaviors are so inherent to her that she was not aware of how some of them would not be accepted nor understood by her partner, Bryan. When Bryan acted in a way that challenged her values, it was not just that she did not know how to accept his ideas, she felt threatened and overridden. For example, one of her core values was that children should be disciplined. When they misbehaved, they will have clear consequences such as time out or reduced screen time. This idea never came up when they were dating, dreaming of raising a family together. Bryan was "shocked" by the anger and discipline Elsa would routinely dole out to their children. He had grown up with parents who were, in his words, "totally hands off."

Bryan (who, growing up as Caucasian in a homogenous middle-class neighborhood in Connecticut) didn't recognize there was an overt cultural value (Dominican Republic) associated with Elsa's decisions about discipline, but when Elsa was able to verbalize how she experienced life in her parent's home, he could see there was a great difference in how each of their upbringings had influenced them. Elsa believed the punishment she received from her parents gave her the mental toughness to move from the Dominican Republic to New York and to be self-sufficient.

Now, in their culture of two, they discuss how they have been influenced by their cultural backgrounds and how they might find a middle ground for raising—and disciplining—their children that makes room for both of them. This means they both recognize that neither of them wants to be overtly hurtful to their children, but that "not doing anything" when they misbehaved could be interpreted as parental indifference, which neither of them wanted to convey.

Exercise: The Culture of Two Trees[5]

The Individual Trees

Each person will draw a tree that represents their personal culture. Fill in the terms that represent different facets for the following three parts of the tree, writing them down next to the tree:

- **Roots:** origin, sense of belonging to cultural groups (e.g., American, German, European, or other cultural groups like regional cultures, family culture, fan culture, etc.).
- **Trunk:** values you find important in your cultural context (e.g., tolerance, discipline etc.).
- **Leaves:** visible signs of your cultural background (e.g., a certain meal, a language or a way of communication, values, mottos, traditions, a symbol, etc.).

Now reflect on the following questions:

- Was it easy to define the cultural group you belong to? Have you chosen several groups?
- Do you feel the values you have chosen are known to you and your partner?
- Do you feel comfortable with the visible part of your cultural background or do you prefer to keep your culture hidden? Why? In which situations?

The Us Tree

Work together to find terms that represent the ways each of your cultural backgrounds influence a new Culture Tree that represents your *culture of two*. Your culture tree is representative of the third entity and the hard work you've done to establish and maintain it, regardless of the conflict you are in right now.

---

5.   Adapted from https://practice-school.eu/exercise-1-cultural-tree-exercise -for-self-reflection/.

Let's now see how—or if—each of these trees overlap. What are the similarities? What are the differences? What would the cultural tree of your us-ness look like? Consider drawing it together in whatever creative way you can come up with—using the same diagram—for the *culture of two* as you currently experience yourselves:

- **Roots:** origin, sense of belonging to cultural groups (e.g., American, German, European, or other cultural groups like regional cultures, family culture, fan culture, etc.).
- **Trunk:** values you find important in your cultural context (e.g., tolerance, discipline, etc.).
- **Leaves:** visible signs of your cultural background (e.g., a certain meal, a language or a way of communication, values, mottos, traditions, a symbol, etc.).

After having completed this part please reflect about the following questions:

- What are the major similarities between the culture(s) you were raised in and the *culture of two* that is your partnership?
- What are the major differences between the culture(s) you were raised in and the *culture of two* that is your partnership?
- Can you see, feel, and experience the influence and effects of your *culture of two*, including the various cultures and cultural groups that constitute this culture?
- What kind of challenges do you see in your *culture of two* that come from the cultures you each bring with you into this relationship?
- What helpful, creative contributions do you see in your *culture of two* that come from the cultures you each bring with you into this relationship?

PART II

The PACER Model

CHAPTER SEVEN

PACER: The Route Back to "Us"

Most people think couples therapy looks like a court hearing with a judge who determines who is right and affirms that the other is just a big asshole. If only they would just stop being a jerk, everything will be fine. Yet that's not what therapy is or what it is supposed to accomplish.

Instead, therapists like us are here to help each person in the relationship take ownership of their part of the problem, so that they can both contribute to the solution. The PACER model really is about this insight. It's a model that takes you from rupture to repair. Using the insights from the first half of this book, you will see how in some areas of your relationships, your culture of two is functioning well. Yet, there are also aspects that are not working in synergy, leading to conflicts.

By this point you should have a better understanding of the issues that lurk behind the ruptures in your relationship. You may have even begun to see your role in conflicts. But keeping the focus on yourself is not enough to get to repair. Instead, you need to know how to best express what you've learned about yourself, and your relationship to your partner, so that together you can forge a path forward to the third entity that is "us."

The paradox of every good relationship is that only by being able to have the boundaries of me and you are able to create and maintain an awareness of the third entity that is "us." You don't want to lose yourself in the us, which is probably more a state of codependency. However, you don't want to look at your relationship, and the ruptures that occur, as something that is just yours to resolve. Your relationship belongs to your partner, too. The PACER model makes room for both people in the relationship to resolve their issues together.

The goal of PACER is not to have one person take responsibility for everything they contributed throughout the course of their relationship. Instead, we see it as a tool to address one rupture at a time. You will learn how to break down each rupture to see what's really going on in the moment, and then start to detect patterns, and where they may be coming from. We have used this model to save our relationship many times. Each time we use the model we get better at it and are able to move quickly through the stages and reach a repair.

The point is not about who is right and who is wrong. It's about creating an increasingly safer place together to claim our own insights into our contribution, not only to whatever conflict is at hand, but to the dynamic we keep playing out together. And most importantly, to creating other options for relating to intimacy, empathy, vulnerability, and emotional investment, which are the big four relationship ideals ("pillars").

And because it is a process, you can put it to use at any time and instantly take the temperature of the room down a notch or two. Some couples use the PACER model as a cue to send a message to their partner that "I want to talk to you and listen to you constructively." If you and your partner apply PACER model to your conflict often enough, when you request PACER model, you will both feel the mutual commitment and willingness to talk from the position of "I" or "me" and also to listen to your partner.

PACER will help you identify, claim, own, and maintain your contributions to your relationship. One of the tools we developed to raise this conscious awareness is called the 40-20-40 Model.[1] By using this model, finger-pointing, blame, and criticism have no place in conflict resolution. Instead, the 40

1.   The 40-20-40 was developed and used as a tool to take a *couple's inventory* and was adapted from work done earlier by Mark in a community revitalization/empowerment program that he called *Group Process Empowerment*. (Borg, Garrod, & Dalla, 2001; Borg, 2010). Mark found that it is an extremely effective means for helping people during difficult times in their relationship. In this work, though we won't necessarily have the active and overt participation of "the world," we can use the 40-20-40 to establish safe places for ourselves to come to terms with what in the world and in our lives, we can and cannot do something about. (Borg, 2002, 2003, 2004)

percent on either side of the equation represents what each person thinks and experience as *their part* of a problem. The 20 percent in the middle represents shared ownership of the issue and space for the culture of two—and ultimately of the relationship itself. We feel this model allows both partners to be truthful and feel heard, as well as respected and safe. In essence, it is an opportunity to get a relationship back on track, together by reestablishing peace. This setting provides the space so couples can:

- Learn new ways to manage anxiety, tension, fear, sadness, rejection, misunderstanding, and anger.
- Grasp their contribution to how their relationship functions.
- Analyze how current styles of interacting developed in families of origin.
- Learn to stop yourself and your arguments from escalation.
- Learn to forgive yourself and your partner.
- Feel and acknowledge emotions that distancing and destructive routines keep at bay.
- Break out of stultifying relationship patterns.
- Expand relational options by welcoming previously dissociated experiences and feelings.
- Create a new freedom to accept one another as you really are.

While PACER works in times of crisis, we've also found that it provides a framework for having difficult conversations surrounding the often-uncomfortable topics that feed conflicts, avoidance, escalation, rejection, anxieties, and fear: sex, money, immediate and extended family members, problematic friends, and even daily chores. Haruna and Mark don't only use the PACER model when things are bad. Sometimes we use it because there's something tricky we need to talk about or want to talk about. There may be some question of what we're going to spend money on or question of who's going to camp or travel. And so we'll use the model just to have a potentially difficult conversation.

The point is, you don't have to wait for an argument to use PACER: each of these topics can be addressed with this tool rather than continuing to avoid them. For instance, our clients Harry and Amy used PACER effectively to divvy up household chores—an issue that used to drive each other nuts. With PACER, they were able to come up with a weekly plan that was easy to implement, didn't put additional burden on either one, and get the tasks done in a manner that was acceptable to both.

There are five steps to the model. Each step takes time and practice to master, and you may not get the hang of all five steps at once or at the same pace as your partner. But you will learn how to increasingly gain insight into your contributions about what makes your relationship *go*. This will lead to clear understanding of what each person in the relationship is going through. Being able to understand your partner and being understood by your partner can lead to more empathy and compassion.

Some couples may find they are already doing parts of the process, but not all of it, and not in this particular order. For us, the order of the model is important because each lesson builds on the previous insights. Our order allows us to build a consciousness of what the process can actually do for us.

In the following chapters, you will learn how to master each of the five steps of the PACER model:

> **Pause:** When a conflict gets too hot, you need to walk away. But let's use that time to our advantage. Rather than shutting down or escalating arguments when life gets tense, you will both create an empowered Pause, where each person puts down their weapons of offense and defense and takes a break. Pause is not an "adult time out"; it's not a punishment, but it does require a collaborative set of rules. For instance, Mark and Haruna each have different timing for initiating the PACER model. Typically, Mark wants to get through it as soon as the fight begins. Haruna needs a longer pause and wants to take a break and come back to the discussion later. In Pause, we agree to an amount of time before we enter the next stage.

Accountability: Accountability allows each partner to take responsibility for their part in the rupture. In this step you will be guided to think about the provocative statement: "If my actions are not part of the problem, there is no solution." We believe Accountability is the most difficult part of the PACER model because this is where you will be taking the risk of owning your part of the problem using the 40-20-40 Model. Yet in Accountability there is real power: we begin to also see and feel how we can contribute to our own healing.

Collaboration: The Collaboration process is based on a unique, deep kind of listening. Each partner takes turns to speak and to listen. By creating a *meeting in the middle,* each partner is able to share what they discovered in Accountability and sees how their parts contributed to the rupture. Ultimately, Collaboration creates an opportunity for empathy, and a safe space where each is more likely to forgive. "Meeting in the Middle" is our Family-Systems-Meets-Interpersonal-Psychoanalysis term for a way of doing a couples' inventory that was developed by Chapter 9–Couples In Recovery Anonymous called a "Meeting of Two." Chapter 9 is a twelve-step program, a fellowship of people who share their experience, strength, and hope as couples so that they may solve their common problems and help bring harmony to relationships in recovery from addiction and substance abuse. A "Meeting of Two" is described as a way of addressing conflict through a process with a "formal meeting structure, with no crosstalk or inventory-taking, guarantees being heard, helps us learn to listen, and can bring us a new understanding of our partner."[2]

2.   Chapter 9–Couples in Recovery Anonymous (https://www.chapter9couplesinrecovery.org).

Experiment: The goal of Experiment is to rewrite the narrative of your relationship. You will create a new agreement where each person presents their needs so that their partner can respond to them.

Reset, Repair, and Renew: Couples can take a deeper look at what is lying underneath the initial rupture. It allows couples to gain a new insight, connecting the dots in a different way to allow for the possibility of finding other unresolved issues that are lurking below the surface. Ultimately, Reset leaves participants with a new level of accountability and a healthier view of their relationship. If the experiment did not go well, you will be coming up with a new action collaboratively. And although the results were not something that both of you were looking for, you can each acknowledge the other's efforts to try a new action. This effort requires love, care for the other, willingness, and commitment. You will have the opportunity to look at your part in the process of repair and ask yourselves, "How did it go? Could I improve? Can I give myself credit? Can I give you credit? Can you take credit? Can you give me credit?"

Inviting Your Partner into the PACER Model

Most of the time, both people in the relationship know that they're in rupture. There's something they both sense is not right. So how do you initiate the conversation so that both of you are equally invested in the PACER model and agree to give it a try?

We cannot count how many times we have seen couples linger in resentful procrastination as one of them tells us they are the *only* partner "who always makes the first move toward reconciliation," or "is the only one who ever really tries to deal with any kind of a problem." Yet more often than not, there is a true power struggle afoot. If your relationship has an appointed makeup conversation initiator, that needs to change. You need to think about this less as a matter of "conversation initiator" and more as an unconscious agreement about roles and power dynamics. It might seem "more powerful" to be the initiator, when, in fact, there is great power in withholding your willingness to makeup.

We have found the only way to extend the invitation into the PACER model is for one partner to come to the other and acknowledge their part of the problem. First, pick an easy issue and acknowledge that you have been fighting. Then come the two rules: keep the focus on yourself.

You can say, "I know that we've been fighting and I acknowledge and accept my part in it. I'm not sure if this is going to work, but I would like you to join me in resolving this problem together. I would like us to give this a try. I know the very first step to resolve our issue is to bring my willingness. I am willing to listen and discuss this with you. Could you bring your willingness?"

You can then show your partner this book and explain how this new program that you both can try together is about healing.

Having willingness is not the same as having desire or motivation to solve conflict. You might not feel desire or motivation to solve the conflict with your partner. And this results in you not taking actions for reaching out to your partner. While you may feel no desire or motivation for resolution, you can ask yourself, "Am I willing to resolve this with my partner?" If the answer is "yes," then you are trusting the repairing process will show that both of you are invested in repairing and connecting as a couple again. Your relationship is already helped by showing each other your willingness to repair.

We know you cannot control how your partner will respond. So we recommend that you surrender to how your partner responds. In this case, surrender means an acceptance of what your partner contributes (good, bad, and everything in-between) to your relationship. This includes a reluctance or an actual decline to work on the relationship right now. If your partner says, "NFW, not doing it, not changing, happy the way I am," then keep the focus on yourself and reveal why you want to do this work. You can say, "I'm serious; we have a problem and I have a way to address it, but it's going to require the two of us and our willingness. It's going to be uncomfortable at times. I think our relationship deserves a chance."

If your partner declines, you can still do the work. You can use the individual aspects of the PACER model to figure out how to take responsibility for yourself and make the changes in the things you don't like. You're still going to learn. You are going to own your contribution to the conflict that's dividing you and your partner, and at the same time you will come to understand that your contribution is not the only problem. Even if your partner is not willing to participate, at least you will learn to dissect your conflict (40-20-40), understand it constructively, and process it with empowerment. Along this process, you are going to regulate yourself. You will learn to acknowledge your own pain and anger and not act defensively or act out on it. Then you can take care of yourself and your vulnerable feelings with empathy and compassion. One of our clients said, "My partner did not join me today, and I was sad and angry. But because I did PACER model on my own, I have a better understanding of how I contributed to the conflict. It was not easy to do but I did it. There are times that people don't respond to my apology or to my desire to talk about what happened. This misalignment happens sometimes. I want to give myself lots of credit for this! I am proud of myself!"

Learning to speak from the position of "I" is a useful communication tool for any relationship. If your partner doesn't respond well to this communication style, you may feel vulnerable. And it is going to be a "learning process" for you and your partner. Sometimes they are not going to respond well. Learning to register and respect your vulnerable feelings is a process, and it takes lots of empathy and compassion. And it takes practice. And if your partner continues to refuse, you might start to think about taking another action.

For instance, even in our couples peer group, people are allowed to come solo. Christian has been coming for eighteen years without his partner, Felicity. They had started together but about four years in she stopped coming. That's okay with Christian because he's still working on his part. The work helps him be a more loving and caring partner, keeps the focus on himself in the relationship, and maintains a good perspective of what is happening in the relationship.

Max and Sean Enter PACER

Sean and Max used the PACER model to create a sense of joint ownership of the distance that their pain—and their avoidance of pain—had quietly crept into their relationship, and to understand that distance itself was a legitimate rupture that the two of them would have to join forces to repair.

Max's marriage to Sean was the perfect hiding place—hiding from vulnerability, intimacy, empathy, and investment. For years, Max carefully managed the image of an orderly relationship and household by avoiding conflict through distancing behaviors. "I was sealed up tight. All anybody knew about us was that I always kept my cool. Nobody suspected—least of all me—that I had no idea how to be there for Sean. I didn't even know what that meant. Even when his mom's Huntington's disease got worse, I may as well have been a deaf mute. I had no clue what I could do to help Sean get through it and wasn't about to ask."

Keeping an emotional distance was how Max had managed his own mother's decline and death four years earlier. "I didn't want sympathy, compassion, none of it—not that I knew what any of that really was. I was going to be a tower of strength in the middle of everybody else's sadness. Sean tried to be there for me; he always waited up for me when I went to the hospital. But I ignored him and pretended it was nothing special that he was staying awake for me. So I'd go to bed immediately telling him I had to do this or that for Mom in the morning—whatever to prevent Sean from knowing I was actually feeling anything. Nobody was going to know how afraid I was of losing my mom."

"At first, it seemed legitimate. Sean's mom never hid her homophobia, while my mom loved Sean—always remembered his birthday and our anniversary. No way could you compare losing my mom to losing his. So I pretended he couldn't possibly be suffering the way I had—or told myself I had. Well, as it turned out, keeping the whole thing at arm's length had nothing to do with how angry I was at Sean's mom: it was a hedge around the pain of losing my own mom. And somehow, I knew that if I validated Sean's pain, it was going to bring me face-to-face with my own.

"Strangely, Sean's pain became my moment of truth: I suddenly could see that keeping my feelings shut down was killing our marriage. If it was going to be saved, I'd have to revisit my mom's death and my feelings surrounding it.. It was the only way I could be useful to Sean. Up to that moment, I'd never had even an inkling of what intimacy actually is and does."

"It was so strange thinking about creating a formal pause in our relationship because I thought we were on constant pause," said Sean. "But then Max came home one night and said that he needed to 'hit pause' to not reject the care that I was offering him. He asked if we could account for the distance between us, and I was shocked—how could I have anything to do with Max's refusal to let me into his life? But I was finally able to see that I have always been relieved when Max refused my care, my attempts at compassion. We had what he called a meeting in the middle and each saw how we contributed to what had become a cold and painful distance. We then collaborated on new ways of trying to accept what the other offers—especially related to the loss of our mothers. We experimented with these new ways of relating, we use them to reset when we find ourselves slipping back into distance."

Conflict Is Not the End of the World

When you have a conflict, catastrophizing it does not help the situation. We all get into a conflict and argument once in a while because our relationship is built on "us-ness" and not "me" alone. And there will be disagreements and misunderstandings along the way. It's okay to disagree and understand that marriage is not always about being on the same page. Just something as simple as acknowledging that we are not on the same page often leads to a sense of relief and compassion—for each other and ourselves. We're trying our best every day, but some days are better than other days. All relationships have conflict because you cannot and, in truth, probably don't really want to be controlling the other person all the time. There's always going to be some differences and sometimes pushback. It's how you do the pushback. It's how you engage in the conflict that's going to make the difference.

Before you apply the PACER model, remind yourself that conflict, and even loud, messy, fights, are a part of every couple's relationship. This is a self-grounding reminder that you are living your relationship in real life. There is always room for disagreement, but catastrophizing conflict is a distortion based on perfectionism that makes it more difficult to even imagine that the conflict can be real and resolved. However, it's how you address these conflicts that makes the difference between repair and continued resentment. And if you can accept that there will be conflict, resolving them will become easier.

Empowering the "us-ness"—that is, caring for the relationship itself as a discrete entity that the couple values and nurtures—is based on an increasingly conscious, and shared, commitment to using ruptures to:

- Make use of the two rules—to focus on ourselves.
- Better understand how you are contributing to what is working—and what is not—in your relationship.
- Use this understanding to take inventory of ourselves and use this information to better and more effectively navigate conflict, and, ultimately,
- Repair.

CHAPTER EIGHT

Pause: Creating the Space between Thought and Action

For us, a pause is a deliberate, agreed-upon action that you take as a couple when you are in the heat of an argument. The point of pause is to create an opportunity for thoughtful response. It gives both individuals the time and space needed to de-escalate, think, then act, as opposed to what people usually do when they fight: react, act, then think.

The action inside a pause may seem like "no action" on the surface, but in fact there is a lot going on. First, a pause creates the space so that both partners can take a break from the conflict and recover. Heated, escalated arguments can create emotional and physiological reactions. When you are in conflict, your anxieties, fears, and insecurities can feel like they quadruple and can make you feel thrown off or *dysregulated*. These emotions can create a visceral experience, one that you can actually feel in your body: you might find that you are sweating or holding your breath. What's more, if you are dysregulated, it's hard for your partner to hear your concerns or point of view because their emotional state—and their psychological defenses against being overwhelmed by it—are triggered by your reactive state. Their own defenses inadvertently block their ability to take in new information (especially when it can be anxiety or fear-provoking). The result: lots of yelling, or avoiding, and very little ability to take in what's happening. A pause addresses this inevitable emotional dysregulation so that you and your partner can stop the overheated rhetoric, calm down, and recharge your sense of "us." Think of a pause as an opportunity for taking care of one's emotional health in the moment.

By pausing, you and your partner are also acknowledging that you don't want to say anything more hurtful than what has been said already. Perhaps you wanted your partner to listen to your ideas, yet you lost your ability to listen. When we say too much in conflict, we often say mostly hurtful things and can even lose perspective of what we were fighting about. You might end up overgeneralizing your partner's actions by saying something like, "You always do this to me!!!" Or when the escalation happens, each partner starts attacking the other, adding more fuel to the proverbial fire. Escalating your fight can potentially become pure attack, the arguments become no longer connected to what you started arguing about at the first place. Pause will save partners from saying the last word that can devastate your partner and the relationship and at the same time, provide the opportunity to think about how you were communicating during the fight.

Pause will not be easy at first. Let's face it, there's a lot of high-power ammunition we're surrendering when we pause. We are giving up a degree of feeling right, maybe even righteous. We lose the ability to win a fight or place the blame completely on our partner with the conviction that "It is always all your fault." Some people get secondary gain out of attacking their partners, which could be a gratuitous sense of high-mindedness or the ability to project their uncomfortable feelings about themselves onto their partner.

However, there is much to gain during pause, which is why we think it is so important. Within the space of pause, you can start to do the Accountability work: reflect on the conflict and figure out why and what you were fighting about in the first place. It provides a framework for you to open your mind and access a willingness to take responsibility for your part. Pause allows you to take the first shot at the rule: "keep the focus on *your*self!" And by doing so, pause will be a gateway to regain a healthy sense of self. By pausing you will recognize that you and your partner are derailing from the relationship path. This will prompt you to keep the focus on yourself and put your derailed relationship back on course.

In this way a pause is a joint effort that requires hard work and commitment from both partners. Ultimately, a pause allows couples to revisit what they have already built together—their history, commitment, and love—as we consider what our options are for dealing with conflict. By taking a pause, we can connect to our values and ethics, invite in wisdom, guidance, and grace, practice empathy and compassion as we discern the right action and find the right words. It's a time to remind yourself that you need to stop fighting for the sake of your relationship. Your relationship needs a pause, not an escalation.

As basic as pause seems to be, it has profound effects on our relationship and the couples we treat. In our own relationship pausing has allowed us to grow both as individuals and as a couple. We have learned to bring awareness and intention into our relationship, which has made us both better partners.

A Pause Is . . .

The most effective use of Pause is not to avoid continuing the conflict, but to:

- Decrease the length of active conflict.
- Reduce the intensity and heat—perhaps the harm—of conflict.
- Increase awareness of triggers that result in you being drawn into conflict.
- Expand awareness of your part in the conflict.
- Have compassion and empathy for yourself and your partner. Conflicts are inevitable in long-term committed relationship.
- Check in with yourself to see whether you are ready to speak to your partner in a constructive manner (from the position of "I") and to listen to your partner.
- To recognize that winning the fight is not the goal. Resolving the conflict with a plan to move forward is the goal.

Stonewall vs. Pause: A World of Difference

A pause is the exact opposite of a stonewall. As you learned in Part I, stonewalling is a unilateral decision where one person shuts down or freezes out the other. It is the refusal to engage when there is a conflict; where one partner takes all the power in the relationship and punishes the other with their silence. Even if you stonewall by refusing to argue, your spouse might want to have a conversation with you about what transpired. You think you are doing them a favor by not engaging; however, you might be hurting your partner who wants to process what happened.

We believe people who stonewall have difficulty processing intense feelings such as anger, sadness, disappointment, rejection, and pain. We also think people end up using stonewalling as a way of not being able to forgive a partner, especially if they become micro-focused on a small rupture, or they simply don't know how to digest their pain, ease their resentment toward their partner, and be able to forgive someone.

Stonewalling can take many forms. It could look like shutting down or not engaging or not participating. And it can also look like you are overly busy or engaged in activities that do not include your partner. It could look like any compulsive, obsessive, or addictive behavior. No matter what form it takes, if it is used long enough, the underlying message is to express pent up resentment and then punish your partner. In a stonewall, one partner is effectively saying, "I'm walking away and not talking to you," and it could go on for an hour or a week or longer.

Some know that letting a conflict escalate is going to make the repair work a lot harder so they try to extinguish even a small fight by disengaging. This generally creates a bypass where more vulnerable feelings—sadness, hurt, fear—are covered up and avoided by an anger reaction.

If one partner stonewalls and walks away, and then comes back and says, "Now I'm ready to talk," it is not considered a Pause because the decision to come back to the discussion was not consensual. Instead, a Pause is mutually decided upon and provides the opportunity for each person to experience their more vulnerable feelings before they react to them with anger. Most importantly, a pause allows us to put the brakes on our stonewalling impulses.

Characteristics of a Stonewall	Characteristics of a Pause
• React to a conflict by shutting down. Conduct oneself as if they are not in a relationship. • Unable to self-soothe or comfort. • Unable to communicate. • Flooded with overwhelming emotion, often anger and hurt. • Cold and unkind. • Shutting everything/everyone out, isolation, have difficulty thinking about any aspect of the relationship. • Unable to be self-reflective. • Righteous, defended against repair. • Unforgiving.	• Verbally ask for a pause. React to a conflict with a willingness to respond when able to do so with a better ability to assess one's own part in the conflict at hand. • Able to access self-soothing and recall a history of accessing comfort from others—including a partner. • Open to communication when both parties are willing to doing so; willing to check in with the partner to determine when both are ready to communicate. • Upset, yet able to consider that overwhelming emotion is a reaction to more vulnerable feelings like pain and fear. • Cool, but able to access thoughts and memories of kindness and compassion toward the partner. • Uncomfortable, but open to being vulnerable and working together to resolve conflict. • Self-reflective. • Desiring repair. • Open to forgiveness.

Tracey and Frank: Masters of the Stonewall

We once worked with Tracey and Frank, a couple who ended up mastering the art of stonewalling. Tracey constantly felt disappointed and hurt: she couldn't believe their relationship had so completely crashed and burned. Sometimes the fighting would start on a Friday afternoon and Frank would not talk to her until Monday night. Tracey would keep asking, "When are we going to talk?" but Frank would simply not respond.

When they came to see us for counseling, we explained the difference between stonewalling and pause. We then discussed why we couldn't help them resolve their issues without setting up ground rules for a Pause that each could live with, instead of using avoidance to punish the other.

Using Pause, Frank was able to start taking ownership of his need to get away from Tracey when conflicts were too painful or disappointing. The first step was for Frank to learn how to say, "I need a moment. I need a break. I need a walk. I need a day away," so Tracey would know that there would be a definable end to what had been experienced as "Frank's hostile silence." It's not quite that Frank's silence was instantaneously acceptable, as it still felt hurtful and shocking to Tracey because distance and shutting down were not her go-to strategies when she was hurt. However, over time she was able to see that healing could—and did—occur whenever they utilized a formal Pause. Without the anxiety of wondering when Frank would come back and talk, the time during Pause became more tolerable. Frank saw that the time he needed to reset became shorter. Since it was no longer experienced by either as a "pure punishment," each of them was better able to use the Pause to consider how they had each contributed to the conflict at hand.

There Really Is a Bad Time to Have a Fight

It sounds ridiculously simple, but being hungry can makes us irritable and impatient. Perhaps asking for a Pause in an argument until you eat a proper meal can help you focus on the issues brought by conflict.

We also suggest to our couple clients that they don't engage in serious conversations that could lead to conflicts after 8:00 p.m. After a long day of work or parenting, each partner is tired, no matter how old they are. And because you are tired you are more likely to misinterpret what your partner is saying or perceiving.

Arguing at night goes against our circadian rhythm, which is the body's innate mechanism that regulates all our internal systems. Around 9:00 p.m., our body secretes the hormone melatonin, which gets us ready for sleep. When your body is naturally winding down and preparing to sleep, you are not capable of explaining ideas well or listening to your partner.

When we find ourselves in a heated argument, one of us might say to the other, "We're too tired to have this discussion right now. It's 8:00 p.m. We are hitting our circadian time limit. Let's take a break and we'll talk about it in the morning."

Reaction vs. Pause

Pause is an option to immediate, knee-jerk defensiveness (rage) and allows us to consider what it is that we are defending ourselves against. In Pause, we can discover that underneath our defensiveness lies a fear of being hurt, rejected, and abandoned. However, when we are willing to pause, we have a greater capacity to work through these issues, address our own anxieties and

- Remain in pause long enough to stop reacting, self-soothe, and eventually offer a more thoughtful response to each other.
- Consider the possibility that our reactions to our underlying pain and fear have been expressed in actions that can put us in a position to be hurt or hurt others.
- Consciously let go of defensive behavior and consider having a discussion from a position of "I" where you are able to share your contribution to the rupture.
- Live more comfortably in your own skin, accepting each other and yourself *as is*.

Most of us are full of historical examples—even, perhaps especially, in our current relationship—of what our lives have looked like *without* Pause. If you are anything like we were, then the insertion of a Pause just might be among the most wonderful gifts you could possibly offer that third entity— your "us"-ness.

Exercise: Substituting Pause
Where Reaction Once Was

Fill in the chart below following the two samples. Write down two or three reactive behaviors that you have justified based on your partner's behavior. Alongside these responses, write down what their responses were to your reactions, and describe what the outcome typically looks like, or how it might be different if you had taken a Pause.

A reaction I justify based on my partner's behavior.	How my reaction is typically received.	The outcome following my reactive behavior.	What this conflict could look like with Pause.
Example A: I constantly criticize and attack my wife for her spending.	My wife feels ashamed each time we try to talk about this issue—and then my own financial issues are thrown in my face.	I increase my criticism and become more vigilant about monitoring my wife's behavior, leading each of us to refuse to talk about anything related to money.	Instead of criticizing and fighting, I could acknowledge how afraid and financially insecure the spending patterns in our family make me and attempt a productive conversation with my wife explaining my truth.
Example B: My husband micro-manages my interactions with our kids—so I take them on elaborate outings without him.	My husband feels hurt and estranged from the kids and me.	We wind up living in what feels like two different families.	We could attempt to discuss that we have different ways of interacting with our children so that he could rejoin "our" family.

A reaction I justify based on my partner's behavior.	How my reaction is typically received.	The outcome following my reactive behavior.	What this conflict could look like with Pause.
1.			
2.			
3.			

Now think about the following:

Looking at your answers in the chart, how did you feel about your reaction to the original conflict? Do you feel justified about your defensive behaviors whether they are distancing or destructive behavior? If you felt justified, what's underneath your justification? If you don't feel justified, how do you feel about the original reaction you had in the conflict? Does it sit well with you? If not, how would you like to change your reaction with Pause?

- How does your reaction to conflict—your actions—connect to and express your part in patterns of distance and destruction in your relationship? Does your counter-reaction to the brewing argument create more hurt in your relationship?
- Using the fourth column above, what are some other ways of responding to each other when hurt? What does this look like?

How to Pause

A Pause should be co-created, co-developed, and co-maintained. A Pause usually means that two people stop talking to each other altogether, but it doesn't have to. They may want to physically walk away from each other or put only this one conversation on hold until an agreed upon time. On the way to getting to this joint use of Pause, however, most of us could use a good reminder of what a Pause looks like when we commit to it ourselves—with or without the participation of our partner. We agree with the practical implementation of Pause suggested by conflict resolution consultant Marina Piscolish, which involves three key elements: noticing, relaxing, and reflecting.

1. First, *notice* what is happening in your body in the moment of rising stress or when conflict is at hand. Where are you holding your stress: in your neck, chest, fists? What sensations do you feel: tightness, warmth, or numbness? Is your heart beating fast? Does your face feel flushed? Has your breathing become shallow? Having noticed any bodily change, ask for a Pause where you cease engaging further in the conflict until you have gone inward and feel ready to emerge, more prepared.

2. Next, find a space where you can intentionally *relax* those areas of your body where you are holding tension. Drop your shoulders, release your jaw, shake out your hands. Place your hand over your heart to feel it beat and remind yourself that you are safe. Then, see if you can have compassion for yourself and your partner. Having conflict is an inevitable part of being in a committed, long-term, intimate relationship.

3. Finally, slow down so that you can experience your thoughts as they arise. Get curious. *Reflect* on the messages running through your mind. Acknowledge the emotions you're feeling, the rage, fear, disappointment, heartbreak, or all the above. Allow and accept them as valid, rather than pushing them away. Investigate each emotion and try to uncover the source. What are you believing? What unmet need explains that rage or fear? How might that need be met by you? By another? This final step offers the specific information

needed to prepare yourself and to find the words your partner needs to hear.[1]

It's a good idea to set up the ground rules for how you and your partner will Pause when you are *not* in conflict. Every couple can establish their own rules as long as they agree on the length of a Pause. For instance, some couples cannot take a twenty-four-hour Pause because it makes one person feel abandoned. On the other end of the spectrum, five minutes isn't enough time for two people to completely cool down. And within your relationship, each person may require more or less time to be in Pause, which is true for us. Mark can be done with Pause (so he thinks!) in just a few minutes, while it generally takes Haruna a bit longer—at least fifteen to thirty minutes. Mark has a harder time calling for a Pause because he intrinsically believes that he can fix any situation before it gets to the point where we need to Pause. Haruna on the other hand, usually needs a Pause to collect her thoughts.

Respecting your partner's rhythm and timeline is a way of respecting each other and is just another part of being in a long-term, committed relationship. However, we know that sometimes it is not easy to respect your partner's timeline, especially, if you are thinking, This Pause has gone on long enough!!!

If your Pause seems uncomfortable, then you are doing it right! It's perfectly normal to feel uncomfortable when you have an unresolved conflict. It can be uncomfortable to know that you hurt your partner and have to wait to resolve the conflict. Others are uncomfortable because they cannot trust that there will be a discussion and a resolution after Pause. In this situation, the waiting time during a Pause can be even more painful and upsetting than the initial conflict.

Lastly, discomfort can signify that one partner has a moment of clarity where they can see (maybe for the first time) their part in the rupture and has already developed a willingness to return and resolve the conflict. It's no surprise that each of our *Pause-Clocks* is actually calibrated to our ability to sit with discomfort, as it is the discomfort itself that will start to draw people

1.   https://sjquinney.utah.edu/news-articles/the-pause-closing-the-gap-between-our-best-intentions-and-our-actions/.

back to each other. When you master de-escalating with Pause, you might end up taking a shorter pause than before. You learn to comfort and regulate yourself in conflict. And you might experience a feeling of calmness and self-reflection. When you do, you might not feel discomfort. You might feel inner peace, calmness, and self-acceptance. You might even gain some sense of humor about your reaction, *I criticized him again! I better apologize!* And one of the things that we regularly experience as the Pause-Clock winds down is how we each end up feeling calmer than before and recognize that we can make a new loving and caring contribution to our relationship—our us-ness—when the Pause is over and it's time to get into the repair.

If one person says, "Let's pause," and the other person relents, then that's enough for both partners to understand that you are in a Pause. But to make it crystal clear, when one partner asks for a pause, the other has to acknowledge it, otherwise you have a stonewall. If the agreed upon time is not enough for one of you, check in with your partner and share that you need more time.

The "My Dad" Code

In our marriage, we start a Pause by using an obvious code word: "moratorium." Plenty of our clients choose words that are meaningful to them.

"You know," screamed Naomi, enraged with her husband—and, ironically, with her husband's recent angry outburst, "It's true what they say, you do marry your dad—I sure married mine!"

Her husband Vince looked at her and said quietly, "You know, I married your dad, too!"

"Wait! What?" said Naomi as her lid began to flip, "What did you say?"

"Ummm . . ."

Then Naomi burst into laughter. Vince, hesitatingly at first, joined.

From then on, "my dad" became their Pause code word. Naomi and Vince would use it whenever one of them was offering the other a chance to Pause before tumbling into rage. Just using the code word took the temperature of the room down immediately, and both reported that they could regain a sense of humor. Naomi told us, "Saying it reminded us both to not take ourselves so seriously."

Exercise: How Do You Want to Pause?

Work with your partner to develop your style of Pause. Whatever works best is the right answer, as long as it is agreed upon and meets the goal that you will both be able to keep the focus on yourself, regulate your emotions, and return to resolve the conflict.

When developing your rules for a Pause, think about the following:

- Do we need to physically separate ourselves into individual spaces?
- Do we need quiet time without engaging in any form of conversation?
- Can we talk about other things while we are in a Pause?
- Do we need to eat? Do we eat together or separately?
- Do we need to engage in some physical activity? Together or separately?
- Is there an agreed-upon initial Pause-clock?
- What do we do when one of us needs more time? How do we check in with each other?
- What about the kids? We need to take care of them as a team while we take a Pause.
- What other questions might we want/need to ask and answer in order to tailor our Pause to suit our relationship?
- Like Naomi and Vince, do you need to use humor (in their case "my dad") to ask for Pause? Or do you need to use kindness to ask for Pause ?

The Saturday School Showdown

Saturday School is a New York City institution. Because the city is so diverse, people from various cultures send their school-age children for language and cultural education—we send our kids to Japanese Saturday School.

One of our most frequent ruptures occurs on Friday nights—the dreaded battle over completing all of the homework for Saturday School. It typically goes like this:

Haruna came home from a dinner with her friends and Mark and their younger child were sitting at the table playing games and eating snacks. Haruna asked, "You two look like you're having a good time. Did you finish your homework?"

Mark immediately became defensive and replied, "We did a lot of the homework together, but we're getting tired, so I thought it was time to put the homework aside and have fun. Can you just calm down, Haruna?!"

"Okay, I'll calm down," Haruna blurted. "If you can explain to the teacher why our kid didn't complete the homework for this week."

These fights tended to escalate into screaming matches where both Haruna and Mark feel thoroughly justified in their respective positions, leaving no room for understanding and compassion, and are potentially weekend-ruining for the whole family.

Lately, instead of attacking each other, we snapped right into the PACER model, beginning with Pause. Haruna kept the focus on herself and went into the bedroom and changed clothes. Mark could still feel the anger in the room and exerted great energy to resist being defensive about how he was parenting their child. Instead of reacting to that feeling, Mark used his time in Pause to create a plan with their child to get the homework finished in the morning.

This was a relatively brief Pause, but in the short time, Mark could see how complicated and painful Haruna's feelings about children's Japanese education was. Mark could respect all the effort that Haruna had put into ensuring that our kids spoke Japanese. When we paused on Friday night, Haruna could take a breath and realize that her fury—though it felt justified—was creating distance between herself and her child and Mark. In Pause, Haruna could better see what she needed was not acceptance of her rage, but an understanding of how important this education was to her. When she communicated this to Mark, and felt like he heard it, she felt much more supported and cared for. There was simply no way we were going to get past this argument without Pause.

Exercise: How to Calm Down During Pause

During your Pause, you want to regain a sense of centeredness and empowerment. In Pause, you are going to keep the focus on yourself and learn to comfort your vulnerable feelings. This exercise, based on the teachings of Dr. Kristen Neff, can help you reestablish emotional regulation.[2]

- Sit in a quiet, comfortable place where you won't be disturbed or distracted, or go for a walk, preferably in nature. Meditation, taking a warm bath, getting a massage, all of these activities or doing something else that you really enjoy, can ease your dysregulated self.
- Take a few deep breaths to clear your mind. If you are filled with difficult, intense feelings, such as anger, frustration, despair, sadness, or feeling misunderstood, be kind and compassionate to yourself in order to calm down. People in relationships experience conflicts that result in aggressive behaviors from time to time. What you are experiencing is a human emotional reaction to being in conflict within a committed relationship. Fear and worry are also typical emotions to experience in conflict.
- Place one hand on your heart and offer yourself kindness, understanding, and compassion for the suffering you're experiencing. Remember what you're feeling is an integral part of the human experience: you are not suffering alone.
- Pay attention to your breathing. Take a few deep breaths in and long, slow breaths out. If you are still overwhelmed by emotion, continue this breathing pattern as a way to soothe and calm yourself.
- When you're ready, slowly resume your normal activities, knowing that you can return to this exercise at any time.

2.   Kristen Neff, *Self-Compassion: The Proven Power of Being Kind to Yourself* (New York: William Morrow, 2011), 56–63.

After completing the self-regulation exercise, ask yourself, "Am I ready to talk about what transpired in the fight with my partner? Am I in a good place to do this, where can I keep the focus on myself, let go of the blame game, and be able to listen to my partner?" If you are in a good place, then you have experienced—with or without realizing it—a sense of the basic safety that you need to move forward toward a healthy and healing conflict resolution. If not, it is okay to inform your partner that you need more time.

CHAPTER NINE

Accountability: Keeping the Focus on Yourself

Once you've calmed down, the real work of Pause begins. You're not just going to sit by yourself twiddling your thumbs, waiting for your partner to calm down, hoping things get better. You're going to be actively thinking about what your role is in the conflict so that you can understand your contribution to both the problem and its solution. Accountability gives you something to think about instead of ruminating on how you're going to get back at your partner for hurting your feelings or enraging you.

You will be working on acknowledging your contribution to the rupture, the pattern your contribution represents, how the same issue plays out in other areas of your relationship, and ultimately, how these issues are connected to your deeper fears, doubts, and worries. Accountability is the relational version of putting your weapons—your go-to armor of blaming your partner and/or defending yourself—away. In effect, you are disarming yourself and learning to speak with clarity so that you can safely expose your vulnerabilities, become fully seen and heard, and accepted by one another. The psychoanalyst Dan Shaw, in his study of traumatic narcissism, observed that "recognition is a *constantly renewed commitment* we make, working together, creating a dialogue with others that moves us toward mutual liberation."[1] It's quite possible that you may have spent years not knowing how to speak to your partner in this

---

1.   Daniel Shaw, *Traumatic Narcissism: Relational Systems of Subjugation* (London: Routledge, 2013), 4.

manner, a way of recognizing and seeing each other, and have felt lost in the relationship. If you are reading this book, you may have hit your own version of a "bottom," and are just now willing to end the defensive distancing and/or destructive behaviors. The good news is that all of us can learn the tools of Accountability and begin to start a new version of your relationship.

Without these defenses, you can begin to build new behaviors and change your reactions to conflict without resulting in a *regression to the mean,* which we discussed in Chapter Five. Instead of bracing ourselves for attacks, counterattacks, offensive and defensive behaviors, when we change the mean, we gradually come to build a new trust in our partner. This trust is built on the joint recognition that each of you will be doing your part of the work necessary to heal the relationship. Lastly, we have found that when each person can keep the focus on themselves and take responsibility for their actions, they will then be more open to listen to their partner with compassion, calmness, and clarity during the next step of the PACER model, Collaboration.

Just like Pause, Accountability is one of the biggest gifts you will ever give yourself. You will now have the power to contribute to fixing your relationship when it goes off the rails because the only way to achieve that power (and sense of empowerment) is to become open to seeing your contribution to what went wrong. If you can see where you're accountable for what went wrong, then you get the reward of being accountable for what goes right in your alliance.

Accountability Is Not about Discovering Who Is at Fault

We believe every conflict is co-created: it's never just about one person's poor behavior. In Accountability, the goal is to move away from the blame game because when you put the blame on your partner or take all the blame yourself, the outcome is that we unintentionally protect ourselves against the things we want from love. In rupture, we lose that sense of "us," and blaming keeps us isolated and separated from each other and from recreating a sense of unity (that third entity that is us).The PACER model will be the mechanism that reunites us and brings us together, from rupture to repair.

In Accountability, you are creating room for accepting the idea that we all make mistakes. This process leads to a new connection with the larger concepts of forgiveness and empathy—starting with yourself. Adopting these attitudes leads to developing a deeper connection with your partner, where you learn to accept human errors and treat each other with compassion. You are also going to learn how to show up for your partner with compassion, which leads to more trust, love, and connection with your partner.

Couples are often surprised to find how isolating it is to be either always right or always wrong. When you are acting as a judge and deciding who is always right or wrong when conflict erupts, you never have to resolve the conflict because you don't need your partner—or anyone else—to help you interpret where the blame lies.

It is possible that two people could be wrong at the same time, or that you and your partner can be right at the same time. If you stay in your silo of righteousness, you are missing out on the opportunity to work together and decide, *This time, I was wrong, too* or *You were also right about that!*

If your partner told you all the ways in which they were at fault, and you responded by saying, "Aha, I knew it was you," with coldness and judgment, then you have maintained your isolation and divisive righteousness. And you lost the focus on yourself. If you can see how you contributed to the rupture, you can respond by saying, "Thank you for your honesty, and I believe that I contributed as well." Growing your alliance allows you to experience the benefits of what Esther Perel refers to as *together* and *apart*. Acknowledging being apart allows us to recognize and affirm the process—that we come to the relationship as individuals—and that we grow together as we understand and claim our contributions. The together is that us, the third entity, is also growing.

It is easy to act like a judge and take 100 percent credit when things go right and assign 100 percent blame when things go wrong. Yet this state is really a combination of a few major *cognitive distortions*,[2] what cognitive behavioral psychologists call:

---

2. Cognitive distortions are internal mental filters or biases. Our brains are continually processing lots of information. To deal with this, our brains seek shortcuts to cut down our mental burden. Cognitive distortions are irrational thought shortcuts that can influence our emotions. Generally fueled by anxiety, they can simplify the ways we experience, perceive, and interpret ourselves and the world (especially thoughts, feelings, and actions). However, they tend to do so at the cost of fueling our anxieties.

- All-or-Nothing Thinking: Using absolute vocabulary such as "always," "never," or "every," as in "Every time we have a date night, we fight."
- Disqualifying the Positive: Recognizing only the negative aspects of a situation, while ignoring the positive, as in "It doesn't matter that we got along for most the trip, when we disagreed at the end, you ruined everything."
- Overgeneralization: Making broad interpretations based on a single event, as in, "We had a fight; we always fight."

These cognitive distortions result as a consequence of being in a state of conflict. The anxiety of threat blocks the brain's higher functioning, leaving the older and simpler parts of the amygdala, or reptilian brain, in charge. In this state, we are more vulnerable to respond to conflict in either the fight, flight, or freeze reactions covered in Part I, and we will have a hard time accessing Pause, which allows us to make use of these lessons.

Even if you are so convinced that you are blameless in a specific conflict, we ask that you leave open the possibility that you are not. First, this line of thinking (I'm 100 percent right; they are 100 percent wrong) is not doing you any favors. You're handing over all the power to mess up your relationship, along with the power to fix it, to someone else. When you sit in this certainty that you alone are right, it is a powerless position because you can only hope that your partner can change, gets better, and doesn't do it again. In essence, you have given away all hope of contributing to fixing what's wrong. What's more, finding "blame" may be your signature way of expressing and revealing your responses and reactions to IRL or the intimacy of everyday life. Because when conflict gets heated and escalated, it gets heated by two, not one. So looking at your contribution is very important to the process of resolving conflict.

If you can't see even an inkling of what your contribution is to a conflict, and you are stuck in the blame game no matter how much your conflict escalated, you are essentially scapegoating your partner. Blaming, scapegoating, and any other attempt at avoiding accountability is a rip-off for both partners because when either one of you fall for the delusion that it is just one individual who is to blame, then you both lose the chance to learn the lessons that comes from:

- Recognizing the fact that you made a mistake.
- Reconciling your mistake with compassion.
- Accounting for the reasons underlying your behavior.
- Owning your part of the conflict.
- Course-correcting (amending).
- Learning to not do it again.
- Knowing that an acceptable outcome does not have to be a perfect outcome.

Your contribution to a conflict may very well be the fact that you are holding onto your rightness and setting up your partner for a fall. For instance, when we first met with Zeke and Madelyn, all Zeke could say was "I'm a good guy. I didn't do anything."

Mark quickly replied, "There's always something that we have done in a conflict. In your case, you set up a dynamic in your relationship where you are the good guy. You're so wonderful that you inadvertently make your wife the scapegoat for everything awful in your relationship. You have ended up convincing the whole world to think that she's the asshole because you're so nice."

Zeke's understanding was fueled by passive aggressive behavior, and his wife, Madelyn, was comfortable taking on the bad guy role until we mentioned how isolating, divisive, and limiting that can be. When Madelyn and Zeke fell for the one-person-to-blame delusion they effectively cut themselves—and each other—off from the process of rupture and repair that would allow them to fix their problems together.

Haruna said, "Why does one of you have to be the good one, and the other has to be bad? Can't you see how you are both good and bad sometimes?" Blaming one person for being a bad cop is not going to unify your relationship. This strategy creates isolation, division, and power differentiation. The "good cop" needs to learn to look at their actions and say, "I can clearly see what my partner (the bad cop) did. But what's my part in it?"

A wonderful quote from Alcoholics Anonymous addresses this sense of how our anger feels justified, that we've found a loophole, yes, but we've wrongly ignored how we triggered an aggressive reaction. It is how we convince ourselves it's "me against the world" (i.e., my true love). When we cannot see our part in a problem, naturally we feel under attack:

> Driven by a hundred forms of fear, self-delusion, self-seeking, and self-pity, we step on the toes of our fellows and they retaliate. Sometimes they have hurt us, seemingly without provocation, but we invariably find that at some time in the past we have made decisions based on self which later placed us in a position to be hurt.[3]

Once you can see your role in a conflict, it's going to be easy to drift into thinking, Yeah, I did that, but what I did was nothing compared to what my partner did. We call this line of thinking a *loophole*, the rationale of what has been done to us is so bad that it excuses our bad behavior, or the idea that we deserve to stay in a victim role. You measure your behavior vs. what your partner did, and if your damage was less destructive and distancing than what your partner did, you elect yourself to be both the winner of the argument and a victim at the same time. In essence, you created an escape route. However, in conflict there is no grading (who got the A+ worst damage) or competition. If you participated in an escalation, you are not a victim but had a part in it.

When it comes to loopholes, we all get to choose our own—it could be that our partner had an affair, that they've been in some way abusive, that they use foul language or scream. The loophole allows us to slip into righteous indignation; it's that "one thing" we believe we cannot, should not, must not, tolerate. It's also the "one thing" our partner does that allows us to take their inventory—and not our own.

We turn to the loophole to excuse ourselves from the terrifying, painful, and seemingly impossible task of finding our part in what we experience as our partner's very worst behavior. We're not looking to make it seem like you are the cause of your partner's bad behavior. But maybe there is something you need to uncover, some motive that makes it feel unsafe to keep the focus on yourself when your partner gives you what seems like such a good reason

---

3.   Alcoholics Anonymous World Services, *Alcoholics Anonymous* (New York: AA World Services. Inc. 1997), 62.

for doing so. As tempting as this may be, it will make it impossible to use your us-ness to repair when you—your relationship—ruptures.

When you are thinking, Of course I'm allowed to yell when it comes to money; of course I'm allowed to leave you when you've lied to me. I'm okay to start this rupture right now. What you are really saying is "You did this all on your own; I'm just a victim of the rupture that you perpetrated upon me. That means there is no us to turn to, no us to collaborate on a solution, and no us to repair."

In effect, your loopholes are giving you permission to avoid accounting for your part in the rupture. There might be times where you need to stand your ground and protect yourself from the ways your partner has treated you. This is always the case with abuse and often the case with infidelity. But if you are willing to keep the focus on yourself and ask, "What's my part in it?" you can use the PACER model to repair even the worst kinds of damage. In our many years of working with couples we have seen terrible trauma to relationships repaired when each person is able to take full ownership of their part.

Lastly, don't beat yourself up by claiming—proclaiming—that this conflict, or any or every conflict, is all your fault. Accountability is not a *mea culpa*, (i.e., coming to the conclusion that *it's always all my fault*). "It's all me" is no better than "It's all you." Have empathy for your mistakes. If you are letting go of blaming, criticizing, scorekeeping, one-upping your partner, have the same compassion for yourself. All these coping tools covers up our vulnerable human traits. You are co-learner of in real life relationship.

I'll Be Your Mirror—and You, Mine

Why is it so important to own your contribution to the conflict dynamics with your partner? Mostly because in genuine intimacy, we need to be accountable for all our behaviors our partner sees that no one else does. Without our (conscious) permission, our partners become mirrors for us to also see things about ourselves that we'd prefer to not see. If you can't be accountable for the ways you react when you are at your worst, then you can only hope you will not be abandoned and rejected for your terrible behavior, rather than experiencing that these same bad behaviors can be amended and deeper levels of acceptance and intimacy can be achieved when you work together with your partner to repair. In this way, you are doing a disservice to yourself.

Accountability allows you to create a deeper acceptance of yourself, of your core characteristics, traits, and identity. Blaming your partner for all that goes wrong, along with conflict avoidance, are just other ways of seeing that harsh look from your partner when you are at your worst.

The Four Phases to Accountability

Once you have calmed down during Pause, it's time to start working on Accountability. In each of the following phases, you will be asking yourself questions to get to the heart of what your part was in the conflict and consider your own feelings and motivations. Give yourself time to really do these exercises as thoroughly as possible. We know the process can be a bit scary: you are going to see some aspects of yourself that make you uncomfortable, parts you may not like. You may find that you are ashamed of your behaviors. No matter how bad your actions were, you will benefit from understanding yourself. And ultimately, you get to find out where these behaviors come from.

As we learned in Part I, in IRL it is inevitable that our interactions with other people will go off the rails, resulting in ruptures. And, as painful and scary as this is, each and every rupture is an opportunity for repair. In turn, each repair is a chance to increase our vulnerability, empathy, intimacy, and emotional investment in each other, our developing sense of us-ness. Repair is our best shot at *welcoming our unwelcome parts*, allowing us to see exactly how our own history, the dynamics we grew up with, and the core conflicts we now have are interrelated. Everything we learned about culture and identity—and all the exercises we completed—have prepared us for having a more accurate Accountability, so that we can use the PACER Model to repair each conflict.

In Part I, you also learned how you and your partner have dealt with conflict in the past. Being either defensive or offensive did not help resolve the conflict. Think of Accountability as a better, more helpful tool in your conflict toolbox that will actually strengthen your relationship through vulnerability and compassion. In this collaborative repair process, you might end up having transformative experiences. You are listening to your partner's vulnerability and your partner will listen to yours. In doing so, you transform your inner judge to an inquisitive collaborator. You will be changing your inner dialogue from, Let's figure out who was right and who was wrong! to We can both be wrong. We can both be right. And we are both willing to repair it. Instead of Why did you do that to me? you will change your thinking to What really happened? Why did I respond and react?

Remember, you are not doing this work for your partner. You are doing this for you and your relationship so that you can learn to be a better trusting, caring, loving partner, and to understand how you have brought and recreated certain dynamic patterns from your history. These behaviors may be causing you, your partner, or your relationship, real harm and disconnection.

Phase 1: Information Gathering: Recollecting My Part in the Problem

While it is easy to spot what your partner did wrong, it is difficult to spot your contribution. Think about what just happened from only your point of view. Just by doing so, you will calm down. If you start with a polarized view, a guilty-innocent model, remember this is just a starting point and rarely (if ever) the case. At the very least, whatever the conflict is, there are probably underlying issues you need to consider. Take note if you start looking for a scapegoat.

Write down the answers to the following:
- What just happened? What was being said by me? Did I start a conversation from the position of "I?"
- What was my tone? My demeanor? My posture? (The way I delivered my message.)
- Can I see ways that my partner might interpret my behavior/actions in ways I did not intend?
- Can I see ways that my actions might result in my partner feeling hurt/scared/defensive?
- What was my part in it (context)?

- Have I contributed to this problem only right now?

For instance, Brendan walked into our office fuming because he just had the same fight with his wife for the nine millionth time because she didn't put away their child's toys the way he has told her to do it.

We told Brendan, "You think you're angry at your wife, but let's put the focus back on you and see what role you play in this fight." Then we went through this same set of questions. Brendan came to a new realization pretty quickly.

Brendan told us, "I blow my stack when my wife doesn't do what I tell her to do. Now that I'm calm and reflecting, I realize that I was actually reacting in anger to feeling hurt because she wasn't listening to me. I felt disrespected. Every time I've been in a rage with my wife, my wife runs, ducks, and covers, which ensures that we're actually not going to have any resolution. That's the history. In the past I tried to repair the problem by telling her how mad I am and correcting her. But, because I've been so enraged, she doesn't hear that. All she hears is a scolding. I really haven't contributed to repairing our conflict because I have not actually been communicating my fear and feelings of being disrespected."

Phase 2: Keeping the Focus on Myself, without Blame

Using the answers from the questions above, take your personal inventory again. Remember, taking inventory is a process that involves:

- Creating a record of what was being said by me.
- Thoughtful assessment of your motivations and intentions (for example, I wanted to confront my partner or I wanted to talk to my partner) as well as the underlying feelings/thoughts that your behavior (tone, demeanor, posture,) expressed.
- Careful consideration of "my part in it," (as in I ended up slamming the door at the end. I yelled. I justified my defensive and offensive behavior because I have been upset that my partner was spending too much money on our credit cards).

This time, you will be using the inventory model to identify your part in a conflict and potentially see your motivations for destructive behavior. We want to get answers to the most direct questions about our contributions so that we can better understand them, make use of them, and empower ourselves to repair.

Some people have trouble taking their own inventory. Remember, it's important not to criticize, attack, feel guilty, or be ashamed when you see the answers you come up with. Keep an open mind and have compassion for yourself: this is an exercise to be approached with curiosity, kindness, and compassion. Taking inventory is an opportunity to get to know yourself, and this will not happen if you are under assault, even from yourself!

Write down the following:

- How did the conflict leave you feeling? Primary emotions tend to be the ones that make us feel vulnerable: pain, fear, sadness, disappointment, rejection, etc.
- What is my history with this problem? Dealing with it, avoiding it?
- How have I contributed to repairing it in the past?
- What am I willing to offer to help repair it now?
- How does that issue play out in my relationship?
- How do these issues serve to cover up my deeper fears/insecurities?
- What contributions have I made to the ways these issues/problems play out in my relationship?
- What contributions have I made to resolving these issues/problems as they have played out in my relationship?

Exercise: Taking Inventory #3:
The Loophole Inventory

Reflect on the conflict you just experienced.

The Issue _____

How I've attempted to close the loophole by accounting for my part of the conflict.	
How have I become aware using loopholes to justify my feelings about my harmful/ unhelpful contributions?	
How did I use the loophole to justify my pain and take my partner's inventory?	
How did I use the loophole to avoid Accountability for the conflict at hand?	
What loophole was created in this conflict? Who was hurt, and what is the nature of this harm?	

Phase 3: Owning Only Your 40

Once you own your part in the conflict, leave room in your mind for the other person to take some responsibility for this same problem. Leaving room means *not* taking all the responsibility for problem.

How do we leave room for someone else to take responsibility but not take their inventory? The answer is the 40-20-40 Model. Escalation is always co-created.

Imagine you and your partner are sitting at a table ten-feet wide. A line bisects the table at the exact midpoint, leaving five feet between each of you and the midpoint—ten feet apart. Imagine a line in the exact midpoint between you—a 50 percent line. That leaves five feet between each of you and the middle.

You	Mid-Point	Me
0 Feet	5 Feet	10 Feet
0%	50%	100%

Now imagine expanding the width of the midpoint so that it occupies an area that's 20 percent of the width of the table, leaving 40 percent on each side of the midline for both you and your partner.

You	Co-Created Relational Space Expanded Midpoint			Your Partner
0 Feet	4 Feet		6 Feet	10 Feet
40%		20%		40%

If all we were asking you to consider was where you should split the responsibility for what happened during the conflict, the task would be much easier. However, there are many causes that can contribute to each result, outcome, or event. For example, the causes contributing to an automobile accident might include: design of the automobile, manufacture of the automobile, maintenance of the automobile, design of the road system, weather conditions, a variety of things to do with the driver and the passengers, debris on the road, and so on. The point is, the usual way people assign responsibility is too simple, trying to figure out whether it was your fault or your partner's fault doesn't work for relationships—part of the relationship is unique and not about either of the two people alone. The relationship is an entity in and of itself, and as the saying goes, the whole is greater than the sum of its parts.

The 40-20-40 model lets each person account for their contribution to each and every conflict that arises. In the process, each partner can only take no more than 60 percent and no less than 40 percent of the responsibility for any given issue. This leaves a 20 percent space where you and your partner will *meet in the middle* during the next step of PACER, Collaboration. This is a space of shared contribution to the issue/conflict/problem at hand—and also acts as a space that symbolizes "us." That's when you will each safely account for their responsibilities to this conflict without blaming. This nonjudgmental validation of each other's experience places the couple on a better footing for mutual understanding and shared problem-solving.

The 40-20-40 can be used both as an inventory of your part in what is going on in conflict and as a "rapid intervention" tool whenever you're in any kind of situation that makes you feel uncomfortable. Escalating emotions can be tamped down by identifying what's going on. This by itself is often enough to restore rational thinking and choice-making. With practice, examination of painful or scary experiences will empower rather than trouble you, and self-understanding will replace reactive self-protective behaviors such as distancing and destruction.

The following describes the structure and ground rules for using the 40-20-40. This exercise is a practice, so getting the knack of it will take time. Remember the purpose of this practice is to promote taking co-ownership of your relationship. But go easy on yourself: most of us require practice to learn to remain within one's own 60-percent zone.

Exercise: Practicing the 40-20-40

Sit in a quiet place and write down what was going on and how you felt at the time. Be objective when assessing what happened during the conflict. Divide responsibility among yourself and your partner based on how their actions or inactions affected the result. That is what would amount to each of the 40 percent columns (your contributions to the problem and the solution to those problems when they arise). Then, think about how the conflict escalated (I said this and he said that, and I said this and she said that). The way I communicated (tone, facial expression, and gestures). By acknowledging each partner's contributions, you might begin to see the shared 20 percent in the middle.

It seems like a paradox—we think we are shouldering the burden, but by accepting responsibility for more than our fair share, we aren't doing any favors to anyone. We are actually depriving our partner of the chance to meaningfully contribute to the relationship, and we are holding the relationship back from fully blossoming.

- Rewrite "You" thoughts to "I" thoughts. "She is making me uneasy" could be "I felt uneasy when she said X." "He shouldn't talk like that" can be converted into "I want him to talk to me with kindness. I felt criticized when he said Y."
- Feelings don't have to be justified or excused. They are simply part of what happens in you—let's be careful about being critical (of ourselves) here. If judgmental language toward yourself comes up, include it in your column of the 40-20-40.
- If you start writing the words "always" and "never," stop. Those words, the righteous indignation, the feeling of massive unfairness, the sinking feeling in the pit of the stomach, the tight breathing, the desperate need to save oneself from being screwed again, is a sign that you are defending yourself, not looking at yourself, leaving yourself isolated in your relationship. Remember to have compassion for your vulnerable feelings.
- If you use threats, blame, criticism, and name calling, rewrite your narratives. For example, if you wrote, "You screwed up our rental agreement with a rental car. You didn't return our

car on time. You don't care about us. You are an idiot!" Instead, rewrite a narrative by keeping the focus on yourself and bring your compassion. What you wrote may be connected to your deepest wishes, fears, doubts, and worries. You can recast the same experience as "I wanted (you are speaking *your* wishes) you to return our rental car on time and now we have to pay a penalty for the overtime. I feel frustrated about needing to pay the penalty (you are speaking of *your* fears and worries). I am not criticizing you. I am just looking after our finances (*your* worry and solution)." Here you are learning to translate your anger into expressions of needs and wants.

The problem (my part)	How I think my partner felt	Taking my proportionate (40) responsibility with compassion	My solution
Example 1 I called my partner at the last minute and told her that I could not show up for our dinner appointment with our friends.	She was very hurt by my actions. I embarrassed my partner and pushed her away. I feel extremely guilty. The reasons why we are not talking is all my fault. I blame myself.	I embarrassed my partner, but we were not getting along. So, without checking with my partner, I told myself that showing up for the dinner would have added additional drama into our existing fights and made our friends very uncomfortable.	Next time we can talk about existing dinner plan with our friends. I can also call her earlier and tell her that I won't be able to come to dinner. I can also call our friends and apologize.
Example 2 I have a low tolerance for how my husband talks to the kids when they are doing homework. I feel like he is stern and angry, and he sometimes yells at them. When it goes "too far" I come out and "intervene." Sometimes he gets defensive, and I yell at him.	My husband seems very hurt by my actions. I embarrassed my partner in front of the kids and pushed him away. And even though I am very unhappy about his actions toward the kids, my behavior makes me feel extremely guilty. The reasons why we are not talking feels like it is all my fault.	I embarrassed my partner but we have not had a discussion, yet, about our very different approaches to dealing with our frustration with the kids. When I attack him for what feels like attacks on the kids, I wind up taking all of the blame for our homework battles.	Before the next time I believe that my husband and I would be best served if we could each look at our contribution to these homework battles, see how it is that we—as a team—might best be able to help our kids do their homework and help each other deal with our frustrations about it. I can also talk about my feelings toward doing homework when I was a child.

The problem (my part)	How I think my partner felt	Taking my proportionate (40) responsibility with compassion	My solution
Your example			

Phase 4: Accounting for the Unwelcome Parts

Review your answers to the questions in Phase 1. It should include your contributions, good and bad, to the issue at hand, and not your partner's. Then, add in how your relationship can incorporate the unwelcome parts of yourself that you've seen in the mirror of Accountability and in Part I. These are most likely the characteristics and behaviors—especially patterns of behaviors—that you thought you had best keep hidden, perhaps because they could be used as ammunition against you. As you claim ownership to these traits, you are in fact getting to your 40-60 percent Accountability of all that goes on in your relationship. Because when Accountability for these traits is avoided or blocked, you wind up inadvertently protecting yourself from being close to your partner.

This is the information that you're bringing to Collaboration.

Accountability Ends: Coming Back Together

You end the Pause when you are ready to talk about your contribution to the conflict. When you've at least looked at the accountability exercises, then you can either offer or accept the invitation to the meeting. Then when you feel like you come through enough of the Accountability work, then you can invite your partner.

In our relationship, one or the other of us will request a meeting in the middle, which means we are ready for Collaboration. We hope the other has done their Accountability work, but that's not always true. In fact, the nice thing about the PACER model is that the questions that are coming up in the Accountability stage are actively allowing us to pause and keep the focus on ourselves. We try to be compassionate with ourselves when thinking about our contributions to the conflict.

Or you might feel like you are not entirely ready because you are afraid of having another conflict. Then you can say, "I am ready, but I am afraid of having another argument. At least, can we try? I am willing." If you are afraid of having a big conflict again, you can have a very short meeting in the middle. "I want to talk about it, but I am not sure about how to communicate it. Can we briefly talk about how we both are feeling for five minutes each?"

What happens if you don't accept? Then you're not ready yet. You can stay at Pause until you both offer and/or accept the meeting. One of the things that couples need to remember is to not judge each other for their readiness to engage this mind-bogglingly risky task. Be careful of statements like, "I can't believe she's not ready. I am so ready. She's withholding." That itself could become a power struggle and might indicate that you're "not ready" to really buy into the underlying notion of this book: conflict—and its solution—are cocreated. When you get upset at your partner not being ready to talk, you can do more self-compassion work. You can say to yourself, Waiting is very difficult for me. So while I wait for my partner to become ready for talking, I will focus on myself with self-care. Because waiting for your partner to become ready can be a difficult experience, learning to have compassion for your waiting period is necessary. We all have a unique rhythm and some of us have a slower pace of digesting a conflict.

Remember, it's you and your partner against the problem, you are not working against each other. Not only are you suffering, but your partner is also suffering. If your Pause-Clock is faster than your partner's, respect their rhythm. Waiting for your partner to do the Accountability work might be difficult. The ones who have a slow Pause-Clock need to communicate this need with their partner. For instance, saying, "I need more time to reflect on my part in the issues," might help ease their partner's waiting period. And if your Pause-Clock is a lot slower than your partner's, remember to bring your willingness. Your feelings might communicate to you that you are *not* ready for the meeting in the middle. You might have fear and dread of talking to your partner about the issues. If that's the case, check your willingness. If you are scared to have a meeting in the middle, it's okay. Your desire might be elusive, but if bring your willingness to repair and your compassion for yourself and your partner, you can begin the meeting in the middle.

CHAPTER TEN

Collaboration: Meeting in the Middle

Typically, people use the word *collaboration* to mean working together, yet in this step of the PACER model, couples collaborate primarily through listening. Their joint effort in deep listening allows them to hear their own thought-out perspective as well as their partner's. Then, they can not only resolve the conflict but create a new, more accurate inventory of their relationship. Ultimately, what is said during Collaboration becomes a part of the foundation of a new "us."

The main event of Collaboration is an exercise we call a *meeting in the middle*,[1] during which each partner agrees on a formal discussion structure to address the conflict/issue/problem by answering only one question: What was my part in it? Collaboration has nothing to do with getting feedback or being heard through crosstalk, criticism, blaming, or even acknowledging that your partner's inventory is registering. It's just a formalized opportunity to let each person speak from their heart and be heard. We have seen countless times how Collaboration transforms intolerable escalating fighting—or insufferable

---

1.   To reiterate a point made in Chapter Seven, a "Meeting in the Middle" is our term for a way of doing a couples' inventory that was developed by Chapter 9–Couples In Recovery Anonymous called a "Meeting of Two." Chapter 9 is a twelve-step program, a fellowship of people who share their experience, strength, and hope as couples so that they may solve their common problems and help bring harmony to relationships in recovery from addiction and substance abuse. A "Meeting of Two" is described as a way of addressing conflict through a process with a "formal meeting structure, with no crosstalk or inventory-taking, guarantees being heard, helps us learn to listen, and can bring us a new understanding of our partner."

silence, isolation, and distancing—into productive conversations. You can then come to respect your partner's experiences and have your partner respect yours. And you will learn to speak as allies and over time, develop deep empathy and compassion for each other.

The dividend of Collaboration is that you will learn new things about yourself and your partner:

- **Alliance:** You will learn how to form a healthier connection that furthers your common interest in and commitment to caring for your relationship, each other, and yourself.
- **Commitment:** It will be more comfortable to treat your partner with respect, even when you are hurt, frightened, upset, or angry. You will see more clearly how to support your partner and, as commitment is a two-way street, offer your partner clearer information about how they can support you and your relationship.
- **Vulnerability:** Authentic relationships begin when you can reveal your true self to each other. That means being genuine and vulnerable in your communication and interactions.
- **Availability:** The ability to have meaningful conversations that get to the root causes of your emotions, so that you can comfort each other during an emotionally difficult time.
- **Meeting Needs:** You can nurture each other and offer help when you see the other struggle. It is healthy to have and express needs in a relationship, even though "needy" is most often used against a person expressing needs by one unable—or unwilling—to meet them. The most essential relational needs are: 1) Willingness—the need to feel like we are showing up and effectively caring for each other; 2) Autonomy—the need to feel like we have control over what we do, that there is healthy separation and balance of you and me, and the unit that is us; 3) Relatedness—the need to have meaningful relationships and interactions with each other and other people.
- **Openness:** Being open to change. When you are emotionally open, you are more likely to accept, and if needed, seek out new experiences. You are also more likely to pay attention to your feelings and inner experiences, to respect them, and share them with each other.

- **Decision-Making:** As you try to make decisions together, you will be better able to explain your points of view, listen to your partner's, and come up with a solution that is agreeable to everyone.
- **Following Through:** You will be able to consciously follow through, accomplish what you commit or plan to do for and with each other, in the best manner and within a set time.
- **Stay in the Present:** You will work together at each rupture to repair your relationship. Even if you are holding onto something your partner did five years ago, you will become increasingly open to hearing what your partner is saying in the moment. You are learning to correct the mistakes in the present so stay here and now, so that wounds—old and new—will be healed.
- **Gain Compassion:** You are going to listen to each other with compassion. We all make mistakes. By communicating with the awareness of the here and now, you will accept each other's mistakes and repair through forgiveness. As a result, you will increase your compassion for each other.

Collaboration Is a Two-Step Step

Collaboration is a paradox: the only way to empowerment is to take individual accountability for your joint problem. The real secret of power in a relationship is knowing how you broke it so you can figure out how to fix it. And this meeting in the middle is where you actually do that. This is counterintuitive; it is countercultural. This is total revolution.

And while it sounds deceptively simple, we advise our clients to be ready to absolutely fail: being completely open and honest about our role in a rupture is not what we have ever been taught to do (or seen role-modeled throughout society). We are much more accustomed to blaming the other as a defensive strategy, which is what often happens when couples try the meeting in the middle for the first time.

Not getting Collaboration "right" may likely mirror other difficulties you have in your relationship. For instance, if we start our meeting in the middle with one of us saying, "I know that I need to keep the focus on myself, but . . . ," it reveals how hard it is for us be vulnerable with each other. It's still easier to fall back on old defensive styles (getting in that final dig before resigning ourselves to actual Collaboration). We know most of us are not taught to be vulnerable, and that's why this is a learning process, even for us.

The underpinnings of your relationship may include a history where acknowledging your part has been used as a weapon to prove your partner's point, as in, "See, I am right; you are wrong." At first your partner may use your insights as ammunition against you; and you might use theirs against them. If this happens, you've returned from Accountability only to create another battle, instead of a collaborative chance for repair. You may need more time to reflect with what's happening to you emotionally, psychologically, and to calm down.

If either of you are still feeling angry or defensive, you're both not ready for Collaboration. In our marriage, there have been many times when Mark wants to get started on the meeting in the middle after only a brief Pause (and remember, Mark doesn't always believe that we need to Pause at all). He'll say, "Come on, Haruna—let's get this thing started; we have tools to fix this!" But Haruna usually needs a bit more time. If Haruna can't collaborate at the time Mark is ready to collaborate, Mark then has trouble reaching out for Collaboration for a long time. Sometimes, the fact that we are both not ready at the same time starts another conflict! When we do go back on Pause, the second pause tends to be shorter because we know the last attempt suggests a willingness to collaborate, or we wouldn't have initiated the first meeting in the middle.

If you do have to go back to Pause, go through Accountability as well. Check in with your willingness to see your role in the conflict, and what is blocking you from sharing it. Are you still hurt or scared? We know that admitting your part in a conflict puts you at great risk. You may have to air the shameful, painful, vulnerable, unwelcome parts of yourself that are linked to your understanding of your contribution. Owning these mistakes and feelings, and acknowledging them in the presence of your partner, can be a humbling experience: when you acknowledge that you can try to do better next time, it is an admission that you are not perfect. Our answer to this dilemma is simple: we all have flaws, and we believe that no one can be in a relationship with perfection as the goal. Instead, focus on *progress, not perfection.* This allows us to accept our own and each other's humanity as we *actually are.* We learn from our mistakes about how to be a better partner.

Sharing

The first part of Collaboration involves sharing what we learned in Accountability about ourselves. We believe that repairing the relational wound with a partner by owning your part in the conflict is an act of love. The actual repairing process itself generates vulnerability, trust, and love, which is why it is worth the risk of sharing your part in a conflict. Learning to speak without blame, shame, criticism, or catastrophizing leads to the creation of a loving, wholesome, healthy relationship.

In the meeting in the middle, you will be taking turns, each admitting your part in a conflict from the position of "I." Speaking from the position of "I" aligns with our mantra to keep the focus on yourself. It is also a means of empowerment as it allows you to own your thoughts, feelings, and position on the issue at hand. However, it is not okay to say, "I have told you a million times that I don't like it when you _____" or any variation of "I know for a fact that you were wrong."

If you are accustomed to saying to your partner, "You did A, B, and C, again!" it may feel scary to start a conversation from the position of "I" without blaming the other. Because the vulnerability necessary for successfully speaking from the position of "I" is rarely taught or modeled for many of us, if you start your turn with a "You" statement, take a deep breath, and just start over. You can start over as many times as you want. And if you really, really can't share your feelings from the position of "I," then you're just not ready for this stage. Instead, we advise that you both go back to Pause without dwelling on the idea that you have in some way failed.

Listening

The second part of Collaboration involves deep listening. If you can hear what your partner has to say with empathy and compassion, you are allowing your relationship to have room for the inevitable mistakes we all make. You will be listening for the ways that your partner might share their feelings. This can include "difficulty and struggle" with a particular topic, as in, "I'm uncomfortable thinking about my salary. In my mind I make very little. And I feel ashamed of that. And I never wanted to talk about it openly with you."

You might hear your partner express "fears and worries," as in, "I was never in a consistent, steady relationship before so I never had to talk about sex and sexual intimacy with my partner. I am scared to talk about it with you."

Or your partner might share feelings of "guilt," as in, "I know it was my fault when I hit the car in front of us when I was parking. I wasn't watching where I was going."

Any of these expressions show that your partner is trying to be vulnerable, open, and honest with you. As you listen, do not interrupt. Instead, think about how you can be sensitive to each other and to yourself. You may come to understand what hurts and scares your partner, and yourself. This listening will pave the way for deeper and more connecting repairs; repairs that often result in ruptures that are less intense and resolve quickly.

The right kind of listening is going to take some time and practice. There are simple rules for this that mostly require the most essential ingredient for listening: attention. Anything that interferes with this (cell phone, social media, books, TV shows, obsessive thinking about work, etc.) put aside; everything that enhances your attention (sit down in a comfortable place, eye contact, an open heart and mind, gently hold each other's hand) include. You are learning to embrace your experience as well as your partner's. By focusing your complete attention on listening, you are unable to create a comeback filled with blame. You might find it difficult to fully listen to your partner if you are used to interrupting and quickly moving into heated arguments. Remember, you are not listening to win the conflict or determine who is the guilty or bad one or even to resolve the conflict. At this point you are simply listening so that your partner feels heard and you can understand your partner's inner experiences and perspectives.

We have found that receiving blame, or dolling it out, collapses any productive conversation. When we are blamed, criticized, or attacked in any way, our psychological defenses take over and we unconsciously protect ourselves by blocking out—literally *not hearing*—what is being said. However, we are affected by the attack, and we wind up protecting ourselves to a greater degree by shutting ourselves off from each other and creating a scenario in our minds that only one of us can be right, and then the other must be wrong. As we each fight for the "right" perspective, if we can't convince our partner, at least we can hold onto this belief ourselves.

Yet when we are really listening without holding onto the idea that we are the one who is right, we can recognize that two perspectives of the same situation can coexist, and both may be valid. We refer to this as the *and/both mindset*. This mindset is described by the psychoanalytic term *multi-determined*, in which there could be many different experiences, drives, motivations, and even conflicting and contradictory emotions and thoughts, all existing at the time of the rupture and all contributing to the event. And/both thinking will generate synergy rather than division. It helps couples avoid the power struggle of whose idea is better, and helps you come to a better solution, together.

The "and/both" mindset means there are many different ways to be "right." Inside many conflicts there are numerous motivations—some of them contradictory, but often, both are well-intentioned. We often don't check our own motivations, much less each other's. But if you are open to listening, you may uncover each other's underlying feelings instead of focusing on nursing a growing resentment.

For instance, Penny believes good parents are supportive, loving, and help their children discover their passions. Alex believes good parents, the ones who provide structure and discipline, are helping their children be self-directive and responsible. This couple knows their individual parenting values are at odds with each other, which often lead to fights about the children. We explained to them that both of them are right, and that they had to figure out a way to respect the other's idea when appropriate. In Collaboration, Penny and Alex promised they would each listen to the other and in the moment, accept each other's idea. Then, together, they could determine a compromise or set rules for the children that they both could live with. They both shared the reasons for their parenting styles; the "and/both" thinking made room for both of their experiences.

Trust the Collaboration Process

When we ask our partner to keep the focus on themselves, we cannot control what they will say, what your partner has done, and what they will do to get to repair. We can only control how we respond to our partner, or what we are ready to share in collaboration. We do this again, by keeping the focus on ourselves. In so doing, we come to trust the intentions and the motivations of our own actions, including our willingness to join our partner in a process of genuine healing.

Starting the Collaboration

Collaboration begins when both partners are ready to engage in conversation: it is the official end of the Pause stage. If your conflict has left you both feeling raw, angry, or hurt, you both have to be open and willing enough to hear what the other person is willing to share. If you are not, then you can go back to Pause until you are both ready to be open and willing enough.

Create a Safe Space

At the time of conflict, couples can forget they are meant to be allies. In order to bring that sense of "in it together" back, you both need to feel safe: an understanding that you will not be blamed, criticized, or attacked. The safer we feel when we share our inventories with each other, the more likely it is that we start recognizing the patterns we fall back on that caused the conflict in the first place. For instance, you will be comfortable sharing formative experiences and assess the ways in which old family patterns are being played out unconsciously in your current life.

To create a sense of safety, explain out loud what your intention is. You can hold each other's hand and say something like, "We are going to create a safe space so that we can talk about what happened between us, each from an "I" position. We are going to take turns speaking by keeping the focus on myself and listen to each other."

You can customize starting your meeting in the middle by coming up with your own creative rituals. Some people take a deep breath together or prepare a snack or warm cup of tea. Your ritual is meant to send a message that "you are allies." It is also meant to create a form of coregulation. You can say to each other: "I make a pledge that I am not going to judge you."

The Meeting in the Middle

Now you are ready for the meeting in the middle. First, set some ground rules. The basic structure and ground rules include:

- Decide who will be the timekeeper and who will speak first. Collaboration is most successful when strictly timed. Five minutes is plenty of time for each party's initial share, and then three minutes for each share thereafter. Each person can have additional times to share until they feel that they have been heard.
- More often than not, the "topic" will be evident—as it will be *the* issue/problem/conflict (i.e., rupture) that you are currently in the process of repairing. These tend to be acute conflicts.
- Each person only talks about their own feelings and their contribution to the issue.
- Each person only shares what they are feeling and must be able to do so without fear of blame, criticism, or having what they say used against them either during the meeting in the middle or at a later time.
- Each person must be able to safely acknowledge their part in what's happening, both good and bad.
- Interruptions and arguments are out of bounds. This rule is especially important if what you are hearing is drastically different than what you have experienced.
- Topics like sex, money, or parenting may need numerous meetings in the middle in order for each of you to understand the different perspectives and feelings about the topics. And perspectives and feelings about sex and money can change as you age.

You can start the meeting in the middle by saying something like, "I'm going to tell you how I feel. I contributed to this problem when I _____."

Then, your partner takes a turn, also speaking from the position of "I." You can respond to their sharing by saying, "I felt _____ when this issue arose, and I see my contribution to this issue as _____" as this keeps the focus on yourself, accurately reflects what is going on (in your opinion) and reflects your thoughts and feelings. Continue with this open exchange, and while you are doing so, take note of feelings and thoughts your partner reveals that you identify with, and share these in your next turn to share.

If you are having a hard time listening, voice your feelings, as in, "I have trouble accepting your ideas due to my own strong attachment to my ideas. I am trying to listen. I want to be open to compromise. But it's hard." By doing so you are staying in the process and leaving the door open for differences, discussion, and negotiation. Listening and speaking without pushing for an answer helps you both stay in the process of understanding each other.

After completing three turns each, assess what you talked about with your partner. At this point, you are not trying to solve your conflict or come up with new strategies for the future. All you want to get through is a clear understanding of how you both felt and what your contributions were to the conflict.

Discuss the following questions, focusing only on your part: finger-pointing and criticism are out of bounds.

- How did you initially understand the issue?
- How do your own feelings, such as hurt, shame, anger, or fear, get in the way of your communicating honestly about your contribution to the conflict?
- Have either of you brought distance and/or destruction into the relationship? Do you have a better understanding of what brings this about?
- Were you able/willing to be vulnerable with your partner? What does that feel like?
- Were you willing/able to be compassionate and empathetic with yourself and your partner? Did you get to talk about your experience and explain your difficulty/struggle, worries/fear, first time experience,

shame, guilt, hurt, and pain? Did you feel like your partner was able to be compassionate and empathetic toward you? What is that like?

- What was your experience of intimacy like during the meeting in the middle? Do you feel more (or less) accepting of and accepted by your partner? Did you feel heard?

- Assess your level of emotional investment to the relationship as an outcome of having been vulnerable enough to share your contribution to the conflict at hand.

Exercise: Addressing Chronic Issues through a Meeting in the Middle

It is also possible that you are carrying chronic conflicts in your relationship, and you can call for a meeting in the middle at any time to work on the resolution of such conflicts. Or you may find that one issue requires more than one run-through of the PACER model. When this happens, it is likely the issue you are addressing—though acute in the fight—is representative of more chronic issues in your relationship.

Jointly think of problems in your life together—either interpersonal or related to your roles and shared responsibilities (work, parenting, household issues, etc.)—that you have both identified and tried unsuccessfully to solve that are outside of the immediate conflict. Chronic issues don't always require solutions; sometimes they just need to be aired. For example, money or sex are topics that couples need to discuss and reevaluate over the course of the relationship.

Next, each of you should write down your answers to the following questions:
1. How each of you perceives that issue.
2. Your own history with that issue.

3. How you've tried to fix it in the past.
4. Did you force a solution to the issues? Did forcing a solution create other unintended issues in the relationship?
5. What has historically stood in the way of fixing it?

Next, complete the following exercise alone. Write down your answers to the following:

1. Who is affected by this issue?
2. How is your relationship affected by this issue?
3. How long have you been dealing with these issues?
4. Are you personally affected by this issue?
5. Which vulnerable feelings do you experience while dealing with this issue? (For example, shame, guilt, feeling abandoned, not feeling understood, not feeling heard, emotional pain, sadness, isolation, etc.).

6. What have you done, or continue to do, to take care of your vulnerability?
7. What did you do to repair or work on the issue individually?
8. What did you and your partner do together to fix or work on the issue?

You and your partner are now ready for a new meeting in the middle where you can discuss your findings regarding this issue. Remember, the goal is not necessarily to find a solution at this moment, but to use the meeting as a means to develop an understanding of what things do and do not work for you as a couple when you encounter this particular problem. The same rules for the meeting in the middle for an acute conflict apply here: clearly state your contribution from the position of "I," and listen to what your partner has to say. Openness to this kind of sharing is the essence of interactive repair and forms the impetus for emotional connection.

Sheila and Nick Pause, Account, and Collaborate

Sheila and Nick are both entrepreneurs who, since they got married and began filing jointly, had been audited by the IRS—twice. They both recognized that the discussion of their taxes was going to be a hot topic (as each historically had blamed the other for the audits), so they decided to use the PACER model during their initial attempt to talk about this year's taxes.

One night, Sheila, asked what she believed was an innocent question, "Nick, how much, do you make each week?"

Nick replied, "I really don't know. I've never looked at my income that way before."

Sheila thought Nick was either joking or lying. And she was not only pissed-off, but now sure that it was, indeed Nick's fault that they got audited! Shelia was becoming increasingly furious, feeling deceived, while Nick, who felt like he had taken a great risk by being honest, was defensive and equally enraged. Rather than hashing it out immediately, they called for a Pause. Each stormed off into their part of the apartment.

After cooling down in Pause, they each started doing their work, privately accounting for their own contribution to this issue. In Accountability, Nick realized that he had never shared his deep sense of financial insecurity, nor had he ever told Sheila that he heard his parents talking about money a lot when he grew up. He interpreted his parent's relationship with money that one would have to "be an idiot" to accurately account for their income because it only led people to "get ripped off by the government." He realized this mindset influenced the way he covered up his earnings from his own understanding of everyday accounting.

Sheila realized she was carrying into their relationship a deep sense of what seemed like financial responsibility but was actually a state where her parents were ruled by financial insecurity. Her parents "counted every penny" and spent nothing on themselves. They firmly believed that they "sacrificed everything for their children" and though seemingly proud of Sheila's accomplishments, they also worried about her hubris. Therefore, *not asking questions* about Nick's finances allowed Sheila to disavow how much better she and Nick were doing than her parents had and deny the truth of her parents' harsh criticism.

When Nick and Sheila agreed on a Collaboration, Nick shared his thoughts first. "I admit that I feel very insecure about money. I didn't know how to talk about it and I still don't know how. But I am willing to talk about it with you one step at a time. I want to learn."

Sheila said, "I am sorry for getting immediately upset and running out of the room. I did not listen to you nor I was ready to discuss money with you. I am insecure about money, too. I wanted you to take a lead on everything related to money, like my father did. I expected a lot from you. I am sorry."

During their meeting in the middle, they both realized they had different insecurities about money, and they didn't know how to talk about them with each other. They both ended up apologizing during the meeting. Nick acknowledged that his financial insecurity was extreme and that he was "intentionally not looking" into his own finances because he feared he would find that he "did not earn enough money to take care of Sheila." Sheila could see how she had brought with her a sense of being an outcast from her family of origin as a result of how "well" she and Nick were doing financially.

They both reported to us that this part of the PACER model was eye-opening. Sheila said it was the "most intimate" conversation they had ever had and felt much closer to each other—and aware of their own insecurities—than before. Then they were able to continue through the model to get to a resolution. Their solution was to have conversations about money on a monthly basis so that they get used to talking about money. They decided collaboratively that in order to deal with their own insecurity and fear around money, actually talking about money would help them overcome those feelings. At least that's what they agreed on for the time being.

A Checklist on Us-ness

How do you know that collaboration—your meeting in the middle—has worked? How do you know if it is successful? The first, actual experiential sense you will have is *connection* to your own feelings and each other. Others include:

- **Alliance:** In what ways have we used our couple assets to create a strong alliance?
- **Commitment:** How have we discussed our individual parts in our conflicts with each other?
- **Vulnerability:** How have we experienced and shared the vulnerability of the other (the vulnerability together)?
- **Availability:** How have we experienced the availability of the other (each other) and had quality time?
- **Meeting Needs:** How do we nurture each other and offer help when we see struggle?
- **Decision-Making:** What decisions have we made to keep our relationship foremost in our minds?
- **Openness:** Are there new, unexpected events happening to you and your partner? If so, how often are you discussing it while you are dealing with this? How do you share your feelings with each other and to others? And when does that happen?
- **Following Through:** What commitments have we made together to our relationship? Have we followed through on those commitments?
- **Allow Growth:** What are you doing to accept mistakes made by you and your partner? (For example, reflecting on the significance of the mistakes. If it's a small mistake, you let it go. If it's significant that it is affecting your relationship, then you talk about it in the meeting in the middle.)
- **Have trust in the process:** you might not find the solutions or answer immediately.

Stay in the present not the past: Are you checking in with yourself to see whether you are reflecting on the past difficult events more than being present with your partner in the present moment. By being in the present with your partner, you are staying in the repair and working together to find a solution.

The degree of expressiveness (feelings-wise) is depending on your cultural upbringing. If your expressiveness is through act of services or quality time, take note of how much you are doing them instead of expressing feelings with your partner. You can also add appreciation here.

After the Meeting in the Middle: Collaboration Ends

It is a good idea to assess the outcome of your Collaboration immediately after the meeting in the middle, so that you can document the crucial insights in case a similar rupture occurs in the future. Consider the following questions.

- How do you feel about letting go of your protective/defensive/ destructive/distancing state?
- Do you feel like you are becoming a better partner? If so, in what sense? If not, what is still missing?
- How does the change you agreed to feel frightening or bad (e.g., I'm a bad person because I am selfish and too expressive of my own needs.)?
- How does the change you agreed to feel like a relief or bring an otherwise good result (e.g., I feel compassion toward my partner)?
- How has distance and/or destruction made you suffer or feel hurt, sad, fearful, anxious, or angry, and how do you feel about seeking peace and joy with your partner in the future?
- How has distance and/or destruction made the other person suffer or feel hurt, sad, fearful, anxious, or angry, and how will you think about this in the future, so you can be more active and engaged, still a great listener, but not disengaged in unhealthy ways?
- How much willingness to be open and compassionate did you bring to the meeting in the middle? Were you able to make a request instead of making a demand?

CHAPTER ELEVEN

Experiment: Replacing Defensiveness with Openness

The next step is the Experiment, where we will begin to find and implement solutions that resolve the conflict and get us closer to a full and lasting repair. During the Experiment phase, couples will use the data gleaned from every phase of the PACER model—the outcome of taking a personal inventory, ownership of their part through the 40-20-40 assessments, and the meeting in the middle—to brainstorm new decisions and behaviors they can use to resolve the rupture effectively and develop a roadmap for repair. Then, you will put the Experiment into action and begin to experience us-ness as a *culture of two*. By having a better understanding of your relationship, you will be able to:

- Gain new awareness that usually what you are fighting about is just a single piece of the conflict, and that neither partner is the problem, and that "the problem is the problem."
- Understand that how you were communicating with your partner was "the problem" and you and your partner were not the problem.
- Become allies who work together to address "the real problem."
- Bring willingness (your commitment) to repair your love relationship.
- Bring willingness to discuss ideas generated by both partners and negotiate them.
- Have a new kind of intimacy that reflects both of your ideas.

- Take risks and try our new behaviors.
- Make new attempts at vulnerability.
- Increasing willingness to empathize with each other individually and as a couple.
- Open up to new levels of intimacy.
- See, feel, and experience the emotional investments that can be made toward the third entity, which is your relationship.

We have found that when couples share their vulnerability during Collaboration and have each owned their part of the conflict and make clear what they truly need and want, there is a natural tendency for them to drop the weapons of distance, destruction, and inventory-taking of their partner altogether, and come to a new sense of empathy. Finding solutions to even chronic conflicts can be easier at this point.

You may need to try a few experiments before you come up with the solution that fully addresses the conflict. Unlike the repairing of ruptures that comes with each successful meeting in the middle, solutions developed in the Experiment phase may take days to implement and see results. Yet each attempt/experiment is a piece of the repair because experiments are risks taken together that actively create a new state of co-ownership—and, in this sense, they are transformational and lead to a renewed relational environment.

By finding new solutions to each conflict as they come up, the Experiment also provides the opportunity to discover what other problems might contribute to both acute and chronic conflicts, and how they might more effectively be solved. When you and your partner start to Experiment, you may discover that you're ready to talk about other issues that are upsetting or smoldering underneath the surface. You may even find this conflict was about something else entirely. For instance, a conflict about parenting may be related to stress about money.

The Experiment Is the Solution

Psychologist Michael White's perspective that "the problem is the problem," which we discussed earlier, is a crucial mindset to hold onto during the

Experiment phase because it allows you to address a problem together, instead of each of you trying to blame your partner for the problem and trying to fix your partner. When the conflict first occurred, you may have thought your partner was the cause, and therefore, they were a bad partner. Or you may have felt that you caused the conflict, and you were the origin of the problem. But as you've learned, both parties contribute to every rupture; it is how you communicate and address the conflict that needs to be fixed, not you or your partner.

The Experiment is limited to the specific conflict at hand: do not try to address, resolve, or change every tiny aspect about our partners that rubs us the wrong way. We are here to fix the problem, not each other. We constantly hear our clients say, "I agreed to try the PACER model believing that all I had to do was fix my partner and everything would be fine." But that's exactly what we're working to dispel. The Experiment is not about fixing your partner; it is a way to heal your relationship by repairing each rupture, one at a time.

By letting go of old defenses and seeing conflict as an opportunity to get to know yourself and your partner, and strengthen your relationship, you begin to use your alliance to address and resolve problems rather than trying to fix your partner. That is the core difference between taking either a defensive or offensive approach to conflict compared to the PACER approach.

Defensive/Offensive Approach (My partner is the problem)	PACER Approach (The problem is the problem)
• Seeing the partner as an enemy. • Needing to win: conflict is a battleground. • Blame/criticize/judge/attack • Dismiss/don't listen/avoid. • Make demands.	• Choosing to remain as allies. • Open to co-developing solutions, negotiate, and compromise if necessary. • Speaking with compassion, love, kindness, and respect. • Listening with empathy. • Make requests.

The solutions you may develop with your partner can take different forms:

- Come up with a new, practical idea for issues such as taking care of children, sharing household chores, wants/needs related to living together.

- A solution may mean formally scheduling another conversation to explore the issue further. Ongoing conversations are appropriate for topics including money issues, sexual intimacy, or cultural conflicts. If you are a biracial/culture couple like us, you might have conversations about how differences can impact the relationship time to time throughout your relationship.

- A solution may involve bringing in outside resources. If you or your partner has a difficult time hearing what the other is saying regarding a particular topic or topics (sexual intimacy, infidelity, money), think about bringing in an expert to help you get to a resolution. Experts can share their professional views about the topics and pinpoint things that you can't understand. An expert can be topic-specific: a financial planner, accountant, real estate agent, infertility doctor, or even a couples therapist. Remember, you are figuring out your life as you live it, and so is your partner. It's okay to acknowledge, "I don't know about this topic and want to hear from a professional" or "I can't think straight since my partner cheated on me." Not admitting that "I don't know how to talk about this," can prolong the distancing and destructive state and can significantly impact your relationship.

How to Experiment

In the Experiment, you will still keep the focus on yourself. This time, try keeping a mind frame of not only openness, but a genuine willingness to establish peace. A mind frame of peace allows you to put down your weapons and listen to each other. If you are able to have a conversation in a caring manner, you will be creating a safe space for each other, and develop greater empathy toward your partner and, most likely, yourself.

We understand there are many relationships that have a well-grooved dynamic, where one person can easily express their needs, and the other person has a much more difficult time. If you are the one who has trouble expressing your needs, think of the Experiment as an opportunity for you to grow. It's also an opportunity for the person who more easily expresses their needs to make room for the other person to do so.

EXPERIMENT

Step 1: One Partner Expresses Their Needs

Using the information that each person has learned about their own contribution to the conflict, the Experiment begins when one partner asks for the help they need, by specifically using the word "need" in a calm tone.

While the word "need" infers a request, what you are actually offering is your vulnerability. Vulnerability is what we see when we look into the proverbial mirror that reflects our relationship back to us.

But conveying your needs alone does not mean "we both win," or that "neither of us wins," or "one wins and one doesn't." What it provides is an opportunity for one partner to share and be heard, and the other person listens with as much empathy as possible. When one person says, "You have to. You should. We should. We need." it sets up a power imbalance where one person is "right" and the other is by definition, "wrong." And words like "have to" and "should" send a message that the other partner is "obligated" to meet the other's needs and therefore does not leave any room for options. Yet when you use the word *need* in the context of keeping the focus on yourself, as in, "I need to feel that you're listening to me," each person is able to experience that they have something of value to offer the other person (one person shares their vulnerability while their other person shares their acknowledgment and empathy), and, in so doing, cocreates a sense of equality (we each can give and receive something of great value to us: our alliance).

Try to express your needs in a way that will reach solutions that you and your partner can actually attain. We do not want to experiment with ideas that we can't deliver, as in, "We need to make our debt disappear, tomorrow, and if we could, everything in our relationship would be perfect." Instead, make your needs clear:

- "I really need to sleep until nine o'clock, and I really need the room to be as dark as possible."
- "I really like to wake up first thing in the morning and get going, and that's why I need to open the shades."

One of the best need statements to start the Experiment could be, "I need you to hear me." It's not, "I need you to take out the garbage," because it is unlikely that the state of your alliance will be immediately thrown into

219

regressive battle based upon doing a household chore. Also, this need is only your idea. On the other hand, "We need to figure out how to more fairly divide the chores" is a very good need statement because while on the surface the request is mundane, it may be emblematic of the problematic dynamics in your relationship. Here, you are creating an environment to discuss a way to figure out the problem *together*. You are co-creating a system that works for both of you. By running this experiment, you may be able to resolve other similar issues at the same time.

Step 2: The Other Partner Hears the Request

The partner listens to the request and responds by acknowledging they have heard your need. You have been heard and your partner can now make use of their understanding of, and compassion for, your position. If you have been truly vulnerable in your expression of your needs, then you have given your partner an opportunity to care for you by meeting your needs. When your partner acknowledges your needs, it becomes an opening into each person's vulnerability because your partner has the chance to drop their defensive position as part of the process of hearing what you had to say and relating to it.

Step 3: Rinse and Repeat: From the Other Perspective

Now it is your partner's turn to express their needs, and for you to acknowledge them. Once you have both acknowledged that you have needs, especially ones that are in conflict with the other's, you can take an inventory of each person's needs, together.

The Needs Inventories

Who was hurt and the nature of this damage? What does each partner need to resolve this damage?	How do you each relate to and empathize with each other's need(s)?	What experiments can you implement together to meet your needs?	Document each attempt to make room for both of your needs and the results.
Example **Partner A:** I need to feel heard. Every time I have any kind of issue, my partner tries to fix it (that is, fix me). It enrages me, makes me feel condescended to, misunderstood, and unheard. **Partner B:** I need to feel that I am making a viable contribution to this relationship. It hurts me when my partner reacts to my attempts to help with anger and criticism.	**Partner A:** I do listen and empathize with my partner, but when I share my vulnerability and they try to fix me, I realize I don't set boundaries, and my need to be heard gets misunderstood. **Partner B:** I see that my need to help can be overwhelming. I really do empathize with my partner, but I realize it doesn't come across that way when I'm giving advice and trying to fix a situation.	**Partner A:** I need to set better boundaries *and* state exactly what I need. I need to leave room for my partner to actually provide help and support. **Partner B:** I need to understand better how my empathy affects my behavior. When I'm overwhelmed by my feelings, I need to pause before reacting so that I can hear what my partner is really saying and asking for.	We have been conducting meetings in the middle and are discovering a lot about how we each have been feeling resentful about the way we interacted, without realizing why. Now we can see that our previous way of dealing with issues made us both feel unheard and unappreciated. Going forward, when we present an issue, we are going to ask each other what kind of help we are actually looking for: listening vs. making suggestions.

Who was hurt and the nature of this damage? What does each partner need to resolve this damage?	How do you each relate to and empathize with each other's need(s)?	What experiments can you implement together to meet your needs?	Document each attempt to make room for both of your needs and the results.
Fill in:			

There may be times when even with the best efforts and intentions, you wind up in a standoff, agreeing to disagree, with whose needs will be met this time. But often, after having listened to each other with deep vulnerability, empathy, and care, you as a couple will be able to decide whose needs are more urgent right now. When this decision-making is done together, you can also agree that the other person's needs are important, and a plan of action for meeting those needs at a later time can be developed.

The goal of any Experiment is to create a dynamic of *mutuality*. Mutuality is the practice of each party's accepting what the other has to offer and opening the door to feel emotional connection, which is another way of putting our empathy into practice.

The way each need is expressed and responded to defines where we stand right now in terms of the four pillars of true love. This need-meeting by your partner is then a powerful means of experiencing the action of love, the offering, taking in, and making use of what each has to offer—beginning with acceptance of you as you are. In essence, each need met is a profound incident of intimacy and a legitimate *repair*.

The way we make use of our newfound vulnerability is to express, share, and meet our needs as individuals and as a couple. Take another inventory of your relationship together and explore how being distancing or destructive has interfered with the sense of safety and security between you. Use these results as a model to delve further into your Experiment.

The Issue/Conflict
(Has it changed after you completed the first step of this exercise?)

How you each shared your vulnerability (i.e., being hurt, scared, or upset)?	Is there a shift in feelings of empathy and intimacy with each other?	Assess your current level of emotional investment—your us-ness.	How has our relationship changed since our needs have been met?
Example: We shared how we each felt unheard and unappreciated. **Partner A:** I stated that I felt hurt—that my partner didn't care about me because he didn't try to understand what I need. **Partner B:** I was "afraid" that my partner would reject every attempt I made to help her.	By stating our needs and becoming vulnerable with each other, we are increasingly willing to really hear what the other wants and needs. We have opened ourselves up to relate to each other, and we are more empathetic to and with each other. In doing so, we are more intimate—we know each other and accept each other as we are.	As a result of being vulnerable, opening up about our needs, empathizing with each other, and accepting each other—and ourselves—as we are, we find ourselves more invested in our relationship and each other.	We are having fewer destructive conflicts because we are getting better about expressing our needs in the moment and allowing each other to meet these needs.

Candace and Dino Experiment with Giving and Receiving

So many of us overlook the fact that we confirm our partner's value when we accept what they have to offer in terms of meeting our own needs. Yet if you are cast in the relational role as "the giver," you may be inadvertently rejecting what your partner has to offer and unintentionally conveying the message: *you have nothing that I want or need, nothing of value to offer me.* Being the giver puts us in a one-up position and allows us to circumvent our vulnerability while suppressing our own needs and creating a dynamic where we unintentionally defend ourselves against accepting what our partner has to offer. Putting ourselves into a dynamic of give *and* take allows us to create a more equal dynamic and a space for our vulnerability to be present and addressed.

"If I'm not in control," says Candace, "then who'll run the show?" Dino looked at us just a bit cross-eyed, until Candace said, "Just kidding!" But the truth was, she was not.

A few months earlier, Candace dragged Dino, her partner of fifteen years, into our office because in her words, Candace was "sick of hearing me say to my friends that I was finally, this time, going to break up with Dino—and then, not dump him."

"Many of our efforts could be called 'cosmetic psychotherapy.' And that was not necessarily because of the therapist or even the type of therapy, but because of how I was using it. We were band-aiding our heartaches and denying the fact that together we were a love-dodging machine," proposed Candace. Yet somehow, the "hope" they both felt about the work of the PACER model was filling each of them with dread. But when they looked at this fear together, it also created a window of opportunity that allowed them to begin to be honest with each other and agree to earnestly take on this work—no matter what the outcome would be.

Both Candace and Dino were in their mid-fifties. Candace had been married throughout her thirties in what she referred to as a failed attempt to "disown her identity and desire." Dino had been in relationship after relationship with women who he felt, as he often does with Candace, needed him to need them. Both of them, it turned out, had become experts at being absent, avoiding conflict by sidelining their own needs and desires.

Dino was from a large Puerto Rican family living on the Lower East Side of Manhattan. He'd spent his whole upbringing acting as if whatever kind of care his numerous family—and extended family—members had to offer actually worked. He did have some mild curiosity about why it was that he kept attracting—and being attracted to—women like Candace who thought that Dino needed some serious *help* that he himself was unaware of, but that, if he didn't play along, the relationships tended to go kaput.

Candace grew up in a small Midwestern town, the only child of white, lower middle-class parents who met rather late (for the time) and, as she said, "had me last minute." Her father had trouble making ends meet, and her mother struggled with alcohol. Candace sometimes felt like her mother drank to punish her husband for not meeting her expectations. Both of her parents were miserably unhappy with their lot and took it out on each other. Candace played Switzerland in their long-term battle and excelled at just about everything she endeavored to do, making them genuinely proud of her, and providing a distraction from their raging hatred of each other. It was, at least consciously, their pride in her that made it impossible for her to divorce her first husband while they were alive.

So when Candace told all of us in the room that she was running the show, we were not at all surprised. She went on, "Listen, we've been doing inventory, having those meetings in the middle together. We've been listening to each other, relinquishing our defensive distancing stances, and stating our needs, just like you suggested."

"How's that going?" Mark asked.

"Well, I had no idea how thoroughly committed I was—okay, I am—to my position as a giver and not a receiver. It is amazing how tortuous just admitting how much you matter to me is," said Candace, " . . . and you do!"

This acknowledgment began a series of experiments we worked on in their couples' sessions where the primary challenge was for Candace to clearly articulate her needs to Dino and give him a chance to meet them. The Experiment also included becoming more open to not just accepting what Dino had to offer (such as doing more work around the house), but also taking his help in as a gesture of his love, making use of it (taking a break, scheduling time with friends, for instance). Over time, we found the Experiment helped them develop a subtle kind of safety: Candace learned that she could count on someone else to take care of her; Dino learned that he could contribute to a relationship in a meaningful way and feel valued. In learning that giving and receiving wasn't a threat to their safety, Candace and Dino were able to achieve a new sense of mutuality, trust, and intimacy.

Candace told us, "I was always patting myself on the back for how hard I worked for us. And the whole time I wasn't helping us at all. It backfired, creating a wall between us. And there was Dino on the other side of that wall, pretending that he couldn't do anything right so that I could take credit for everything that was holding our life together. We both said what our needs were. Mine was the need to challenge myself to drop my defenses of being the absolute giver and take the risk of allowing someone to care for me. Dino's was to refuse the idea that he had nothing valuable to offer me and could help me out with lots of things."

Then Dino said, "But what was even weirder was doing that part somehow got us back in touch with the person we had each been crazy about when we first met. Even though there were no fireworks, no grand and glorious dreams of what we wanted to do with each other. It was just—each other. Experimenting was like those late-night conversations in Starbucks that we didn't want to end. Back then, no one was controlling or being controlled, we were too busy just falling in love."

Experiment #2: Adjusting with the PACER Model

The second experiment assesses the PACER model to see if it is working for you and your relationship, and what can you do next time to make it more effective. Specifically, this time the Experiment focuses on tinkering with the meeting in the middle. Your own PACER model might come up with a rule that says, "We do not have a meeting in the middle first thing in the morning," or "We do not have a meeting in the middle right before we go to bed."

For instance, Haruna and I have learned that we can't have a meeting in the middle thirty seconds after the start of a fight. We also know that if Pause goes on for too long, we don't ever get to repair.

Discuss the following questions with your partner:

- What seemed to go well when you were conducting the meeting in the middle?
- What was the hardest thing about it?
- What would you do differently next time?

Exercise: Joint Compassion Meditation: Observing Thoughts and Feelings

Observing thoughts and feelings nonjudgmentally—known as *mindfulness*—is a technique that can be used during stressful situations. This practice can be used at any time, even when the work in this book becomes anxiety-provoking and overwhelming. You and your partner may find that you can do this exercise together; in other instances, it may be necessary to do this exercise in separate rooms or even at separate times.

These instructions can help you see how your mind responds by having a way to step back from your thoughts and analyze them. Keep in mind that you are learning to observe your thoughts and feelings. It is going to take some practice.

- Start in a comfortable, seated position with your feet flat on the floor, your head slightly tilted down, and your eyes partially open, focusing on a spot a few feet in front of you.
- Set an initial time limit of three to five minutes. Sit quietly, giving attention to your breath while observing without judgment the stream of thoughts passing through your mind. When you notice your mind wandering, bring your attention back to your breath.
- After your session, no matter how brief, make notes about how it felt:
- What did you think about?
  - How did this practice relate to learning how to be present in your relationship?
  - How did it feel to observe your thoughts and emotions without reacting to them?
  - What suggestions or reflections can you offer one another about observing thoughts without reacting to them?

CHAPTER TWELVE

Reset, Repair, and Renew

The R in PACER officially stands for Reset. Reset doesn't mean that you have to go back to where you were before the conflict. Instead, resetting pulls together all the work you have done in the PACER model to get to a new way of relating to each other. Once you both understand your individual contributions to the conflict, and link them to your history, cultural patterns, and defensive strategies, then you can get to a place of forgiveness, for yourself and your partner. Each completion of the PACER Model fractures how you both used to be in your relationship and establishes a new set point. This shift occurs regardless of the severity of the issue at hand, its acute or chronic nature, as well as its manifestation as destruction or distance. You as a couple have succeeded in making maximum use of a specific rupture to work all the way through your conflict and have achieved a deeper, more connected, reciprocal, and mutual experience of your relationship.

You have discovered your vulnerability and empathy through the Experiment phase. And all along the way, as you have been getting to know each other better, you may now be able to see how you can become more accepting of each other. For example, now that you've seen each other through anger, you can put a finger on what was beneath the anger, and what the anger was protecting you from, which is often vulnerability and intimacy. Sometimes, this means that you or your partner will be open enough going forward to show each other pain, fear, sadness, or grief.

With each traverse from rupture to repair, you will integrate the previously unwelcome parts of yourself (all of you) into a more fully integrated *culture of two*. It is this culture of two, representing an increasingly comprehensive acceptance of *you as you*—both singular and plural—that is the us-ness you have been building through the PACER Model. And it is this us-ness that makes you increasingly invested in each other and your relationship. And like any other investment, the more we put into it, the more we have to lose. In this case, the investment is one where we increasingly allow ourselves to love, care for, and count on each other. It is an immense investment; one that we all know can be lost. Why take the risk? Because to *not* do so is to live in isolation—even when, perhaps especially, we are in long-term relationship.

Emotional investment is a by-product of cultivating and maintaining vulnerability, empathy, and intimacy in your real-life relationship. As you allow yourself to be vulnerable, empathetic, and intimate—close and connected in a genuinely accepting manner—with your partner, you will create a deep sense of love and trust. The emotional investment that lives in deep love can help you securely attach yourself to your partner and therefore, secure the relationship.

Reset Feels Like Revitalization

Reset involves reflection. You've dropped your guard and you're able to notice valuable things about your partner that you hadn't noticed before. When both of your defenses are down, you may even expose or portray a part of yourself that you've never shown before. What's more, you may see parts of yourself that you've never seen, which could be liberating. The net result of Reset is a greater acceptance for who you are, who your partner is, and who the "us" is. It revitalizes your relationship and gets you back to the place of, *oh that's the person I fell in love with.* You notice your partner in a new light, where you like this person, just being next to them. Your relationship is in a very good place.

Seeing yourself and your relationship more clearly may also be scary. When you acknowledge that you are invested in your partner and your relationship, your previously "unwelcome parts" can put you at risk for losing something now experienced as invaluable. Yet rest assured, if you feel scared when you experience something new, whether it's new tenderness, new vulnerability, or new empathy in you and your partner, that is a sign your feelings are now being welcomed back into your relationship, rather than being acted out in distancing or destructive ways. In other words, it is the best, most valid current evidence that you are achieving relational growth.

R Can Also Stand for Repair

Every rupture is an opportunity for repair. And every repair is a victory. In fact, every repair successfully accomplished—every time that a couple goes through the PACER Model, implements the Meeting in the Middle, and realistically takes inventory (using the 40-20-40)—there is a challenge to their *culture of two.* And while this might not feel comfortable while we traverse the PACER process, every challenge creates more room for us to experience an ever-increasing acceptance of who we *really are and who we are becoming.*

Ultimately, Repair requires a willingness to give each other, and the relationship, attention. It requires the openness to keep co-creating the "us." The more we put in, the more we are at risk to be vulnerable, the more bonding and strength we gain. The increased emotional investment feeds back into an increased willingness to take the risk of vulnerability.

Don't be surprised if you need to try various experiments before you come up with the solution that leads to a full repair. There are benefits in both the outcome and the process. Though, of course, we might all be justified in wanting to cross the finish line, bask in the relief of the hard work endured, and take in the accolades of completing this (PACER) process, we find that it is in the process that we come to find a sense of faith in what we have built together: a living, breathing, and thriving experience of "us" in the relationship combined with a deeper acceptance of ourselves as invaluable contributors (40-20-40) to our "us-ness!" We find that it is often during this process that couples experience themselves as both an individual and a couple—a me and an us—for the first time in a long while.

Exercise: A New 40-20-40 for Accountability and Interdependence

The following practice helps couples build and expand safety and intimacy with one another by focusing on developing empathy. As you build a new alliance as partners, you can use the 40-20-40 to cocreate a safe space wherein you can feel that, yes, there is you, and yes, of course, there is me—but in this 40-20-40 space there is a third thing: co-created us! Now you use that us-ness as a middle ground for negotiating issues. In the middle ground, you first learn to accept a partner unconditionally through active listening, and then hear what they offer without taking up space within their side. At the same time, you maintain responsibility for what you bring to the table—your 40 percent. This leaves a 20 percent space in the middle—a collective for the ongoing process of developing and expanding us-ness, which is your relationship. Remember, this middle space is a relational place for connection, acknowledgment (whether you agree or disagree), discussion, negotiation, and reciprocity.

Also remember, the purpose of this practice is not to identify points of criticism or blame but to promote Reset and Repair by taking coownership of your relationship. Go easy on yourselves: most of us require practice to learn to remain within one's own 60-percent zone.

- Sit down and face one another. Let yourself become conscious of what it's like to be present and attentive with your partner.
- Next, try to empathize with how this experience is for your partner to be here with you, especially the emotions they may be experiencing.
- Reflect together on the following questions:
  - What's it like to think about accepting your partner *exactly as they are, first?*
  - How has your vulnerability, empathy, intimacy, and emotional investment changed through the work you've done in the PACER model?

- How can you agree to show up for one another without trespassing into each other's individual 40 percent of the 40-20-40?
- What would it be like to commit to this agreement unconditionally (one rupture at a time)?
- What is it like to tell your partner about your needs and wants?
- What is it like to have your partner tell you about their needs?
- What do we notice about one another as you reflect on these questions or techniques?

Use the following categories to assess your practice of 40-20-40, looking for strengths and areas you can work together to Reset and Repair. We have seen couples who have used the PACER model have dramatic shifts in the following three areas:

Empathy	
Before PACER	**After PACER**
• I felt there was a distinction between what I thought and what my partner experienced. • I felt criticized and unheard. • I felt uneasy and unsure about my ability to reach my partner.	• Listening to and hearing one another felt natural. • I wasn't confused by my own feelings. • The practice of listening and being heard felt "caring." It was an opportunity to learn from each other.
Interdependence	
Before PACER	**After PACER**
• I felt I could manage my life on my own. • My partner's attempts to help or contribute felt like an intrusion. • We have so many problems that we'd probably be better off splitting up.	• Though we have problems, I feel that talking about them strengthens our relationship and makes our life together better.

Independence	
Before PACER	**After PACER**
• I felt disturbed and even put down when my partner made attempts to help me. • I tried to fix our problems by myself and coerced my partner into following my suggestions. • I was easily swayed by my partner and had a hard time asserting my thoughts.	• The PACER Model promoted a mutual reciprocity—a focus on giving and receiving. • Reciprocity allows us to accept—even appreciate—our differences. • We can now see how we can maintain an individual sense of self and feel connected at the same time.

Take five to ten minutes to focus on the Reset and Repair goal of this exercise. If you are feeling distressed, consider hitting Pause (to stop, think, feel, reflect, and regulate with self-compassion), and do something compassionate for yourself, which shows accepting and/or receiving something—generosity, kindness, gentleness—that will soothe you. Remembering how your history of conflict—acute and/or chronic; distancing and/or destructive—worked to block receiving and/or accepting, where reciprocity is the goal of Resetting and Repair, that is, the whole of the PACER Model.

Then discuss the following questions with your partner.

- What seemed to go well when you were doing the PACER model with 40-20-40 sharing of accountability and interdependence in mind?
- What was the hardest thing about it?
- What would you do differently next time?

Exercise: Take an Assessment of Your Progress

Consider the following questions:

- By letting go of your defensive position, taking your own inventory of your contributions (no more than 60 percent, no less than 40 percent), are there differences in how you experience yourself now in this relationship?
- Seeing that your partner has also released their defensive position, take your inventory again of your contributions (no more than 60 percent no less than 40 percent). How does this affect how you view yourself in this relationship? How does it feel for you to own your accountability in your relationship?
- How does this new and/or expanded sense of yourself contribute to how you experience and express your part of your us-ness? How does this expanded sense of yourself contribute to how you experience your relationship?
- What has your relationship become? How is it for you to be in this relationship while being accountable for your actions and owning your contributions to the conflict in front of your partner?
- How does this change feel frightening or good or mixed? Do you have bad thoughts about yourself when you are in conflict (e.g., I'm a bad person because I cannot overcome my anger at my partner.)?
- How does this change feel like a relief? What are the good thoughts you have about yourself when in conflict (e.g., I feel compassion toward my significant other, but I understand that it isn't helpful for me to suppress my own needs until I am ready to burst.)?
- How has the ways that you assessed your part in your conflicts made you suffer, feel anxiety or anger? How do you feel about seeking the peace and joy of Repair and Resetting as you move forward?
- How has the ways that you assessed your part in your conflicts (taking too much or not enough accountability) made your partner suffer or feel anxiety or anger? How will you think about this in the future so you can be more active and engaged?

Exercise: Taking a Final Inventory, Together

Take an inventory of your relationship together and explore how destructive or distancing behavior has interfered with the sense of safety and security between you. Use these results as a model to deal with issues as they arise.

The Issue/Conflict _____

How you each contributed to the issue/conflict: "What's my part in it?"	
How you each felt: hurt, scared, or upset.	
How you each justified the destructive, unhelpful behavior and avoided addressing your role in the problem.	
Your feelings on having destructed each other and the relationship.	
How you each contributed to repairing the damage, and the results so far.	

R Also Means Renew: Getting Back to IRL

Now that you're done with your *Love. Crash. Rebuild. rehab*, creating a parenthetical space for your relationship to Repair, when do you go back to your real life and renew your commitment to each other? How do you transition back into real life and carry the lesson with you?

When we get to Reset and Repair, we can offer each other an affirmation of our appreciation: this is the work towards renewal. The net result is a greater subjective experience of accepting and being accepted. Because we're seeing each other more clearly, we're seeing both the good and the not so good (but real) stuff, which is what this whole model is really about. An affirmation can be the one time where you're allowed to take the focus off yourself. As you repair the relationship, you can add to your affirmations and acknowledge what you have accomplished. If you feel safe you can say, "I love you," or "I love the fact that we're spending more time together."

Exercise: List Your Relationship Attributes with Asset Mapping

You can also make a gratitude list of your partner and relationship. The asset mapping exercise will be a kick starter for the affirmations and gratitude list. These assets are labeled—good parents, good lovers, deep friends—which then encourages the new alliance of "us." These affirmations can be the start of a new foundation for how we want to see ourselves and how we want to be in this relationship.

Let's consider the many healthy qualities you as a couple possess. Go back to your answers in the similar exercise in Chapter One. Now, see how you can affirm the answers each of you included there, and express how you feel about your relationship.

Partner A Affirmation of Partner B: You are kind.

You are _____

You are _____

You are _____

Partner B Affirmation of Partner A: You are reliable.

You are _____

You are _____

You are _____

Couple Example: We appreciate the sense of humor of the other and are able to share a good guffaw together.

We_____

We_____

We_____

Putting PACER All Together: Our Story

Well into the development of our model, we had an argument that brought up an extremely sensitive and largely unresolved historical experience (meaning, we fought about the same thing all the time, and it pissed off both of us). The argument took place during a particularly difficult period in our relationship. Mark got caught up in a project that was draining much more of our financial resources than either of us was comfortable with. However, when there was any discussion of how money should be spent in terms of the project, Mark became defensive and began using a phrase to excuse himself from revealing the extent of the money issues we were facing. The phrase was, "After all I do for you," as in, "After all I do for you, I do not need to be completely transparent about what is going on with us financially," (i.e., mind your own business).

Haruna wasn't too troubled by Mark's inability to talk about money, until the day when Haruna went to the grocery store and took out her debit card and was told by the cashier that she had an "insufficient funds" notice. She was humiliated, and it was no longer possible to avoid the fact that how our money was spent was *both of our* business.

When Haruna got home she asked (well, screamed at) Mark, "Where the hell is our money? What did you do with our money?"

Mark, rather than answering the question said, "Look, I've been building a new business and yes, I have been making large financial contributions to that business so that we, as a family, can survive raising a family in New York

City. And frankly, I am shocked that *after all I do for you,* you would question what I do with my money!"

"Your money?" Haruna replied. "It's *our* money, and you building your business does not mean that I am responsible for all of your business expenses!!! I am so upset!!!"

Mark snapped back, "Fine. If you don't want to support my decisions, I understand. I will let this business crash and burn. And let you take over all the finances of our family!"

"I can't believe you did this to me! You lied to me about how much money you were spending on this project! This is not the way we're supposed to handle money as a couple. We need to separate our bank accounts. I can't trust you anymore!"

Mark was stunned: he never expected the conversation to take this turn. "Are you kidding!? I never lied to you. How can I lie to you about how much I am spending on this project when it all comes out of our joint bank account? Go ahead! Separate your bank account from mine. While you are at it, why don't we think about a more serious separation."

However, and perhaps because we'd been working on a nascent version of the PACER Model for quite some time, we were just barely able to yell "Pause" before we walked—okay, stormed—away from each other, barely avoiding the dreaded stonewall and, instead, opting for a moratorium.

What happened next? Mark went to the store, bought a bottle of milk and came home forty-five minutes later.

What *really* happened? On Mark's walk he experienced a decrease in anger and, at first, a deep sense of injustice at what he felt was an unfair attack. After all, he told himself, he had been maligned and he felt compelled to "right a serious wrong." However, he quickly shifted into Accountability.

He started to think about the argument as a rupture and was curious to see what was pushing his aggressive behavior during the argument. He started to think about his own past and his tendency toward self-sufficiency that he felt ever since he was a kid. Where did that need to be in charge and not reliant on anyone come from? I guess it goes back to my parents, he thought. Mark's dad took off when he was a boy, and he felt as if he'd been left behind to act as a parentified child to take care of his wounded and

239

depressed mother. He knew that ever since then he had a problem with being a compulsive caretaker.

There was also the whole cultural thing about men making money, and that a successful marriage meant that the woman, like his mother, would be raising the kids and not talking about money at all. This cultural standard had actually bit him in the ass once before, when his dad, who was really far beneath his mother's financial class, left. It had been a real embarrassment to her family. His mother came from Los Angeles' upper class society, and she never really had a job. She would complain about having no money, but they lived a privileged life in an incredibly expensive house in probably one of the most expensive neighborhoods in the country. So even when he heard his mother say, "We don't have money," they were still living in this incredibly fancy house in this incredibly fancy place, and he went to an incredibly fancy private school. That disconnect meant that Mark could never really understand that not having money really and truly meant that there was no cash in the bank.

Mark looked at the reasons why he became so angry when Haruna confronted him. Because he never talked about money with his mother (too crass a conversation, to be sure), he never expected that Haruna would actually confront him about money. He thought Haruna's family also had money, so that if they were ever in a bind, money would somehow just appear. He was always confused why Haruna would talk about her parents as basically blue collar, sort of middle-class, even though they lived in Japan where in his mind, Japan had a very thriving economy. (Mark recalls that in the 1980s he heard that a McDonald's hamburger cost $25.00 in Japan.) Even though Haruna tried to describe her family as very modest and very cautious with money, prudent, and never impulsive, Mark had this image of the Japanese people as being pretty well-to-do and secure.

Mark now realized that he might have left Haruna in the dark in terms of his spending. He had been the primary earner when their children were younger, so he clung to a belief that he had earned a superior position in the family, which came with the right to make financial decisions on his own. He also thought he earned the right to invest *their* money in *his* project, forgetting that he was going through a major transition at work. Yet he was embarrassed at the amount of money this project was costing him (okay, them), and, partly because of this, he was afraid to openly discuss his experience of what, at the time, felt like failure. Underneath it all, Mark realized he had a fear of getting caught spending more money than they had. Instead of talking about this fear, he dissociated the problem completely. He purposefully left her out of the decision-making. His instinct was to discount Haruna's ability to make financial contributions, even though her practice was coming together. He wasn't trusting that her business acumen was going to actually be as salient as his contribution. Yes, he said to himself, the flow of their money was there to be seen in their joint bank account, but when he was honest with himself, he had to admit that he was much more abreast of their financial status.

Meanwhile, Haruna took a Pause and realized she was feeling a ton of anger. Her initial thoughts were, How could he do this to me!? And to us!? She was fuming for a while. After taking a deep breath and digging deeper into her own Accountability, she realized she had been afraid of, and intentionally postponing, looking at the bank account and having a conversation with Mark about money. Her conflict was wrapped in ambivalence: wanting to know what was happening with Mark's business project with his colleagues, and at the same time, not wanting to know and just wanting to be taken care of financially. She thought she needed to let Mark manage their financial affairs because she had put him on a pedestal with the assumption that as the man, he would take care of their family financially. She felt betrayed because he wasn't living up to her gender expectations.

But the reality was, she avoided looking at the financial activities associated with their joint account. She could have asked Mark at any time to talk about how much money he was putting into this project. However, she was afraid to know because deep down, she too was afraid of financial failure. When she thought about it, she realized this fear was coming from not having enough knowledge about handling money. Her parents had always worked for the Japanese government in civil servant jobs. They had a salary, and never had her experience of being a business owner with her own clinical practice. The only way her parents talked about money was in terms of saving for a future when they retired.

Haruna's fear of not having enough money was complicated by her understanding of limitations that women, and particularly Asian women, experience in the US. Not only did she know about "the glass ceiling," she had heard another phrase, "the bamboo ceiling" that applied to Asians, especially immigrants like herself. She couldn't fathom that there were endless opportunities for her to make money and was relying on Mark, which had been fine in the past because if he was anything, he was a compulsive caretaker. Except now, when his caretaking took a wrong turn toward overspending.

When Mark returned home we met in the kitchen, and almost simultaneously asked each other for a meeting in the middle. We both felt less anxious to talk to each other because of the work we did in Accountability. And we each brought willingness to be open, honest, and vulnerable to Collaboration. We knew that now we could finally open up about how we felt about financial security.

During Collaboration, we were able to express each of our parts in the problem, what had triggered it, and to use this information to reveal what we found frightening and unpleasant about our money, security, and failure. At first we were challenged to explore the related issues surrounding money that previously we were each unwilling to share. We talked about our feelings about finances and how embarrassed we felt when we behaved poorly in front of each other, and how we could see how our relationship was suffering because we were too afraid and defensive to discuss this extremely intimate issue. Mark shared that the consequences of his actions were his alone, as was his sense of failure that he hid from Haruna and increasingly cut himself off from her support. Haruna shared that she cut herself off from Mark by not looking more closely at their bank account, and her blind trust was actually avoiding having a conversation about money and enabling Mark's behavior. The result was the same for both of us: we felt lonely, disconnected from each other, and living in fear about money in our marriage.

When we came to the end of our meeting in the middle, we decided to share what we had each learned about ourselves, each other, and our relationship. We used Collaboration and attempted to reframe how we could be more transparent about "where the money was going" and to use this information as just one way in which we engaged—or avoided—conflict. This was an opportunity for us to reframe our understanding of conflict and Repair the rupture of avoidance we both had fallen back on before the current fight. We also decided to Experiment with having future meetings in the middle just for money issues. We decided that we are going to talk about money on a biweekly basis so that we will continue to communicate about money moving forward. We both acknowledged that we have lots of fear about money, and for the sake of our relationship, we need to learn to talk about money. Eventually, Mark decided to pull himself out of the business. Haruna sought career coaching services for being a business owner. These actions came out of the on-going conversations.

In Reset, we began to feel empowered in our relationship and returned to the "we as a team" model that is the backbone of our marriage. Now a little braver, we reviewed the rupture to see if any of these same feelings were bleeding into other areas of our marriage. This time, the rupture was really pretty self-contained. Then we affirmed the hard work that we had achieved to go from rupture to Repair and now can use this as a source of ongoing reaffirmation of our willingness to do the hard work of being in everyday love.

In the past, our attempts to address, confront, and deal with issues that exposed us to extreme vulnerability—in this case, issues of money, security, and failure—often went off the rails, and we would storm off for hours of avoidance. Our previous attempts led to criticism, blame, and stonewalling because these vulnerabilities made us both defensive and anxious. Neither of us, alone, was able to resolve these major conflicts because we did not know how to even talk about them. It was not until the threat of losing each other—the real threat of separation—was on the table that we used PACER to navigate the risky waters of keeping the focus on ourselves, accounting for our part in the rupture, and became empowered to experiment with what empathy, intimacy, and vulnerability could be as a process of true love.

Just Because the Monkey Is Asleep Does Not Mean the Circus Has Left Town

One of our beloved clients shared this line with us when he described the recurring states of conflict he and his wife experience. He told us, "While we are more often in a calm state, that doesn't mean that we don't have to continue to keep the focus on ourselves and believing— really believing, even after all the hard work we did in couples therapy—that the other person is the cause of all our problems."

We keep this line handy for the times when old clients wanted to see us again for what we call, a "tune up." For instance, a long-ago client called us in a panic just before we were leaving for a vacation. On speakerphone, we hear Natalie say, "The wheels have completely come off the bus. What do we do first? Pause, right?"

"Right."

"Good. We did that. Now I am calling you after having contemplated and accounted for what I did, and Rosa is in the other room, says she has done the same."

"So? Why are you calling us?"

"Because" Natalie went on, "I think Rosa found a 'loophole' and believes that I am the sole cause of this fight, and her believing *that* makes it clear to me that it's really all her fault this time. Here's what happened: we had gotten back into a habit of having breakfast together after our retirement, and I had come to rely on that. When Rosa said that she wanted to attend swimming class a couple of mornings each week, I told her that was fine. The truth is, it really hurt me, it burned me up. So instead of talking about it in the moment, I sat and stewed in resentment for weeks, which then became months. I became increasingly less able to hide my hurts, resentment, and anger. Yesterday, I told her as she was leaving for class, 'You can go ahead and screw your swimming instructor.' She caught on."

In the background, we could hear Rosa saying that she was ready to account for her part of the problem. So now we were in an "official session," a conference call with all four of us.

Rosa chimed in, "I think I knew that Natalie was not happy when I interrupted our morning routine. I felt, on the one hand, that I was taking care of myself while, on the other, I tried to make her feel that by supporting my swimming, she was the one taking care of me. This was wishful thinking—and something we did not discuss. I did not acknowledge the subtle signs pointing to the fact that things were not going well for us."

"See," blurted Natalie, "She's blaming me! You guys—all of you—spent all that time in couples therapy telling me to express myself and when I do, I am labeled the 'bad one!'"

"Are you kidding me?" exclaimed Rosa, "This just proves that when you said that you were 'okay' with me taking swimming classes, you were lying!"

"I wasn't lying, Rosa. I felt that my hurt and anger were not okay because I told you it was okay for you to swim. When I started feeling hurt, I felt like a jerk. The more I felt that way, the angrier I got. I can see that now. It is true I'd been very uncomfortable with your expression of anger for years. Expressing it myself made me feel like a villain."

We reminded Natalie and Rosa that when one partner believes the other is causing *all* the problems, we have absolutely no power to do anything to get to repair. All we can do is wait and hope that they will get better. We acknowledged the hard work they had done with us, that they had been able to share responsibility—and credit—for both the ruptures *and* the repairs, and that it was a "gift" that Rosa, who was initially scapegoated as "the angry one" had offered Natalie by helping her express her pain and fears that had been coming out as passive-aggressive behavior.

"In this case," said Rosa, "you let me know—with anger and hostility— that you're unhappy, and suddenly you are burdened with being a villain? I accept that I hurt your feelings, but you have to find a better way to deal with it. Pushing it down without letting me know was our old passive-aggressive way, which nearly killed our relationship."

"I know," agreed Natalie. "When you joined the swim class I was okay at first, but as the weeks went by I really felt hurt and then I was embarrassed about feeling that way. The Borgs told us that discovering our passive-aggressive behaviors was going to be like a prison-break and, yes, I have found that to be true. I guess I slipped back into my old routine. Suddenly this seething hurt and fear and anger resurrected."

Rosa seemed calmer. "I feel like we've both said our piece. Does this count as our collaboration stage?"

We agreed that the phone call constituted the C—the Collaboration stage—in the PACER model, and we spoke for a while about what the Experiment would look like: each of them exploring with each other how they had contributed to the conflict and sharing the emotions they were experiencing, and then experimenting with new ways of expressing themselves to each other. They agreed to put the Experiment into practice to reset, and then we set up another appointment for when we got back from vacation.

We also explained that conflict is the reminder that in a love relationship, we need to be willing to continuously do the work that keeps our love alive. Natalie and Rosa began to slip back into a dynamic they had used to keep themselves safe from the very things they had wanted—and been terrified of—from long-term love for years: vulnerability, empathy, intimacy, and emotional investment. Their calling in a meeting in the middle with us was their way to actively reengage with the work of rupture and repair.

The Real Lesson of Conflict

Fears and anxieties are often misunderstood. We live lives where, rather than experience our hurts, fears, and anxieties, we have innumerable ways to dissociate—get rid of our conscious awareness of—them, as if they are unequivocally *bad things* whose information, whatever that may be, is to be tossed aside and rejected, as if what our feelings are trying to tell us are unimportant at best and toxic and damaging at worst. The result is that we tend to "medicate" (i.e., avoid) our feelings—and the stronger the feeling (especially pain, fear, anxiety, sadness, and the like), the more effort we—both consciously and unconsciously—put into suppressing them. We also highly misunderstand our mixed feelings—conflict, ambivalence—and generally experience them as if they were telling us: "Hey, if you do not absolutely and unequivocally want this or that (or them), then you must not want it enough." When what it is really saying is: "Hey, this situation (or person) is significant and hence scary, maybe because they are threatening to become a much bigger part of your life."

Without the willingness and tools to listen to and navigate our feelings, we wind up thinking our way through much of our lives—and loves. It's not that we aren't *also* feeling, but feelings often are expressed in actions, behaviors, and the patterns of our lives that are up for our interpretations and/or misinterpretation. In this state, it is much easier to avoid big feelings that are constantly messaging us about what we *really* want, and what we *really* need. Avoiding internal conflict leads us into situation after situation where we wind up avoiding the very things (feelings) that we need to connect with our lives—and each other.

We need to drop our armor of defense and offense and learn to be vulnerable with each other. We listen and bond when we share our vulnerable thoughts and feelings. Being in defense or offense would further divide two partners in committed relationship. Active listening and active reflecting on what you contributed to the conflict would help set a tone in your relationship that you are here to stay no matter what happens in the conflicts of your relationship.

What we have seen through the many years of working with people and couples is that if we refuse to hear what our feelings are telling us, we cannot get to any sort of Repair—as Mark says to his clients, "You can't outthink your feelings." The experiences and feelings that we think are telling us to turn tail and run—ambivalence or conflict—may just be trying to inform us of how grand scale and important (albeit, indeed emotionally threatening and risk-taking) a relationship may be.

The Gottmans believe, as we do, that "feeling unloved" is the most commonly cited reason for wanting a divorce.[1] Rupture and Repair are the actions of love—loving and being loved; being able to give, receive, take in, and make use of the love we create together. Throughout this book, we hope you have come to see that conflict does not tell us that something lacks value, but that it threatens us to our very core with the possibility of being legitimately transformational. After all, there is nothing more frightening than presenting your true self—I am me, I am exactly who I know and am familiar with. Yet real love is such a place where we are constantly challenged to grow and thrive—to become—rather than to simply be.

Conflict is our natural state. Relationships that make room for opposite opinions, differences, and conflicts in each other—and ourselves—are the ones that endure. Why? Because making use of whatever problems, conflicts, failures, mistakes arise—in an effort for us to be who we actually are—is the key to a healthy relationship. Ruptures will continue to happen. Now you know how to Repair. And each time, the relationship will get stronger because you will know what your emotions, fears, and anxieties are really trying to tell you. And you will know how to read the emotions of your partner and live, as allies, in love.

1. John Gottman, *The Marriage Clinic: A Scientifically Based Marital Therapy* (New York: W. W. Norton, 1999), 24.

Acknowledgments

Mark would like to acknowledge:

I love you, Haruna Miyamoto-Borg! You nonstop rock my world! It is true what Isa (the woman who married us) said, "You can fall in love every day"—I have—I do!

Kata and Uta, being your daddy—your *otosan*—and loving you is staggeringly unimaginable joy—joy beyond measure.

Pam Liflander—editor, *par excellence*—you know that this project simply would not exist without your care, your guidance, your love!

As always, Gareth Esersky, my/our agent, has provided the consistent guidance and care for my work—and that of the Irrelationship Group—that undergirds this volume. Thank you, Gareth, for taking me, and now Haruna and me, on. Being represented by you makes me feel like the luckiest dude on earth. Working with you and the Carol Mann Agency is among the greatest gifts of this whole writing sojourn.

Central Recovery Press, especially Valerie Killeen and Nancy Schenck, thank you! Authorship with CRP has been, as was offered when we began back in 2014, a synergistic partnership. I feel empowered by the love, care, and support I received from you as a member of the Irrelationship Project and throughout the development of this *truly* collaborative endeavor.

The raucous band, All Nite Rave (now Oedipus Triple Rex), was my earliest attempt to form and maintain a collaboration that was challenged to survive the clashing of egos of its many parents. Through dozens of members, it wound up being the cherished, idealized lovechild of Jim DeLozier (RIP) and I. We alone survived *it*—the original name of what Freud called "das *Id*," that raging, instinctual component of the unconscious mind that's ever *at war* with the ego, whose job it is to navigate consensus reality. I love you, Jim, as there is no one who sailed with me more consistently and closely toward treacherous shores. Oh, how I miss you.

Chris Borg—we live, Bro (big Styrofoam rafts drifting out to sea notwithstanding)! I love you and am so grateful to have you in my life.

Seal Beach Surf Crew (AKA, Midnight Surf Team): Greg Hex, Mike Dalla, John Turi, Bill Zunkel. Soulmates, the lot O' ya! God, how I love you!

Kristy Matthews, who would I be without you? All these years; Q of S, more and more love and magic. Thank you.

Danny Berry—what can I say? The mystery of the kiss unsolved—I love you!

Terry and Joan DeLozier. The world is not the same without Jim, and I'm disoriented in ways I continue to discover. The love and refuge you gave us Corona del Mar punks still lives inside me.

Matt Stedman, much gratitude for the calming, nurturing counsel on our surf sojourns up and down the East Coast. Cowabunga, dude!

Also, thank you, Dr. Jeanne Henry for taking me under your wing at Newport Harbor Adolescent Psychiatric Hospital, showing me the ropes, and opening the door to the vast, amazing field of mental health care. Thank you, Dr. Ronda Hampton, my professional soulmate, for the years of shoulder-to-shoulder camaraderie on the front lines of community crisis intervention in Avalon Gardens, South Central Los Angeles (1992–1997). Dr. Maggie Decker, I'm so grateful for your guidance, care, love, and supervision at AIDS Service Foundation in the mid-1990s. These three experiences have formed the central core of my professional identity and I carry you with me every day through what often feels like *clinical mayhem*. I love this work, and you three have made that possible.

PR *par excellence*, Kelli Daniel of Dart Frogg—you rock!

Thank you, Charlotte Rolland for giving me a consistent love that proved itself in action. I believe all these years since you've been gone sets the cornerstone of my willingness and ability to love and be loved— *relationship sanity*.

Thank you, Charlotte and Jon Rysanek. Fixing what was broken between us has been among the most miraculous examples of what love can do. I'm so grateful for the love we share, and so happy for the love shared between my beloved Grrrrrrrls—Haruna, Kata, and Uta—and their Nana and Papa.

ACKNOWLEDGMENTS

Thank you, Sandy Borg for an excellent evening of lion-taming. Its benefits express themselves in my life every day, thirty-five years, and counting, later. And thanks, Erik Borg for *also* loving me through all that—and this.

Love and gratitude to you, Mark Borg and Bonnie Mankoff. Your steady thoughtfulness and kindness maintain our connection across miles and years. Dad, I cannot believe you're not here—the world is not the same without you.

I'm deeply grateful for Osamu and Yoko Miyamoto. I love you, and I believe I hit the jackpot in the in-law department. *Arigato gozaimasu* for all the love and generosity you consistently shower upon your NYC family no matter the geographic distance.

Deep, deep appreciation to Thomas Hussey, ("Uncle") Rob Gutfliesh, Gordon Ramsey, and Freddie Stephens—loving you for sharing the road *of*...

American Psychoanalytic Association (APsaA) peers: Barry Wepman, Natasha Lifton, Sheri Ashcraft, Michael Slevin, Caroline Sehon. Wouldn't have made it without you!

Dr. Grant Brenner—*Irrelationship*—let's keep on keepin' on!

Special mention (again) to those mods and punks, surfers, shrinks, black sheep, iconoclasts, colleagues, mentors, supervisors, and soulmates who, from a vast array of time periods and contexts, have loved and were loved by me in ways that still fuel a wider and ever-expanding *raison d'être*. Special thanks to: Bill Defina, Britt Huycke, Karin Nance, Phil Vock, Megan Hardy, Byron Abel, Ken Blomster, Valentine Burlacu, Johanna Rhyins, Vic Ruggiero, Robert Taube, Glenn Parish, Paul Loringer, Steve Torrey, Scott Murdock, Cheo Rodriguez, Liz Rusch, Marty Strom, Emily Garrod, Tom Cox, Emily Damron-Cox, Paco and Maiken Lozano-Wiese, Wil Diaz, Scott Graham, Bobbi Fuentes, Rie Ogura, David Kopstein, Scott Stewart, Jonathan Schnappe, Kumi Hirose, Tim Barnes, Mark Lanaghan, Molly Goldman, Dave Jawor (ANR), Patrick Holert (PRD), Gavin and Kali Selman, Burgos Pangilinan, Richard Polatcheck, Gloria Robotham, Elizabeth Shanahan, Isa Stanfels, John Henry Eldridge, Norman Karns, Shawn Marie Turi, Jimmy Boyle, John Hatchett, Daniel Leyva, Father Michael Lynch, Maureen Kamsi-Storey, Joerg Bose, Sandra Buechler, Jack Drescher, Sue Kolod, Brent Willock, Jack Eppler, Kako Takeuchi, Joshua Horowitz, Phillip Solomon, Zeke and Sheila Zimmerman, John Flikeid, Connie Rolland, Jules Cohen, Hara Estroff-Marano, John Ellert,

Jared Katz, Scott Munsey, Jennifer McCarroll, Chana Pollack, Mike Moore, Chris Adams, Kent (TK) Jones, Ken Robidoux, Mauri Helffrich, David Lester, Gary Ireland, John Lance Harrison, David (Mrs. Smith) Hanbury, Bob Jones (OTR), Rob Lipshutz (PRD/OTR), Chris Ginn, Amy Kerr, Kitty Brazelton, Stan Boyd, Mark Bouthilette, Masaki Matsubara, Tim Couch, Sean Carver, Wendy and Kim Marshall, Paul Tully, Daniel MacNamee, Brendan Rafferty, NYHC (especially Drew Stone, Larry Kelley, Vinnie Stigma, Roberto and Amarù Fenoutt), and, of course, all those dudes at PAX. The combined force of your love, all of you, is what gives me the will to traverse through—and sustains my every step into—whatever it is that comes next, and then after that.

Haruna would like to acknowledge:

I want to thank all of my teachers who have inspired me to write this book. This book could not have been possible without their passion and relentless dedication to enhancing couples' relationships and increasing our understanding of their complex states of intimacy. In my work with my clients, I do feel that I am supported by the community of the incredible thinkers and visionary clinicians.

Special thanks to my mentor, Michele Scheinkman, who has demonstrated thirst for understanding the complex world of intimate relationships and has taught me to become a better couples therapist. Dr. Suzanne Iasenza, who has courageously put words and verbal narratives to the forbidden, unspoken world of sexuality and sexual intimacy. Her courage and dedication have helped me understand the matrix of sexuality and sexual intimacy. Dr. Latasha Smith, who generously has taught me and shared her vast knowledge and experience of working with individuals, couples, and families.

I am very grateful for all of my couple clients who have trusted me to do the work with them and showed me in their efforts that the difficult but inspiring repair work is possible. They are the ones who have really taught me to become an attuned couple therapist.

I want to thank my teachers at Ackerman Institute: Judith Stern Peck, Betsy Witten, Keren Ludwig, Andrea Blumenthal, Silvia Espinal, Miguel Torres. My journey as a couples therapist began by listening to these incredible team of teachers at Ackerman.

ACKNOWLEDGMENTS

I thank my colleagues and mentors: Joyce Caraccioli, Kimi Aoki, Dr. Kenta Asakura, Dr. Takashi Matsuki, Hope Kelaher, Dr. Lisa Orbe-Austin, Dr. Richard Orbe-Austin, Dr. Michal Ginach, and Dr. Faith Bethelard. I have been very blessed to have them in my clinical circle.

And thanks to my friends who support me through any and every challenges I encounter while writing this book: Chris Billias, Rosa Godmundsdottir, Moonli Singha, Sheila Zimmerman, Noriko Matsuki, Ayako Kigoshi, Mieko Ueyama, Minami Yusui, Miko Yasuda, Rika Eisenberg, Rita Coelho, Yukiko Sugawara, and Yuko Nakaya.

I want to thank our incredible editors: Pamela Liflander and Nancy Schenck. I am indebted to our agent Gareth Esersky who believed in us and our work with couples. I can't thank Carol Mann Agency enough for representing us. I want to thank Central Recovery Press, particularly Valerie Killeen, for giving us a chance to publish this book.

Finally, I want to thank my daughters, Kata and Uta, who have supported me and given me love through this book writing. And I am very thankful to my husband, Mark, who has shown me love and compassion. With his love, I am helped to realize how deep and compassionate love is possible—every day.

Bibliography

Ainsworth, Mary. "The Development of Infant-Mother Attachment." In B. Cardwell & H. Ricciuti (Eds.) *Review of Child Development Research* (Vol. 3, pp. 1–94) Chicago: University of Chicago Press, 1973.

Alcoholics Anonymous World Services. *Alcoholics Anonymous.* New York: AA World Services, Inc., 1997.

Alcoholics Anonymous World Services. *Twelve Steps and Twelve Traditions.* New York: AA World Services, Inc., 1952.

Aron, Lewis. "The Paradoxical Place of Enactment in Psychoanalysis." *Psychoanalytic Dialogues, 13* (2003): 623–32.

Borg, Jr., Mark B. "The Psychoanalyst as Community Practitioner." *Psychologist-Psychoanalyst, 22* (2002a): 26–34.

Borg, Jr., Mark B. "The Avalon Gardens Men's Association: A Community Health Psychology Case Study." *Journal of Health Psychology, 7* (2003a): 345–57.

Borg, Jr., Mark B. Psychoanalytic Pure War: Interactions with the Post-Apocalyptic Unconscious. *Journal for the Psychoanalysis of Culture and Society, 8* (2003b): 57–67.

Borg, Jr., Mark B. "Venturing Beyond the Consulting Room: Psychoanalysis in Community Crisis Intervention. *Contemporary Psychoanalysis, 40* no. 2 (2004): 147–74.

Borg, Jr., Mark B. "Community Psychoanalysis: Developing a Model of Psychoanalytically Informed Community Crisis Intervention." In N. Lange and M. Wagner (Eds.) *Community Psychology: New Directions* (pp. 1–66). Happague, NY: Nova Science Publishers, 2010.

Borg, Jr., Mark B., Grant H. Brenner, and John D. Berry. *Irrelationship: How We Use Dysfunctional Relationships to Hide from Intimacy.* Las Vegas, NV: Central Recovery Press, 2015.

Borg, Jr., Mark B., Grant H. Brenner, and John D. Berry. *Relationship Sanity: Creating and Maintaining Healthy Relationships.* Las Vegas, NV: Central Recovery Press, 2018.

Borg, Jr., M. B., Grant H. Brenner, and John D. Berry. *Making Your Crazy Work for You: From Trauma and Isolation to Self-Acceptance and Love.* Las Vegas, NV: Central Recovery Press, 2022.

Borg, Jr., Mark B., Emily Garrod, and Michael R. Dalla, "Intersecting 'Real Worlds': Community Psychology and Psychoanalysis." *The Community Psychologist, 34*(2001): 16–19.

Borg, Jr., Mark B., & Haruna Miyamoto-Borg, "The Borderline Stage of Relationship." *Psychology Research, 2* (2012): 1–13.

Bose, Joerg. "Trauma, Depression, and Mourning." *Contemporary Psychoanalysis* 31, no. 3 (1995): 399–407.

Bose, Joerg. "The Inhumanity of the Other: Treating Trauma and Depression." *The Review of Interpersonal Psychoanalysis* 3, no. 1 (1998): 1–4.

Bowen, Murray. "The Use of Family Theory in Clinical Practice." *Comprehensive Psychiatry, 7* (5), 345–74, 1966.

Bowlby John. *Attachment and Loss: Vol. 1.* New York: Basic Books, 1969.

Bowlby, John. "The Nature of the Child's Tie to His Mother." *International Journal of Psychoanalysis, 39,* 350–71, 1958.

Bromberg, Philip, M. "Standing in the Spaces: The Multiplicity of Self and the Psychoanalytic Relationship." *Contemporary Psychoanalysis, 32* (1996): 509–39.

Bromberg, Philip, M. *Standing in the Spaces: Essays on Clinical Process, Trauma, and Dissociation.* New York: Routledge, 1998.

Bromberg, Philip, M. *The Shadow of the Tsunami: And the Growth of the Relational Mind.* New York: Routledge Taylor & Francis Group, 2011.

Brown, Lucy L. and Helen E. Fisher. "The Anatomy of Love" Know Thy Brain, Know Thy Self, Know Thy Partner." https://theanatomyoflove.com (accessed on 4/29/2023).

Drigotas Stephen M., Caryl E. Rusbult, Jennifer Wieselquist, Sarah W. Whitton. "Close Partner as Sculptor of the Ideal Self: Behavioral Affirmation and the Michelangelo Phenomenon." *Journal of Personality and Social Psychology.* 1999 Aug;77 (1999): 293–323.

Falicov, Celia J. "The Cultural Meaning of Family Triangles," in M. McGoldrick and R.J. Green, (Eds) *Revisioning Culture in Family Therapy* (pp. 37–49). New York: Guilford Press, 1998.

Feist, Jess and Gregory J. Feist. *Theories of Personality (7th Edition).* New York: McGraw Hill, 2008.

Fisher, Helen E. *Anatomy of Love: A Natural History of Mating, Marriage, and Why We Stray.* New York: W. W. Norton, 2016.

Fisher, Helen E. "Cupid in Quarantine: What Brain Science Can Teach Us about Love", *New York Times*, April 13, 2020.

Fisher, Helen E; Xiaomeng Xu, Arthur Aron, and Lucy L. Brown. "Intense, Passionate, Romantic Love: A Natural Addiction? How the Fields That Investigate Romance and Substance Abuse Can Inform Each Other." *Frontiers in Psychology, 7* (2016): 687–97. 2016.

Freud, Sigmund. "Remembering, Repeating and Working Though." in *Standard Edition of the Complete Works of Sigmund Freud, Vol. 12*, 145–56. London: The Hogarth Press, 1914.

Freud, Sigmund. "Beyond the Pleasure Principle." in *Standard Edition of the Complete Works of Sigmund Freud, Vol. 18*, 3–64. London: The Hogarth Press, 1920.

Goldklank, Shelley. "The Shoop Shoop Song: A Guide to Psychoanalytic-Systemic Couple Therapy. *Contemporary Psychoanalysis*, 45(2009): 3–25. 2009.

Gottman, John. *The Marriage Clinic: A Scientifically Based Marital Therapy.* New York: W. W. Norton, 1999.

Gottman, John M. and Julie S. Gottman. Gottman Couple Therapy in A. S. Gurman, J. L. Lebow, & D. K. Snyder (Eds.), *Clinical Handbook of Couple Therapy* 129–57. The Guilford Press, 2015.

Harari, Yuval N. *Sapiens: A Brief History of Humankind.* New York: Harper, 2011.

Harris Emily A., Aki M. Gormezano, Sari M. van Anders. "Gender Inequities in Household Labor Predict Lower Sexual Desire in Women Partnered with Men." *Archives of Sexual Behavior.* Nov; 51(2022): 3847–870.

Hendrix, Harville. *Getting the Love You Want: A Guide for Couples.* New York: Henry Holt & Company, 2008.

Hirsch, Irwin. "The Concept of Enactment and Theoretical Convergence." *Psychoanalytic Quarterly*, 67 (1998): 78–101.

Holmes, Lisa (2021). "Here's Why the Honeymoon Phase is so Intoxicating," *Science*, 2021 https://keeplerapp.com/honeymoon-phase/.

Iasenza, Suzanne. *Transforming Sexual Narratives: A Relational Approach to Sex Therapy.* New York: Routledge, 2020. 47–77.

Jackson, Don D. "The Question of Family Homeostasis. *International Journal of Family Therapy*, 3(1981), 5–15.

Jacobs, Theodore. "On Countertransference Enactments." *Journal of the American Psychoanalytic Association*, 3 (1986), 289–307.

Johnson, Sue. *Hold Me Tight: Seven Conversations for a Lifetime of Love.* Boston, MA: Little, Brown Spark, 2008.

Kluger, Avraham N. and Angelo DeNisi. "The Effects of Feedback Interventions on Performance: A Historical Review, a Meta-Analysis, and a Preliminary Feedback Intervention Theory." *Psychological Bulletin*, 119(1996): 254–84.

Lerner, Melvin J. and Carolyn H. Simmons. "Observer's Reaction to the 'Innocent Victim': Compassion or Rejection?" *Journal of Personality and Social Psychology*, 4, no. 2 (1966): 203–10.

Levenson, Edgar. *The Fallacy of Understanding.* New York: Basic Books, 1972.

Marazitti, Donatella and Domenico Canale. "Hormonal Changes When Falling in Love." *Psychoneuroendocrinology* 29 (2004): 931–36.

Matthews, Gillian A. and Kaye Tye. "Neural Mechanisms of Social Homeostasis." *Annals of the New York Academy of Sciences* (December 1, 2019).

Nagoski, Emily. *Come As You Are: The Surprising New Science that will Transform Your Sex Life*. New York: Simon & Schuster, 2015.

Neff, Kristen. *Self-Compassion: The Proven Power of Being Kind to Yourself*. New York: William Morrow, 2011.

Real, Terrence. *How Can I Get Through to You: Closing the Intimacy Gap Between Men and Women*. New York: Scribner. 2001.

Perel, Esther. *Mating in Captivity: Unlocking Erotic Intelligence*. New York: Harper, 2006.

Psicolish, Marina. "The Pause: Closing the Gap Between Our Best Intentions and Our Actions." *University of Utah, PDR Blog*, September 27, 2021 (accessed 7/18/2023).

Plutchik, Robert. "A General Psychoevolutionary Theory of Emotion," in Robert Plutchik and Henry Kellerman (Eds.), *Emotion: Theory, Research and Experience, Theories of Emotion*, vol. 1 (pp. 3–33). New York: Academic Press, 1980.

Scheinkman, Michele and Mona D. Fishbane. "The Vulnerability Cycle: Working with Impasses in Couple Therapy." *Family Process*, 43(2004): 279–99.

Shaw, Daniel. *Traumatic Narcissism: Relational Systems of Subjugation*. London: Routledge, 2013.

Sternberg, Janine. *Infant Observation at the Heart of Training*. London: Routledge, 2018.

Sullivan, Harry Stack. *The Interpersonal Theory of Psychiatry*. New York: W. W. Norton, 1953.

Tronick, Edward Z. "Emotions and Communication in Infants." *American Psychologist* 44, no. 2 (1989): 112–19.

Tronick, Edward Z. *The Neurobehavioral and Social-Emotional Development of Infants and Children*. New York: W. W. Norton, 2007.

Tronick, Edward Z. and Andrew Gianino. "Interactive Mismatch and Repair: Challenges to the Coping Infant." *Zero to Three, 6* (1986): 1–6.

Tronick, Edward Z. and Claudia M. Gold. *The Power of Discord: Why the Ups and Downs of Relationships Are the Secret to Building Intimacy, Resilience, and Trust*. New York: Little, Brown Spark, 2020.

Tummala-Narra, Pratyusha. "Cultural Identity in the Context of Trauma and Immigration from a Psychoanalytic Perspective." *Psychoanalytic Psychology*, 31(2014): 396–409.

van der Kolk, Bessel. *The Body Keeps the Score: Brain, Mind, and Body in the Healing of Trauma*. New York: Penguin, 2014.

White, Michael. *Maps of Narrative Practice*. New York: W. W. Norton, 2007.

White, Michael and David Epston. *Narrative Means to Therapeutic Ends*. New York: W. W. Norton, 1990.

www.ingramcontent.com/pod-product-compliance
Lightning Source LLC
Jackson TN
JSHW022111190625
86377JS00003B/3